British Fictions of the Sixties

Also available from Bloomsbury

The 1970s: A Decade of Contemporary British Fiction, edited by Nick Hubble,
John McLeod and Philip Tew

Ian McEwan: Contemporary Critical Perspectives, 2nd edition,
edited by Sebastian Groes

Julian Barnes: Contemporary Critical Perspectives,
edited by Sebastian Groes and Peter Childs

Kazuo Ishiguro: Contemporary Critical Perspectives,
edited by Sean Matthews and Sebastian Groes

British Fictions of the Sixties

The Making of the Swinging Decade

Sebastian Groes

Bloomsbury Academic
An imprint of Bloomsbury Publishing Plc

B L O O M S B U R Y
LONDON · OXFORD · NEW YORK · NEW DELHI · SYDNEY

Bloomsbury Academic

An imprint of Bloomsbury Publishing Plc

50 Bedford Square
London
WC1B 3DP
UK

1385 Broadway
New York
NY 10018
USA

www.bloomsbury.com

BLOOMSBURY and the Diana logo are trademarks of Bloomsbury Publishing Plc

First published 2016
Paperback edition first published 2017

British Library Cataloguing-in-Publication Data
A catalogue record for this book is available from the British Library.

ISBN: HB: 978-0-8264-9557-0
PB: 978-1-3500-5419-6
ePDF: 978-1-4411-7616-5
ePub: 978-1-4411-1706-9

Library of Congress Cataloging-in-Publication Data
A catalog record for this book is available from the Library of Congress.

Cover design: Eleanor Rose
Cover image: Getty

Typeset by Integra Software Service Pvt. Ltd.

Contents

Introduction
Revolutions of the Mind

What were the sixties really like?

This book is in various ways a continuation of *The Making of London*, a work that teased out how London's myths and fictions are implicated in shaping our perception of that most marvellous of cities. Whereas *The Making of London* was preoccupied with the British capital as a mythical and political battleground, this book argues that the British sixties are an epistemological hinge moment that is clothed in myths implicated in shaping our understanding of the past, our present moment and the future of our early twenty-first-century world. This book is, as Angela Carter once said of her own work, in the demythologizing business: extending, but also offering new, original perspectives on a body of critical work that includes Patricia Waugh's *Harvest of the Sixties* (1995), the historical works of Arthur Marwick (1998) and Dominic Sandbrook (2005, 2006) as well as the cultural analysis of, for instance, Bart Moore-Gilbert and John Seed (1992), Jonathan Green (1998), Shawn Levy (2002), Marianne DeKoven (2004) and Gerard DeGroot (2008). These works were primarily preoccupied with asking if, or to what extent, there was a cultural revolution during the sixties. In most cases the answer we hear is that, yes, there was; but it was a complex, uneven and subtle process rather than a full-blown revolution.

To assess the sixties, these critics need to demythologize the decade of Spectacle, and the images it burned into our collective memory. Our understanding and interpretation of the sixties is hypermediated and overdetermined by a thick crust of fictions. From Beatlemania and the Stones to Mary Quant's fashion and Vidal Sassoon's haircuts; from the rise of working-class actors Michael Caine and Terence Stamp to seductive beauties such as Twiggy and Christine Keeler; from the pill and 'free love' to hippies and LSD; from the *Lady Chatterley* trial to sit-ins at London's Roundhouse; from JFK's and Martin Luther King's assassinations to the Vietnam War; from Brutalist architecture and Pop Art to New Wave science fiction and structuralist theory; from Paris's 1968 revolution to Amsterdam's Provo movement; from Swinging London to Woodstock; from the birth of the teenager to the Women's Liberation movement – all have contributed to a sense that this period was in many ways special. For many critics the sixties saw the birth of postmodernism, with its playful exploration of a new crisis of representation and meaning. I argue that the decade was not so much the starting point of this crisis as a time in which the epistemological uncertainties which characterize western modernity intensified. The sixties saw the acceleration of this crisis of meaning, which manifested itself after the crumbling of traditional, Enlightened sense-making structures.

Fictional representations no longer vied for dominance with the real; there was, rather, a sense that the two were indistinguishable, resulting in a simulacral amalgamation. The key players, media personalities and events became both mythical and fictional in the sense that their representation on TV and film screens and other media preceded their perceived reality. In *Understanding Media* (1964), Marshall McLuhan made the point that our world was approaching 'the technological simulation of consciousness, when the creative process of knowing will be collectively and corporately extended to the whole of human society' (McLuhan 2003: 5). For McLuhan, individual human consciousness became a prosthesis of mass media, and vice versa. The implication of the Society of Spectacle is, in Guy Debord's words, that '[e]verything that was directly lived has receded into representation' (Debord 1994: 7). This is a point made by, for instance, Michelangelo Antonioni's film *Blow-Up* (1968), in which experience is filtered through the lens of a fashion photographer. The work of J. G. Ballard suggests that the invasion of new media in our world fundamentally reconfigures the way we perceive, know and live. In this sense, the sixties also produced the foundations for our cybernetic age, acting as a catalyst that sped up the shift from the analogue period to a digital age in which, despite the increasing desire for reality, authenticity and truth, our connection with the real has only been diminishing.

Roger Luckhurst has called the sixties 'that much contested denotation of epoch' (Luckhurst 1997: 50), and the period has proven to be an ideological battleground where myths take precedence over historical truth. Writing in the early nineties, Malcolm Bradbury notes:

> 'The Sixties' have now ceased to be a historical decade at all. Probably they never
> were, even at the time – rather a state of mind and body, of political and cultural
> revolt, which could be laid across the historical clock in several ways and at a

number of different dates. But there was a historical Sixties, which both preceded and more or less outdated that Sixties state of being. (Bradbury 1993: 335–36)

Much of the decade's branding was spearheaded by a small group of upper-class entrepreneurs, who led the way for the liberation of a generation of baby-boomers empowered by the brief economic upturn in the late 1950s. This resulted in an intense commercialization of the public and private realms and a commodification of individual identity and the capitalist exploitation of human desire in systemic mass pop culture and the emergent consumer society. At the same time, historical revisionism of the sixties was already taking place during the decade itself, as, for instance, the *Look at Life* documentaries suggest. I will argue that it was literature in particular that, as the art form that comes closest to representing human consciousness, immediately responded with a counter-mythological rhetoric that collectively served as cautionary tale against Spectacle.

Perhaps only Mary Quant, the fashion designer and entrepreneur securely hemmed in behind the walls of her reputation, still promotes the swinging mythology. In an interview with students on the 'British Fiction of the 1960s' module which I taught at the University of East Anglia, Quant kept serving up stories of the revolutionary sixties. My students were respectful because of Quant's achievements; she is after all a stylish, creative and taboo-breaking fashion and make-up icon who allowed the playful mocking of the politico-economic and cultural establishment and who helped women to reinvent themselves. But the students were also highly critical of Quant's narrative: 'Like a scripted robot she talks of unending parties, dancing and celebrities. [...] Her tale contains hardly any hardships or nuance. Her sixties is a story she has told so often she thinks it's true' (Beesley et al. 2005: 17). Quant's happy perpetuation of the mythology is hardly surprising as she was part of the Chelsea Set, a group of creative entrepreneurs consisting of mostly upper-class artists, photographers and writers such as Alexander Plunckett-Green and Nell Dunn, who, together with (American) mass media such as *Time Magazine* (scrutinized in Chapter 4), dreamt up what we now conceive of as the Swinging Sixties. The students concluded that, although Quant's success must have involved more real, hard labour than she appeared to remember, her attitude is symptomatic of the persistence of the rose-tinted image of the sixties she helped to construct and perpetuate.

Already during the sixties it became fashionable to unpick the Swinging Sixties mythology, its images and iconography and, in the process, the wide variety of powerful and sometimes valuable ideas that it generated. Angela Carter's fiction and journalism tried to unstitch the turbulent social changes that were reshaping life, from make-up and fashion to Englishness and counterculture. Upon reflection, she noted:

> Anyway, they'd say: 'What were the sixties really like?' Impossible to answer except, well, it wasn't like they say in the movies. It was the best of times, it was the worst of times, etc. etc. etc. The pleasure principle met the reality principle like an irresistible force encountering an immovable object, and the reverberations of that collision are still echoing about us. (Carter 1992: 84)

Carter here draws on Freudian terminology to indicate, as Debord and McLuhan did, 'the real' was bulldozed by the powerful fictions produced by individual and collective desires. Yet, Carter also acknowledges that the nature, or at least the 'feel', of life had changed:

> I'd like to be able to dismiss it all as superficial and irrelevant to what was really going on, people arguing about Hegel and so on, but I'm forced to admit there was a yeastiness in the air that was due to a great deal of unrestrained and irreverent frivolity [...] there's no denying that towards the end of the decade everyday life [...] took on the air of continuous improvisation [...] *Carpe diem.* Pleasure. It didn't have to cost much, either. (Carter in Maitland 1988: 212)

The attempts to understand what happened has continued to the present day. The Austin Powers films, television programmes such as the BBC's *Why I Hate the Sixties* (2005) and UKTV History's Sixties Season, art shows such as the Tate Modern's *Art and the 60s: This Was Tomorrow* (2004), the V&A's Sixties Fashion Exhibition (2006–7), the fiftieth anniversary of 1968 celebrations in 2008 and a recent photography exhibition 'Swinging Sixties London' in FOAM (2015) have all drawn on the decade's imaginative and creative potency while expressing reservations about its legacy.

Mythologies of loss

We must continue to demythologize, therefore, and continue to dismantle the utopian rhetoric of ideological liberation, unbridled (sexual) freedoms, of hedonism, and of self-transformation and social mobility. One of the major critical problems in understanding the decade is that the period evokes associations and doxologies so strong that we personalize the period, painting it as a vicious charlatan of Dickensian proportions rather than as a space of time containing a complex matrix of events whose meaning continuously alters along with our changing historical context and our individual and collective perception of the past. The sixties has accumulated an extraordinarily diverse multiplicity of complex, contradictory and often hostile meanings and opinions.

In an edited interdisciplinary collection that promises to unstitch sixties myths and clichés, *Cultural Revolution?* (1992), Bart Moore-Gilbert and John Seed also note that the cultural upheaval of the period was a media myth. Were the ostensible political, economic, social, cultural changes really significant and permanent? The editors note that their book 'is part of the work of demythologizing, that there was in these years no monolithic counter-culture or cultural opposition with a coherent programme' (Moore-Gilbert and Seed 1992: 1). They identify and structure their delineation of the contradictions of the sixties around four areas of debate: the ostensible parochialism of English culture (something which Doris Lessing brought to the fore in various writings); the absorption of the counter-culture by mainstream cultural forces; the narcissistic celebration of the self; and the formation of a new cultural elite that worked against the purported impetus of democratization. *Cultural Revolution?* attempts to 'understand the present by bringing it into a critical relationship with the recent past, making intelligible the various histories that shape our present and present crises' (Moore-Gilbert and Seed 1992: 14). The crises Moore-Gilbert and Seed refer to are centred on the rise of the New Right under Thatcher in the 1980s, whose conservatism rejected fully the democratizing impulses of the counter-culture. In our time, we face our own distinctive twenty-first century crises, including the rise of right-wing extremist parties, new terrorist groups wreaking havoc, the persistence of totalitarian states, a renewed racism and xenophobia, global financial crises and conservative attitudes to gender relations.

Moore-Gilbert and Seed's anthology reacts against conservatives such as Peter Hitchens, who claimed that in the 1960s 'the wrong future [for Britain] was chosen' (BBC 2004). In his book *The Abolition of Britain* (1999), Hitchens paints a bitter, apocalyptic picture of the UK in the 1960s:

> The condition of 1960s Britain was rather like the huge scrapyards of the time full of the steam engines which had been such a characteristic part of the urban and rural landscape for the previous century. Those cemeteries of rusting iron monsters were a melancholy metaphor for the state of the nation. Britain had been living on her Victorian inheritance, an elderly but rather grand steam locomotive, hiding her leaky valves behind shiny paint and well-polished brass, obsolete but magnificent. Now the truth could not be concealed any more. In a matter of a few months, a whole way of life was condemned to be cut up with blowtorches and turned into lawn-mowers and tumble-driers. (Hitchins 1999: xi–xii)

Hitchens's post-Thatcherite excoriation refers to the closure of railway lines and the wholesale abandonment of the steam engine, that wondrous Victorian invention that played an important role in the British Empire and helped shape the idea of 'Great' Britain. Rem Koolhaas calls the ruins and remnants that are left 'junkspace': 'what remains after modernization has run its course, or, more precisely, what coagulates while modernization is in process, its fallout. Modernization has a rational program: to share the blessings of science, universally. Junkspace is its apotheosis, or meltdown...' (Koolhaas 2002: 175). Rather than experiencing such ghostly ruins, with their complex temporality, as a conglomerate of paradoxical emotions that involve the uncanny, the sublimely beautiful, pride and embarrassment, critics such as Hitchens embody an irrational response celebrating a singular imaginary – an unquestioning nostalgia for myth – that rejects the pillar of modernity: change.

Herein lies the importance of fiction, with its ability to cut through myths and to give a strong, deep and complex sense of consciousness at a particular point in time. Much of Martin Amis's fulmination against the perils of democratization and moral slackening is a reaction to historical processes and events taking place in the 1960s. In some of his non-fiction, he argues against the increased distribution of wealth and its related cultural democratization that characterized the sixties on the grounds that it generated an 'equality of sentiments' and '[e]motional egalitarianism' (Amis 2001: xiii). The spirit of tolerance that came with the spread of liberal values also entailed the loss of competition and high intellectual and moral standards, as well as an increased passiveness. Amis's eschatological criticism is more complex and subtle than Hitchens's, a difference which becomes clear when looking at Amis's fiction, which also denounces the sixties. Consider his critique of hedonism and greed in the Reagan–Thatcher era, the novel *Money* (1984), in which the narrator, fast-food addict, alcoholic and porn enthusiast John Self, looks at joggers, and confesses:

> My generation, we started all this. Before, everyone was presumably content to feel like death the whole time. Now they want to feel terrific forever. The Sixties taught us this, that it was hateful to be old. I'm the product of the Sixties – an obedient, unsmiling, no-comment product of the Sixties – but in this matter my true sympathies go further back, to those days of yore when no one minded feeling like death the whole time. (Amis 1985: 64)

At first glance, we seem to encounter a rejection of the sixties understood as a time when key values and traditions, some of them elitist and belonging to the upper classes, were irreparably damaged by progress and innovation too much and too quickly. We must, however, take into account here that the voice of Self is itself a composite of many fictional layers that compromise the direct attack we get in Amis-the-critic. We recognize, for instance, echoes of Larkin, whose poems famously lamented and railed against the sixties but in a knowing, even romantic manner. When looking at Larkin poems such as 'The Whitsun Weddings' (1958), 'High Windows' (1967), 'Annus Mirabilis' (1967) and 'This Be The Verse' (1971), however, what strikes you is the ironic tone, which creates a sense of indeterminacy undercutting the confident pronouncements on, and lamentation of, the loss of morality and cultural heritage. There is also a sense of the continuity behind the apparent decline. The narrator of the latter poem may perhaps be fucked up by his mum and dad – in itself a playful pun about biological and social relationships, 'But they were fucked up in their turn.'

Indeed, both Larkin and Amis present us knowingly with mythologies of loss. English literature has been obsessed with loss and decline from its very beginnings; the decline of morality part of the very fabric of its consciousness since the very first Old English tales of knights roaming a deserted world in search of lost masters and destroyed mead halls. Just after the Second World War, the very English connection between literature and morality was cemented in F. R. Leavis's *The Great Tradition* (1948), which stated that the great English novelists – Joseph Conrad, George Eliot and Henry James (with Jane Austen and D. H. Lawrence snuck in) – 'brought an intense focus, an unusually developed interest in life. [...] Far from having any of Flaubert's disgust or disdain or boredom, they are all distinguished by a vital capacity for experience, a kind of revert openness before life, and a marked moral intensity' (Leavis 1948: 17–18). An even bigger influence upon Amis's narrative voice is Dickens, who was a great critic of the damage wrought upon the individual and collective psyche and social fabric by industrial developments in the nineteenth century. This complexity and ambiguity of voice undercuts any unequivocal return to a glorified image of Victorian Britain in the manner of Hitchens or Margaret Thatcher. In this tradition of loss, the sixties embodies not discontinuity but an intensification of continuity in this tradition, just as the Thatcher regime's over-romanticized, mythological image of nineteenth-century England would generate creative, counter-mythological resistance in the 1980s work of, for instance, Angela Carter, Michael Moorcock, Iain Sinclair, Patrick Wright, Maureen Duffy, Ian McEwan and Martin Amis. This book explores what the 1960s means in the twenty-first century.

The multi-layered narrative voice of Amis-the-novelist embodies the idea
that our perception of the present and past is heavily influenced by fictions
and myths. Myths are an important form of knowledge about a people, which
can be useful in attempts at understanding the historical relationship between
ourselves and the world. Alan Sinfield states: 'The 1960s is of course a myth;
but that is an important thing to be, since what we think and do depends on
the stories we tell ourselves' (Sinfield 1997: 283). One of the key figures of
the sixties, the prolific science fiction writer, editor of *New Worlds* magazine
and member of the 1960s band Hawkwind, Michael Moorcock, expresses his
admiration for writers such as Dickens, whose transfiguration of London
'created an authentic myth, more potent than fact' by achieving 'a universal
symbolism' (Moorcock 2001: 239–40). Anthony Burgess too admits to an
increasing interest is myth: 'I think my own novelistic future depends more
and more on digging into mythical roots, the mythical expression of human
behaviour, rather than the naturalistic expression of what we see around us'
(Burgess in Lewis 2002: 266). We hear the same concern in Iris Murdoch's
seminal 'Against Dryness' (1961), in which she fulminates against the new
journalistic way of writing literature in a highly scientific, empirical context,
arguing for a crystalline novel that depicts a metaphysical, three-dimensional
(wo)man immersed in a rich context and 'against a background of values, of
realities, which transcend him' (Murdoch in Bradbury 1977: 26). The interest
in myth around this period is itself a complex response: it is at once a reaction to
the kitchen-sink realism of the writing of the 1950s and a (perhaps regressive)
return to the Modernist interest in classical mythology – one might think of
W. B. Yeats, T. S. Eliot, James Joyce and W. H. Auden – in response to the
mediatized, technological and anti-metaphysical mythologies of modernity,
which Debord, McLuhan and Roland Barthes analysed.

As the human animal is an irrational being that hardly has insight into her or
his self, illusions are necessarily part of our organization of the world; we need
myths to make life bearable. We cannot live without illusions, and illusions can
often make our world more civilized and progressive because they inspire us to
achieve better conditions for ourselves and the world at large. Myths and fiction
fire our imagination, stimulate us intellectually, morally and artistically and yet
can also have a harmful impact on our thought and society. The danger, and,
therefore, the importance, of challenging and destroying mythologies cannot,
however, be underestimated. Often myths become a dominant component of
our consciousness, making us blind to their actual complexity and fictionality;
they often lead to a reductive over-romanticization and misrepresentation of,

for instance, national identity, of ethnicity, gender, religion, etc. In her concise history of England, *England: The Making of the Myth from Stonehenge to Albert Square* (2001), Maureen Duffy acknowledges that myth-making is part of any nation's healthy understanding of itself and that the wholesale reinvention of the nation in violent and bloody revolutions such as the ones in France 1793 and Russia 1917 is in danger of destroying the important images and ideas that tell us who we are. Yet she also warns against myths: 'The danger is that we may come up with [the] militarism, intolerance, xenophobia, that our travelling hooligans choose to express their Englishness' (Duffy 2001: xii).

Writing in the aftermath of events that emerged from utopian acts of myth-making, the Second World War and the Holocaust, Frank Kermode is very much aware of the dangers of myths. In *The Sense of an Ending* (1965) he posits fiction as an antidote:

> We have to distinguish between myths and fictions. Fictions can degenerate into myths whenever they are not held to be fictive. In this sense anti-Semitism is a degenerate fiction, a myth; and *Lear* is a fiction. Myth operates within the diagram of ritual, which presupposes total and adequate explanations of things as they are and were; it is a sequence of radically unchangeable gestures. Fictions are for finding things out, and they change as the sense-making changes. Myths are the agents of stability, fictions the agents of change. Myths call for absolute, fictions for conditional assent. Myths make sense in terms of a lost order of time […] fictions, if successful, make sense of the here and now. (Kermode 1966: 39)

Kermode's argument can be pitted against the end-time thinking of critics such as Hitchens and, to a lesser degree, Amis, who use a rhetoric of the present as a time of an abrupt ending of tradition also employed by various Modernist authors, Yeats and Eliot in particular. Indeed, against their presentation of our age as unique and exceptional in the irrevocable changes we live through, Kermode helpfully notes that the apocalyptic has itself become the very condition of modernity, that a sense of transition is itself endless (Kermode 1966: 91–124).

One of the paradoxes that the 1960s presents to us is that, while we know a great deal about it as a period because of the directness and totality of our access to it, we are also least able to grasp the decade precisely because our access is too vast and undifferentiated. Moreover, it is also difficult to understand because the sources we have at our disposal are to a large extent mythical, fictional and 'Spectacular'. At the start of the twenty-first century, we are more than ever fully immersed in the Society of Spectacle, albeit in different forms, media and contexts. As Marianne DeKoven points out, after 9/11, the sixties have once again become both more and less relevant:

> In the immediate wake of September 11, the sixties seemed to me at once to have receded into a more distant past, and also to have become more present than they had been since the height of the culture wars. The anti-war movement that defined so much of what we think of as 'the sixties,' and the Vietnam War that produced it, seemed to belong to a different world. The violence of much late-sixties radicalism seemed no longer naïve, misguided, and embarrassing, but shameful – an ugly look in the mirror – even for those of us [...] who did not participate in it but justified it up to a point and felt some of its motivating rage. The utopian passions that inspired the sixties political and countercultural movements, assuming the necessity and the inevitability of total social, political, and cultural transformation, seemed to me not just deluded and superceded but also retroactively contaminated by the all-or-nothing fanaticism of contemporary fundamentalisms. (DeKoven 2004: xv)

Indeed, the idea of 'revolution' has returned in sinister ways in our time: not necessarily as a form of culture war but certainly as ideological warfare, driven by violent extremist politics and religious radicalism. Given the intense role of technology and involvement of (social) media, we need to return to the sixties to understand the complexities of our situation.

Against interpretation

This is why I am not wholly convinced that it is only historical analysis that can help us fully understand the nature of the sixties. Historical studies such as Arthur Marwick's fist-sized standard work *The Sixties* (1998), Mark Donnelley's *Sixties Britain* (2005), Dominic Sandbrook's *Never Had It So Good* (2005) and *White Heat* (2006), and Gerard DeGroot's *The Sixties Unplugged* (2008) promise the reader not only to present a nuanced view of the decade but to reveal the truth behind the decade's overpowering mythologies. The frequent references to, and invocations of, literature in Sandbrook's work are particularly problematic, as he tends to assume that art can be used to prove the validity of historical conjecture. In short, reality comes first, then representation – as if the two can be separated easily. The relationship between art and the world out there is, however, much more complex, as Bruno Latour reminds us in *We Have Never Been Modern* (1991). For Latour the distinction between the modern and the ancient and the nature versus society/culture split are false, as is C. P. Snow's

Two Cultures argument or any other distinction between entities in this world, including that between humans and the nonhuman. Human identity is never pure; it is a hybrid construct. Latour points out that Enlightenment structures created a mode of purification or, as I put it, a zone of ontological sanitization, which is based on the fetish of categorization. The sixties are important in presenting us with a rigorous breakdown of the stranglehold of the very ideal of a singular, monolithic identity in favour of a complex, contradictory form of human identity.

One of the aims of this book is to challenge the existence of a straightforward causal connection between socio-historical context and artistic representation. The tendency for literature to be made to piggyback on history, sociology, history, or economics often results in the neglecting of outstanding works of literature (Angus Wilson, Margaret Drabble, Maureen Duffy, Iris Murdoch) in favour of mediocre work that is seen as representative of particular historical events or periods. The 'Angry Young Men' literature from the fifties, such as John Braine's novel *Room at the Top* (1957) or John Osborne's *Look Back in Anger* (1959), are taught because they exemplify their historical era. It is conspicuous that Sandbrook spends various pages on realists such as Osborne and John Wain, while more 'difficult' authors with an intricate aesthetic are mentioned only in passing. Angus Wilson mocked this type of response to *Look Back in Anger* in his own novel *Late Call* (1964), in which the character Sally Bulmer notes: 'It's a clever enough play. But a decent social worker would have cleared up the whole mess within a day and a half' (Wilson 2001: 160). It is helpful to quote Maureen Duffy, who in speaking about her semi-autobiographical first novel, *That's How It Was* (1962), pins down the complex relationship between fiction and historical reality, making use of that quintessentially sixties metaphor, fashion:

> A book is written not in a vacuum but at a precise historical moment which will affect not only the stylistic dress in which it is clothed but its moral and political underpinnings. I hope that twenty years on my first novel can still say something about that moment as well as about the abidingness of its central theme. (Duffy 2002: xi)

Duffy makes a helpful distinction between subject matter and form and style, although she acknowledges that fiction is not divorced from the historical conditions in which the writer operates. Fiction and historical reality are engaged in a dialectical relationship in which it is not necessarily social conditions which fundamentally determine literature; fictions themselves shape our understanding of the past. As we will see, some of the more experimental, avant-garde writing of the period attempts to place itself outside the world in order to think about experience in a new, autonomous way. These fictions resist the alluring tendency to reduce literature to the demonstration of often rather vulgar truism about society, and the making functional and useful, in a one-dimensional way, of literature. W. H. Auden said that 'poetry makes nothing happen'; in Ian McEwan's words, 'we know in our hearts that the very best art is entirely and splendidly useless' (McEwan 2005). Iris Murdoch knew this too, when she spoke of the responsibility of the literary artist: 'It is the function of the writer to write the best book he knows how to write' (Murdoch in Bradbury 1977: 23).

Nowadays, in an increasingly efficient and commercialized academic context, these may be radical and subversive positions. Indeed, even Roland Barthes's ideas about the death of the author and authorial intention have become unfashionable, as the general audience busy themselves with 'finding the author' at literary festivals. Foucault's utopian notion of the heterotopia seems difficult to maintain in a materialist, neoliberal context determined by *Realpolitik*. The radical ideas that created a vibrant intellectual context are the baby thrown out with the postmodern bathwater. Indeed, the attraction of sixties fiction is that it is heterogeneous, conflicted and contradictory, like the finest art in any period, but all the more so.

The title of this book, *British Fictions of the Sixties*, suggests a different relationship between art, human beings and the world. We should not be under the impression that by clearing up the misunderstandings surrounding the epoch that we can arrive at some kind of truth. The nature of demythologization is different for each epoch. The 'truth' this book is after is something more subtle, which plays itself out at the level of consciousness, unconsciousness, mood, emotions and sensibility. It starts from the idea that, if we are to understand our Spectacular condition, we must acknowledge that there is no unalloyed 'real' to be retrieved.

This is what Susan Sontag alerts us to in her seminal essay 'Against Interpretation' (1964) where she points out that art in the western consciousness since Plato and Aristotle has traditionally been framed as being 'in' this world and, as such, is always deficient as a reflection and meditation on that reality. This view of art has returned to us at the start of the twenty-first century through a renewed emphasis on formalist approaches and a revaluation of less easily quantifiable subjects such as affect, qualia (momentary experiences of subjective conscious experience), emotions and beauty. Literature reminds us that our knowing is shaped by unconscious codes and numerous rules of interpretation: 'the knowledge we gain through art is an experience of the form or style of knowing something, rather than knowledge of something (like a fact or a moral judgment) in itself' (Sontag 2009: 22). Art is both autonomous and related to the world as prosthesis, as mental extension of our consciousness. The problem lies in the fundamental paradoxes presented to us by the study of any period in history. One writer who was already starting to think about this in detail in the decade itself is Angela Carter, who published an essay, 'Notes for a Theory of a Sixties Style' in the magazine *New Society* in 1967. Carter analysed fashion, and changing attitudes towards it, by politicizing fashion as a system of signs, along the lines of Roland Barthes's work on semiotics. Fashion provides social identity, for Carter, but it also triggers a subtle shift in our ontological status: 'For we think our dress expresses ourselves but in fact it expresses our environment and, like advertising, pop music, pulp fiction and second-feature films, it does so almost at a subliminal, emotionally charged, instinctual and non-intellectual level' (Carter 1982: 85). Another piece, 'The Wound in the Face', investigates the changing shape of women's faces in the light of new cosmetics technologies, aesthetic tastes and styles, reading this change as a sign of the physical battering women's image took in the sixties – here investigated in Chapters 2 and 7. Carter's writing symbolizes a growth of awareness of humans as semi-agentic, with limited free will.

The study of literature in its widest form – from narratology and discourse analysis to the deconstruction of metaphors, symbols and the analysis of (a possibly changing) human character – has a key part to play in the understanding of these (unconscious) constructs. Narratives of interpretable facts and events take no priority over the experience presented to us by the literary imagination, a creative and critical *Gesamtkunstwerk* that generates its own specific knowledge and energy. The novelistic space allows us to know and see in very particular ways by allowing the human brain to make less obvious yet illuminating connections between people, society and events, and thus it makes us understand consciousness and experience in new and profound ways. This book prefers that approach and attitude over the safer paths walked by colleagues working in historical, cultural and sociological studies by suggesting that literature is not contained by, or subordinate to, this historical period but is both an interdisciplinary product and producer of the sixties as a complex mythological and fictional construct. A decade that saw the birth of the Society of Spectacle – a world in which all social relations between people as well as the perception of the self are mediated by complex and omnipresent forms of representation – can, in fact, only be critically understood and challenged if we study the novel as an art form specializing in thinking about mediation and fictionalization. The study of literary imagination and fictional narratives has, therefore, a special and vital contribution to make in assessing the workings of the personal life and private imagination in relationship to our comprehensively mediated and globalized world at the start of a deeply troubled early twenty-first century.

What is striking about the fiction covered here is that, while it often only obliquely connects with, and underscores, the established historical narratives about the 1960s, these novels capture the sixties at the level of form, aesthetics, imagery, atmosphere, metaphor and symbolism. We set out, then, to show not only that the relationship between historical events and sixties writing is more complex and nuanced than is usually suggested but that sixties writing has a dominant role to play in shaping perceptions of post-war writing as a whole and the literary scene in the twenty-first century. *British Fictions of the Sixties* maps, and catalyses, a renewed exploration of the sixties as a space of affect, attitudes, emotions and specific yet complex forms of energy and of a 'spirit'. These emotions will include discontent with the persistence of Victorian heritage and attitudes, politics, economic and power structures. They will include disappointment with the achievements of the ostensible revolutions the decade is renowned for but perhaps also a residual hope and belief in progressiveness. Taken together, these ideas represent a claim for the decade as a hinge moment that occasions the waning of the realist novel's representative power. We'll see a move away from strictly humanist imaginings to a complexly fragmented mental landscape in which humanism as a reference point is supplemented by late capitalist as well as posthuman subjectivities. This epistemological shift takes place in the sixties, and allows us to understand the decade as a compression of several endings of tradition, and as the catalyst of new beginnings.

What follows are, rather than readings of literary fiction clustered together and placed against historical, social and cultural backdrops, a series of deep cognitive readings of fiction that presents the experience and consciousness of the sixties at the level of literary representation. We should not just look for connections between the 'outside world' or 'external reality' and literature at the level of subject matter, but seek to gain a sense of the epoch through stylistic innovations. This book situates its readings in various cognitive frameworks, and acknowledges that the cognitive turn we are experiencing at the start of the twenty-first century provides the central critical framework for understanding the world today.

Sontag seems to have anticipated this by focusing on memory, cognition and phenomenology in her discussion of the importance of literary form:

> form – in its specific idiom, style – is a plan of sensory imprinting, the vehicle for the transaction between immediate sensuous impression and memory (be it individual or cultural). This mnemonic function explains why every style depends on it, and can be analysed in terms of, some principle of repetition of redundancy. (Sontag 2009: 34)

As I believe that the elusive complexities and paradoxes of the sixties cannot be captured by conventional structuring procedures, it is as much at the level of form that this book aims to say useful things about the decade as a space of time when human consciousness and imagination went through a plethora of fascinating, often minor transformations the impact and repercussions of which we are still getting our head around. What follows are a series of narrative walks through the sixties, taking place on a number of analytical levels, from space, place and time through to political and cultural practices, and changing sexual politics, to name just a few. These psychogeographical walks aim to connect these topics through literary responses and hope to make the reader *feel* and *see* how developments and events changed our thinking and experience in profound and lasting ways.

British Fictions of the Sixties is underpinned by a number of beliefs and claims, which revolve mainly around the death of the conventional realist novel during the decade. This book suggests that the sixties sees the death of the puritan realist novel with its reliance on Aristotelean poetics; a tradition that goes back to Daniel Defoe's *Robinson Crusoe* (1719). This shift in aesthetics and literary sensibility also ensures that traditional forms of realism are and will remain untenable. After the Modernist divorce of signifier and signified and structuralism's linguistic work, which allows us to think of language and literary representation as an autonomous process, fiction releases itself from its presumed duty to imitate reality. This waning of the realist novel comes as capitalism and Spectacle are radically reshaping both the traditional forms of (thinking about) society. Although as a reaction to postmodernism we have seen the attempted formation of a new puritan tradition by and through the thinking about a renewed reality hunger in the work of David Shields, an unalloyed perception of, and relationship to, the real is and will remain impossible. This explains the current waning reputation of writers like Murdoch, Drabble, and Angus Wilson, and the return to the Modernist aesthetic in writers such as Ian McEwan, Tom McCarthy and Nicola Barker, to name but a few. The novel has taken on increasingly creative and vibrant posthumous lives.

Various other arguments are situated within this framework of the death of realism. These include an analysis of the novelistic engagement with Spectacle and the attempt to understand and depict the complexification of our relationship of the real. We shall also bear witness to a marginalization of literature within culture and a lessening of the authority of literary writers as cultural commentators. We also see the dispersal of the novel into a plurality of literary forms and genres such as sf, magical realism and social documentary. The sixties inaugurates a new interest in literary experimentation, which leads to what I call the 'Extreme Sixties', made up of hardcore experiments in anti-novelistic writing by J. G. Ballard, Christine Brooke-Rose, R. C. Kenedy, Eva Tucker, Ann Quin, Elspeth Davie, Alan Burns and B. S. Johnson, whose work radically seeks new literary aesthetics. Rather than being parochial and local in its outlook, the sixties saw a new interest in new forms of space (the internationalizing impetus of the Space Race, the Cold War) and place (the New Town, London's cosmopolitan offerings). In the Conclusion, the ramifications of these analyses will result in this book making a claim for literature as the pre-eminent art forms capable of safeguarding cognition and memory in the twenty-first century.

1

Authenticity and Audiotape

Introducing Nell Dunn

We encounter one of the most harrowing and haunting moments of post-war fiction in the description of a premature birth induced by a backstreet abortion in Nell Dunn's *Up the Junction* (1988):

> Rube was shrieking, a long, high, animal shriek. The baby was born alive, five months old. It moved, it breathed, its heart beat.
>
> Rube lay back, white and relieved, across the bed. Sylvie and her mum lifted the eiderdown and peered at the tiny baby still joined by the cord. 'You can see it breathing, look!'
>
> Rube smiled. 'It's nothing – I've had a look myself.'
>
> 'I reckon she had some pluck going seven times', said her mum.
>
> Finally the ambulance arrived. They took Rube away, but they left behind the baby, which had now grown cold. Later Sylvie took him, wrapped in the *Daily Mirror*, and threw him down the toilet. (Dunn 1988: 65)

The short passage reveals much about the lives of poor, working-class women in South London's slum areas in the early sixties. Their almost childlike wonder at the baby ('You can see it breathing, look!') stands in sharp contrast to the harsh, almost primeval nature of this event. The seeming trivial value attached to human life, the young mother's denial of her child as 'nothing' and the pragmatic manner of the corpse's disposal are particularly disturbing. Yet, at one and the same time the aloof, deadpan narration and the presentation of its grotesque minutiae – the baby's heartbeat, its umbilical cord, the revelation of its gender, the eternity it takes for the ambulance to arrive, the naming of the tabloid newspaper – evoke in the reader an overwhelming sense of injustice while forming an implicit but strong justification for the introduction of the pill in 1962. Simultaneously, we are, as readers, repulsed and outraged by having being manipulated into this cruelly voyeuristic position, prying into this private moment without being able to intervene. The repetition of the word 'look' makes us aware, however, of the necessity of our witnessing this heartrending scene and acknowledging the girls' wider predicament. As Adrian Henri notes in his introduction to the collection, it is the use of the *Daily Mirror* that is so important: this seemingly isolated incident reflects the everyday fate of thousands of girls before 1962. And beyond Henri's point, the reference suggests a serious crisis in representation: their lives are unreported, invisible. Dunn's work offers itself as an artful mirror that 'corrects' this misrepresentation by inscribing the lives of these women into the popular imagination. Yet, it is the reader who, immersed in this book about life, sex, death and everyday survival, is asked to let the horror dissipate into empathy for these girls and their plight. This act is a profoundly moral one and opens up a wider concern with the power of realism, mediatization and the ethics of authenticity. This chapter brings to the fore these issues by exploring how traditional criticism of the sixties has often overlooked the way in which new forms of technology – in Dunn's case, the tape recorder – create a new sense of 'the real'.

Up the Junction is about sexual exploration and desire, and their consequences: pregnancy and abortion. It is rather curious that Deborah Philips includes Dunn's early work in a genre she defines as the 'Single Mother Novel of the 1960s', 'The narrative of the single mother constructs a fictional world in which men are peripheral: the focus is on the choices and experience of a young woman' (Philips 2008: 37). Philips points to Lynne Reid Banks's *The L-Shaped Room* (1960) and Margaret Drabble's *The Millstone* (1965), which indeed are about mothers without partners, but *Up the Junction* does not fit into this category for two reasons. Firstly, while the single mother novel is about middle-class women, Dunn depicts working-class women. Secondly, *Up the Junction* is not a novel, but an experiment with vignette form. This lack of attention to form points to a reductive focus on how fiction needs to affirm the lack of sex education in the late 1950s and early 1960s, leading Philips to argue that the 'raucous exuberance' (Philips 2008: 51) of Dunn's work fits in neatly with the bland, dreary worlds of Reid Banks and Drabble. I argue that pregnancy and abortion cannot simply be read in literal, sociological ways but require instead an investigation of the metaphorical economy and the poetics and rules of representation. These physical states and trajectories signify the very condition of being for these young women – of constantly thwarted hope, of social exclusion, and material-bodily exploitation.

Generated by a restless creativity, Nell Dunn's seminal incendiary sixties texts *Up the Junction* (1963) and *Poor Cow* (1967) contain some of the most powerful and perceptive writing of the decade while opening up a series of questions about new ways in which literature is able to think about changing social conventions and morality. They display many characteristics and contradictions associated with the decade's mythology and provide a useful starting point for exploring representative problems in sixties fiction. At one and the same time, these paradoxical texts offer a didactic Marxist lesson in economy while acknowledging the power of the newly burgeoning consumer society; display a Romantic belief in the possibility of progress while quashing any sense of hope; foreground the importance of selfhood at the expense of a community whose demise is lamented; and embody a destructive obsession with newness while nostalgically longing for that which is lost. Read as part of a genre called 'the modern grotesque' (Minogue and Palmer: 103–28) that has its roots in Bakhtinian grotesque realism, the texts' graphic display of abortions could be said to have pinpointed issues that were repressed by the political mainstream but also to have contributed to the desensitization of the public realm.

Although the works are connected by their subject matter and narrative technique, they are also exceptional in that the growth of the author's mind matches that of the collective consciousness during the sixties. *Up the Junction* is composed of a series of loosely connected semi-fictional sketches chronicling the lives of a group of often unselfconscious, startlingly outspoken and promiscuous young women in Battersea, South London's wrong side of the tracks. Haunted by the ghost of hope, they live in cramped two-up-two-downs around Clapham Junction station – the eponymous junction – do stultifying, repetitive jobs in factories and drink ale in pubs where their lust after men results only in disappointment or, worse, in illegal abortions. Attracted by fifties icons such as Elvis and James Dean, the young men chase dreams too, seeking to purchase elusive consumer goods such as motorcycles and convertible Cadillacs. The girls are in many ways more advanced than their counterparts: they reject the marriage trap in favour of flings with married men, make their own money and are on the brink of claiming their autonomy. The 'novel' received the John Llewelyn Rhys Memorial Prize in 1964 and its controversial success increased when Dunn rewrote the stories into a Wednesday Play directed by Ken Loach, aired by the BBC and screened in cinemas in 1965.

Poor Cow is a short novel that homes in on the ups and joyless downs of a young working-class mother, ironically named Joy Steadman, who at twenty-three could be one of the girls from *Up the Junction* five years later. She has just delivered her baby, Jonny, after which the young family move from Fulham to

Ruislip in suburban West London. Not long after, her promiscuous husband, the petty criminal Tom, ends up in jail, leaving Joy to fend for her son and herself. She works in a pub, turns briefly to nude modelling and prostitution, while her new lover, Dave, is also sent to prison. After her son goes missing, the novel ends with the realization that 'all that really mattered was that the child should be all right and that they should be together' (Dunn 1988 [1967]: 127). This novel too was turned into a critically acclaimed television film by Dunn and Loach in 1967, ensuring her place in the decade's popular imagination.

Dunn's signature lies in her use of a social-realist, documentary mode and her sparse prose. Through a poet's grasp of visual sensation, her sketches acutely evoke rather than spell out atmosphere: 'Snow blew up in white sheets low across the black road and wind blew through the castle gates' (Dunn 1988: 87). She also has a fine ear for the South London dialect, as the following dialogue captures when the girls, after a night out, go swimming with a group of boys:

> Outside revving bikes were splitting the night.
> 'Where we going?'
> 'Let's go swimmin' up the Common.'
> 'We ain't got not swim-suits with us.'
> 'We'll swim down one end and you down the other. It's dark, aint' it?'
> 'Who do yer think's going to see yer? The man in the moon?'
> 'Yeah and what's to stop yer hands wandering?'
> 'We'll tie 'em behind our backs.' (Dunn 1988: 14)

This playful verbal sparring between the girls and boys – a teenage tussle between innocence and experience which gains its erotic dimension by collapsing into a confusing collection of disparate, disembodied voices – gives us an insight into the changing relationship between the sexes. The night is not the only thing being split by the bikes; the machines also, in an echo of Muriel Spark's *The Prime of Miss Brodie* (1961), establish 'a protective fence of bicycle between the sexes' (Spark 1997: 5). The game of seduction that plays itself out suggests that a new structure is emerging in which the girls appropriate a new, independent position while the boys are forced to adjust to and accept the loss of their former privileged position of dominance.

In both form and content, the novels map the wounds inflicted on a society by poverty while presenting intelligent tracings of the stuttering progress of female emancipation. Contrary to Anthony Burgess's *A Clockwork Orange* (1962), which projects the results of the economic and sexual liberation of teenagers into a dystopian, future Britain, *Up the Junction* stands with one foot in the fifties' Mods and Rockers culture – poverty produces a time-lag. Boys wear leather

centres on the question of the authority and authenticity of fiction and the relationship between fiction and reality. ⟋ ʃʊʊ

Dunn's narrating alter ego in *Up the Junction*, 'an heiress from Chelsea' (Dunn 1988: 20), merges, apparently seamlessly and without any ideological problems, with the working-class women she describes. The opening sentence states: '*We* stand, the three of *us*, me, Sylvie and Rube, pressed up against the saloon door, brown ales clutched in our hands' (my emphasis, Dunn 1988: 13). Although the narrator shares the girls' gender, the lack of distance between narrator and the girls in terms of class is potentially problematic. This stands in great contrast, for instance, to Liverpudlian Douglas Dunn's poem 'The Clothes Pit', published in the collection *Terry Street* (1969) – a social realist chronicle of a working-class street in Hull, in which the narrator describes similar scenes. However, here the narrator is keen to keep a clear distance while foregrounding his voyeuristic view into this 'inarticulate paradise' (Dunn, D. 1969: 13). Waugh notes that in Dunn's poems '[t]he divided phenomenological realities of "them" and "us" [...] can never be reconciled through verse, for "they suffer, and I catch only the surface"' (Waugh 1995: 123–24). In Nell Dunn's writing, class and ethnic identities are subsumed, transcended and legitimized by the importance of the genderedness of the subject, and the question is whether we accept this rather demanding premise.

Interventions by Dunn's authorial self have not helped to alleviate potential allegations of misrepresentation. In a Q&A-session moderated by Paul Magrs, Dunn was asked: 'How do you question your authority on the basis of class?' Her answer seems rather weak:

> I don't believe in censorship, therefore I believe we should be able to write about any class we want. Although I am not working class I do write a lot about the working class. That language suited me better than Standard English for what I wanted to say. Also a more odd and sinister reason: as a child I was very much surrounded by working class people and there's a bit of me that wants to remain in that childhood state and does not want to be grown up and deal with a great big world of what's happening in other countries and who's prime minister. (Magrs 1998)

Dunn does not make a political point about how this particular working-class accent could function as a means to bolster the local identity as form of social subversion. Instead, we find a curiously romantic and escapist attempt to recapture an innocent, prelapsarian state which Dunn associates the working class. When Magrs asks whether she sees herself as working class, Dunn replies:

No, I don't really. I think I'm often exploring matters of the heart and therefore, certainly in the mother/daughter relationship thing I wanted to explore, again it seemed a language thing to a large extent. A mother/daughter relationship can be very deep, so I don't particularly think of them as working class. [...] I seem to like describing that and using that. I haven't really got to the bottom of it. (Magrs 1998)

This vacillating answer suggests that beneath the grime and horror of Dunn's fiction, the solution is for a retreat to a middle-class, conservative ideology that reaffirms the need for the bourgeois stability offered by the nuclear family unit. This is most painfully represented in Dunn's allegorical children's fable about love and fidelity, *Freddy Gets Married* (1965), where the canine protagonist seeks, and ultimately finds, a spouse to complete her life: 'HUSBAND WANTED – MUST BE CLEAN AND RESPECTABLE' (Dunn 1968: unpag.). Dunn could then be considered, as Angela Carter says of George Orwell, 'a kind of tourist in class terms' (Maitland 1988: 211). While attempting to represent the working class, Dunn's work is complicit to the selling of the working class *as* the working class by reinforcing a specific archetype of the underclass as without any agency and tragically blind to its own fate. Dunn appears to be complicit in the process of mythification and regressive misrepresentation that Frank Kermode deems dangerous: the multiplicity of working classes regresses into stereotype.

There are various critics we could turn to, however, in springing to Dunn's defence. An early review suggests that Dunn does not stereotype:

At the time when many of 'the reading public' are pretending to be unaware of class distinctions, Nell Dunn and her husband, Jeremy Sandford, have worked hard to introduce us to those lower-class citizens we so rarely know as neighbours. In fact, through paperbacks and television dramatizations, the Sandfords have even managed to give to these citizens an image of themselves that is less misleading than usual. The word 'lower-class' in not meant patronizingly, but as a statement of fact. The surprise is the Sandfords' work is the unsentimental way in which they treat their characters as equals. (*TLS* 1967: 373)

Twenty years later, Margaret Drabble would actually praise the absence of the author and the absence of moral judgement:

Dunn succeeds wonderfully, and never hits a wrong note. She does not moralise: her characters exist, freely, in their own world, without an ideology, without a superimposed interpretation. *Poor Cow* is a touching, truthful and fresh piece of work, written with an unselfconscious elegance that conceals its craft. And far from being saddening and nauseating, it has an exhilaration, a strange joy. (Drabble 1988: xi)

Dominic Head tentatively approves of Dunn's work, preferring *Poor Cow* to *Up the Junction* because of the improved narrative technique. He notes that we are handled by 'a knowing author', which would chime in with the suggestion that *Poor Cow* forms an improvement upon Dunn's earlier mode (Head 2002: 91). For Head, *Poor Cow* also displays a greater sense of unity because of its clear plot structure and its focus on a single protagonist, the interrogation of form occurring through a dynamic interplay of first- and third-person narration and through the new complexities introduced by the use of the epistolary mode.

Deborah Philips is, however, not impressed by such arguments, and even lays a charge of racism at Dunn's feet: 'While there is liberal awareness that racist remarks should not be condoned, Dunn's narration claims reportage of working-class voices and there is a marked reluctance to change such attitudes' (Philips 2008: 51). Rather than depicting a neutral view of her experiences, Philips argues that Dunn should have taken on a more didactic, moralistic role:

> While Dunn does allow the women characters to take pleasure in sex, and she does allow Joy to articulate her dreams, in her 1960s writings she gives them no means of fulfilling them, and offers no way out of becoming the Poor Cow of the title. The women in these narratives are offered no option beyond the menial factory work or financial dependence upon men, whether through marriage or forms of prostitution. (Philips 2008: 53)

What makes Dunn's work so refreshing, however, is that it resists the pedantic moralizing Leavisite tendency, by suspending judgement and handing responsibility over to the reader.

The important question which has not been posed by any of the critics is that the problem Dunn's work presents is not so much about whether or not she does or does not take a moral, judging position (she does not), but whether this absence of judgement is the product of an active rejection of any moral perspective or of a confused indecisiveness. My claim is that Dunn's texts are fundamentally dependent on a consciously constructed narratological and representative indeterminacy that suspends moral judgement and puts the onus on the reader. Dunn's use of new technology is vital for the construction of this subversive uncertainty, yet so is her undermining of classical tropes and traditional narratology.

To demonstrate this textual indeterminacy, let's first look at the way in which Dunn places her subjects within a classic tragic paradigm. Dunn represents these women as Tragic, for instance, in her juxtaposition of images of 'falling' or downward motion with dreams of flight and freedom that indicate their desire for economic liberation and social mobility. Little Jonny's observation that '[p] oor Mum fall down' (Dunn 1967: 107) becomes symbolic of Joy's inability to claim her agency. The biker Terry hopefully states 'I'd like to be a racing driver or a pilot' (Dunn 1988: 15) only to die in a crash. This creates a sense of downward movement towards a grimy, filthy underworld; Joy's life from early on is set on a downward spiral. There appears no escape from the fate allocated to them by their socio-economic context: the men are invariably punished by being killed or ending up in prison. This sense of tragedy is underscored by the tyrannous causality that operates within the text: the chapters that make up *Poor Cow* have a simple and logical 'progression' from which no escape is possible. The sweet factory where the girls work also operates on disciplinary regime that shows that the place is actually a prison: 'My eyes began to ache in the cold electric light. There are no windows in the room where we have been sitting since eight in the morning earning two-and-fivepence an hour—tenpence an hour for the under eighteens. The siren hoots to call tea time' (Dunn 1988: 26). Both public space and private space are fully wrapped up in the penitentiary logic that comes with poverty and squalor. The very furniture of the domestic environment is inscribed with irony: 'embroidered flowers on the lace curtains twisted hopefully up the sunless window' (Dunn 1988: 10) suggests, cruel in its beauty, that resistance to their plight is futile.

The reader's position vis-à-vis this tragic force beneath the textual operations is complicated and undermined, however, by the black humour and potentially cruel irony in the texts, resulting in a curious indeterminacy. Despite this tragic atmosphere of darkness and squalor, there is comedy and optimism everywhere: 'Ah, well, life's not much without a giggle' (Dunn 1988: 41). As the title *Poor Cow* suggests, Dunn's young women are the subject of at least a degree of authorial parody and mockery, not in the least by the ironic commentary provided by the pop lyrics that the girls hear on the radio and in the pub. The narrator of *Up the Junction* visits the Scala with Pauline who 'is pretty in the dirty café; full of ashtrays and dripping sauce bottles; sugar bowls with clotted lumps of white sugar' (Dunn 1988: 24) and the jukebox comments: '*Oh come on, take me by the hand/And lead me to the land/Of Ecstasy – Oh Ecstasy*' (Dunn 1988: 24). When Joy ponders her predicament shortly after giving birth to Jonny, which she experiences as a form of imprisonment, 'the wireless played:/*I shan't be leavin' any more*' (Dunn

1968: 10). If humour and irony are meant to suggest a hardened attitude of the subjects towards their fate, they fail. It is patently obvious that the girls are aware of the predicament and are guarding themselves through humour. And yet, the use of irony produces an awkward relationship between the author and reader: there is no straightforward contract between them and the characters. The irony mediates between the reader and the text, providing a complexity and a sense of unresolved engagement with the girls, which varies from pity to disgust, yet in the end one response wins out: laughing with the girls in order to subvert the hierarchical structures that attempt to keep them in their place.

New Journalism, voice and audiotape

To resolve this investigation into the nature of Dunn's authenticity, I want to bring to the fore two points. The first is that in any investigation of artistic representation – but especially in that of the representation of the working classes – we should be reminded of a paradox pointed out by William Empson. In his essay on the emergence of a new form of art in the then recently formed Soviet Union, 'Proletarian Literature', collected in *Some Versions of Pastoral* (1935), Empson states:

> To produce proletarian art the artist must be at one with the worker; this is impossible, not for political reasons, but because the artist is never at one with any public [...] It may be that to produce any good art the artist must be somehow in contact with the worker [...] but I am sure it will not be pure proletarian art and I think it will spoil itself if it tries to be. (Empson 1935: 14–15)

Although the artist can never be at one with the people, s/he is able to speak *on behalf of* them. This should make us realize that the necessary gap between those represented and their representation is actually an important dynamo of representative power. It's not simply that the bigger the gap, the better, or, that the greater the fiction the more truthful the result is. Quite the opposite: great fiction can, in Martin Amis's words, 'show us what the imagination can do without the corroboration of experience' (Amis 2001: 129). Similarly, literature derives its originality from an aesthetic equilibrium and its truthfulness from its very *necessity*: certain books need to be written in order to have an effect upon the world, while others do not – they are contingent. The point is that there should always necessarily be a representative gap, and it is exactly this distorting distance and refraction that creates artfulness and knowledge.

The second line of inquiry, which was alluded to in the *TLS* review but subsequently forgotten in literary criticism, is Dunn's use of the tape recorder. Whereas the anonymous *TLS* reviewer decried Dunn's use of new technology, we need to investigate the complex renegotiation of the relationship between the real and representation by audio tape. Maureen Duffy's *The Microcosm* (1966) also started from a series of taped interviews about 'female homosexuality which would delineate the state of the heart in the early sixties when we were presumably in the middle of a sexual revolution towards a more open society [...] To this end I took a tape recorder to a number of women forming a grid of age, class, occupation and geographical spread' (Duffy 1988: 288). Duffy also gives the women's voices she collected a certain critical-creative shape that exploits the democratizing basis that the technology's neutrality allows to produce a radical, subversive political form that harks back to Joyce (see Chapter 4). *The Microcosm* acts as an *Up the Junction* for the gay world by inscribing voices produced by women's bodies in physical books. Like Dunn, Duffy quotes the jukebox to root the novel in the present, while her attention to the record as a recording device also makes the novel temporally much more complex: 'The record is spinning a web of remembered sounds that unites the presents and past, binding the room and all its separate elements into a mesh of memory' (Duffy 1989: 8). Duffy's novel not only creates an intertextual web of written allusions but pays specific attention to the democratic and agentic potential of the human voice.

Dunn's and Duffy's sixties writing is the product of developments in the new nature and form of writing at the time enabled by the portable tape recorder. Dunn's collection of sketches emerged from a collaborative project that involved a collection of newspaper articles, interviews and research on the local South London residents that Dunn and her husband had befriended after moving to Battersea. *Up the Junction* and *The Microcosm* can be read alongside the emergence of New Journalism and Gonzo Journalism in America, such as Truman Capote's *In Cold Blood* (1966) and Hunter S. Thompson's *Fear and Loathing in Las Vegas* (1972), in which the journalist was foregrounded as a character that filters subjective experience rather than presenting objective factual evidence. The British poet, writer and filmmaker Iain Sinclair, who started writing in the late sixties and whose work is obsessed with documenting his own experience through semi-fictional narrators, has fruitfully exploited the idea that there cannot be authenticity because of our subjective and partial experience of the world around us, and because any ordering of experience makes it artificial. Sinclair has erased the difference between his fictional and non-fictional writing because any attempt to create narratives in text results in a form of shaping and thus some form of fictionalization. Marianne DeKoven notes: 'The new journalism still believes in both truth and authenticity. The new journalism rejects the authority and claims to objectivity of the profession of journalism not in order to give up on access to truth but in order to acquire it more legitimately and profoundly' (DeKoven 2004: 91–92).

Dunn and Duffy too sought to breathe life into the factual material they gathered and the voices they recorded from the immediate world around them through creative and experimental narration. It is precisely the violation of traditional journalistic authenticity and the challenging of the border between the fictional and the factual that makes these texts exciting and provocative, while their formal features challenge the traditional novel as a comfortable, middle-class form that reinforced bourgeois traditions and values. More importantly, their work also differs from the male, flamboyantly ego-driven work of Capote and Thompson: these women writers use self-effacing modes in order to foreground women as a collective, underrepresented body.

These writers' use of audio tape technology, which transformed both the representative and imaginative processes, raises the possibility of a new feminocentric style that could reclaim women's bodily materiality. As N. Katherine Hayles explains in *How We Became Posthuman* (1999), the development of the magnetic tape and the mass introduction of the tape recorder, first in the professional world of broadcasting but then also as a mass market commodity available for everyone, transformed perceptions of the human condition. Hayles meditates on the idea that '[a]udiotape opens the possibility that the voice can be taken out of the body and placed into a machine' (Hayles 1999: 207–8). The recording, editing, cutting and transposition onto a material information carrier of the human voice had blissfully alienating effects: the ephemerality of the human voice, normally dissolving in the air and lodging itself into the unreliable memory of other people's minds, was now safely stored onto an external memory storage. This causes a 'disjunction between voice and presence' (Hayles 1999: 210), a new self-awareness (as people could analyse their own thoughts) and new temporal, cognitive and memorial complexities. It also changed the relationship between the voice as a direct 'line' of subvocalized sound into our mind and the body:

> When the voice was displaced onto tape, the body metonymically participated in the transformations that voice underwent in this medium. For certain texts after 1950, the body became a tape-recorder. [...] The tape-recorder acts both as a metaphor for these mutations and as the instrumentality that brings them

about. The taped body can separate at the vertical 'dividing line', grotesquely becoming half one person and half another as if it were tape spliced lengthwise. In a disturbingly literal sense, the tape-recorder becomes a two-edged sword, cutting through bodies as well as through the programs that control and disciplines them. (Hayles 1999: 210–11)

These representative complexities and technological revolutions allow us to renegotiate the hermeneutic processes at work in our assessment of literary artists who were using tape recorders. In Beckett's *Krapp's Last Tape* (1958) the recording device acts as a source of alienation whereby the recording of, listening to and commenting on the past self in the present disperses the always already fragmented self, trapping consciousness in labyrinthine spatial and temporal complexities that have a paralysing and regressive effect. *Krapp* can be read as a fearful fantasy of losing male privilege over technology and control over the self. Indeed, the loss of the heteronormative love relationship between Krapp and Bianca runs analogous to the power that technology has over the memory process and which sees the masculine subject cut up, disempowered.

Dunn's and Duffy's use of the tape recorder is diametrically opposite to Beckett's; they use audio tape as a positive socio-political tool that makes the self more coherent through an appropriation of representative power, helping to imagine women as a collective, coherent presence in the popular consciousness. In Beckett's play the tape recorder is a tool that leads to misunderstandings, yet Dunn and Duffy have a much more open-ended attitude to the technology, which they exploit in a markedly more neutral and objective way, creating a new fictional sensibility that denies the history of male-dominated traditions. *Up the Junction* is certainly inventive and original, light, compact and terse. The episodes cannot simply be characterized as short stories, as Clare Colvin has, because the sketches are not self-contained but derive their meaning from the wider structure in which they are placed. A *TLS* review of Dunn's *Poor Cow* notes, more aptly, that '[t]his is a serious and moving little book, but it is scarcely a novel nor, quite, an original substitute for one' (*TLS* 1967: 373). *Up the Junction* presents us with Dickens's classic journalistic sketches illustrative of everyday London life for the *Monthly Magazine* and the *Evening Chronicle* updated by way of Natalie Sarraute's experimental form of writing, part of the *nouveau roman* movement. Sarraute's Tropisms are short, vivid impressions that show 'inner "movements" [...] which are hidden under the commonplace harmless appearances of every instant of our lives [and which] slip through us on the frontiers of consciousness in the form of extremely rapid sensations' (Sarraute 1967: 6). Whereas Sarraute makes visible the human experience of events by creating a 'hugely amplified present' (Sarraute 1967: 7), Dunn stays on the surface of the material world and employs the temporality of the episodic form and anecdotal style. She does, however, share Sarraute's defamiliarizing strategies, such as sparse language and a disjointed relationship between different entries, and the ability to capture the density and multiplicity of experience in highly charged, poetic language.

In Christine Brooke-Rose's novel *Out* (1964) new forms of technology as means of observation of the world remind us that any forms of observation will distort the result, especially making use of an external tool: 'A tape-recorder might perhaps reveal certain phrases that came and went, leaving no track of error in us. Everything that moves increases risk' (Brooke-Rose 2006: 57). The use of the verb 'might' introduces uncertainty into any method of observing, measuring and calculating objects, movements, distance, speed, etc. Brooke-Rose alludes to Heisenberg's uncertainty principle, which states that there is a fundamental limit to the precision with which pairs of physical properties of molecules can be determined, such as position and speed. Although this is not the same as the 'observer effect', which states that in the act of observation changes to the phenomenon or object will take place, the point Brooke-Rose makes is that any form of tool involved in measurement will distort the relationship between observed and observed; Dunn, Duffy and Spark attest to this as well.

Dunn's modus operandi never assumes that technology exists in unmediated form, and her texts indeed work best whenever she consciously exploits the necessary gap that exists between the original material and the artistic creations that resulted from them and the fact that the tape recorder made the representative process much more complex. Whereas Duffy transforms her material into a Joycean experiment, *Up the Junction* is presented as a loosely connected series of semi-fictional sketches that allow us to approach the collection as a valuable document of its time and as a meditation on realism, authenticity and the increasingly uncertain status of the author. The individual, disjunctive episodes of *Up the Junction* make up a loose narrative, and the subtle links between the separate texts create a sense of coherence. For instance, in an early episode 'The Deserted House' we get a reference to an earlier night when the girls and boys went swimming (Dunn 1988: 33) during an illegal party in an abandoned London Country Council house. During this same party Ruth decides to cheat on Terry, leading to the abortion later in the narrative. These subtle interconnections are linked in the readerly imagination.

However, we also find independent episodes, such as 'Death of an Old Scrubber', which are more tenuously connected to the main story. Of these independent episodes 'The Tally Man' feels the most 'inauthentic' because it is, paradoxically, too authentic: the episode feels like a direct transcript of an interview with an actual loan shark, which has not been edited or reworked aesthetically. We have seen, however, this character mentioned a number of times as a rather benign figure, at first presented only on the periphery. When the tally man figure finally makes its central appearance, the unmediated representation has a clear cautionary function, warning the poor against borrowing from such con men.

The influence of the recorder technology upon Dunn's and Duffy's work has an aesthetic effect which aims to unify the multitude, and works against the centrifugal forces of Beckett's *Krapp*, and other male individualist representations. *The Microcosm* is dominated by the rendition of sometimes pages-long dialogue by various characters, in which we lose track of who's saying what: 'a group of two chatters by the platform where drums and piano beat a kaleidoscope of shifting sound patterns into the air' (Duffy 1989: 169). This confusion is a deliberate strategy by Duffy, who aims to dismantle the bounded identity of the self as biological unit in favour of a new emergent process of democracy at the level of a collective voice collected on her preferred recording device, the novel form. The tape recorder acts as a mediating instrument, distorting yet also offering power of control and ownership for marginalized groups. There is a direct link between the dominance of the embodied female voice and the novel's materiality, in which the tape recorder democratizes because its mobility creates an effect that is both ad hoc and interventionist. As the novel's title suggests, its content is occupied with a multitude of outsiders, brought together through the mosaic technique that formally unites these disparate marginalized denizens.

In a story of London debutantes living in a dormitory in 1945, *The Girls of Slender Means* (1963), Muriel Spark also appropriates tape recorder technology to show how audio tape can be exploited for sexual emancipation. Whereas Dunn and Duffy appropriate this technology as the basis for their writing practice, Spark places the tape recorder in her fiction. The love interest of Joanne, Nicolas Farringdon, comes round to the girls with his recording device to interview them about their attitudes to marriage and sex. This man still has power over the girls, through his privileged position of his possession of, and control over, technology. Nicolas has the power to store the girls' vocalizations on a material carrier, making them into an embodied, material memory which could be the subject of power: 'He was adjusting the tape-recorder, and his words were like air' (Spark 1975: 103), but he can capture the girls' bodies, and erase them. As the girls Greggie and Colie gossip away about their sexual explorations and philosophies, thinking they are being recorded, Joanna keeps silent: 'One does miss sex. The body has a life of its own' (Spark 1975: 105). It turns out, however, that his recorder is empty, emphasizing all the more the power of this technology as 'empty threat', and Nicolas notes facetiously: 'It looks more authentic than ever' (Spark 1966: 106). Spark reminds us then that the introduction of the tape recorder itself becomes an intrusive medium that heightens self-consciousness, and thus moves us away from authenticity:

> 'Not a hush from anybody,' said the warden, meaning, 'Not a sound.' – 'Not a hush,' she said, 'because this instrument of Mr Farringdon's apparently registers the dropping of a pin.'
>
> One of the dormitory girls, who sat mending a ladder in a stocking, carefully caused the needle to fall on the parquet floor, then bent and picked it up again. Another dormitory girl who had noticed the action snorted a suppressed laugh. Otherwise there was the silence but for the quiet purr of the machine waiting for Joanna. (Spark 1966: 106)

The self-conscious engagement with this technology by the girls thus negates male power over them through two distinct strategies. Firstly, through the knowing exploitation of silence, that is, control over the vocalizations of the body by withholding expression of thought. This is also Beckettian and Pinteresque, yet here a woman writer appropriates and exposes this technique in a highly self-conscious manner; in short, it's an exposé of a technique associated with male artists at the centre of *avant-garde* culture. Secondly, Spark also employs a surreal strategy: by literalizing a metaphor ('the dropping of a pin'), she brings to the fore a technology associated with women, suggesting that the traditionally female activity of mending clothes wins out over masculine technology. This powerful machine of bodily inscription, and the entire male-dominated scientific tradition that underlies it, is thus itself silenced.

In *Up the Junction*, just as in Duffy's *The Microcosm*, the group dialogue of the girls in the pub confuses the reader: we're at a loss as to who says what exactly, and this has a profoundly democratic effect. Rather than the individual subject driven by ego, it is the anonymous voice part of the powerful multitude which is celebrated. Minogue and Palmer note the heteroglossic and democratic power of Dunn's text: 'From the speaking persons in Dunn's novel comes a flood of language, but one which is made up of many small streams flowing out and into one another' (Minogue and Palmer 2006: 121). We must go further, however, and argue that such proto-modern Bakhtinian pronouncements are redundant so as to accept Dunn's text as a technological text. In the merging of these vocalizations of these individual girls, we find a transactive cognitive entity that is no longer bounded by the singular identities of the individual women; they are joined together into a group consciousness with a collective agency that transcends the agentic self. As Hayles also suggests, there is a metaphorical exchange taking place between, on the one hand, voice and presence, and, on the other hand, the human body and the tape recorder. Indeed, the self-consciousness which Dunn attributes to her subjects is enabled through the use of a recording device, which allows for analysis of and meditations on the self and the self's thoughts. The subject matter of these texts, as well as their formal innovation, is thus a reflection of a new kind of (inter)subjectivity which the girls are still growing into without being fully aware, increasingly embodying a collective force, together. This is the process from which they, sometimes unconsciously, and sometimes consciously, derive their power. The tape recorder allows this new logic to emerge: the human voice is no longer temporary, fleeting and ephemeral but can exist as materiality that can be stored and retrieved in a mobile device. Unlike, let's say, radio drama, which is dependent on various forms of institutional power, the tape recorder liberated artistic inquiry into the world and democratized access to knowledge, science and technology. This allowed Dunn, Spark and Duffy to explore new modus operandi and new forms of representation that allowed women to empower themselves. This technology works against male privilege in artistic contexts and, in more general terms, against male hegemony in the production of knowledge. The sixties should be viewed as a hinge period when the tape recorder allowed women to appropriate, manipulate and broadcast their own voices and, less inhibited by traditional male power, give their words captured in writing a destiny of their own.

2

Reconsidering Realism

The end of a dying tradition

Muriel Spark's *The Girls of Slender Means* (1963) opens up some questions and contradictions in British fiction of the sixties when it comes to capturing that fraught concept, 'realism'. Set in London just before the end of the Second World War, the novel narrates the story of a group of girls obliged to reside at the May of Teck Club away from their families to work in the capital. They take elocution lessons, follow a strict diet that allows them to 'wriggle sideways through the lavatory window' (Spark 1975: 32), pursue trysts and adopt a dress code in order to propel themselves into the upper middle-class echelon. Like Nell Dunn's young women, their poverty forces them to use their minds and imagination as means of breaking free. Consider the following passage, in which Selina Redwood walks down the staircase in their penitential Victorian residence to meet her date for a night out:

> Poise is perfect balance, an equanimity of body and mind. Down the staircase she floated, as it were even more realistically than had the sad communer with the spirit of Jack Buchanan a few moments ago floated up it. It might have been the same girl, floating upwards in a Shiaparelli rustle of silk with a shining hood of hair, and floating downwards in a slim skirt with a white-spotted blue blouse, her hair now piled high. The normal noise of the houses began to throb again. (Spark 1975: 89–90)

Spark appropriates a cliché from the history of narratology – the Cinderella fairy tale in which a poor, plain girl transforms herself into a mesmerizing beauty – and injects it with Hollywood iconography. Selina's conditioning of her mind and body by means of discursive and bodily discipline gives her the power to project an enchanting image of herself that translates itself into the momentary suspension of the laws of gravity. Spark's fiction exposes how the human mind's conditioning by gendered narratives, whether they be fairy tales or Hollywood films, predetermine our experience.

The reference to Buchanan, a film and musical star and dancer renowned for playing the quintessential Englishman, injects a different mode, and mood. This set-piece indicates that the world constructed within the novel is rooted in a modified form of traditional realism that stands outside the rules of realist representation. Whereas her housemate Pauline, who needs to dress up and act out fairy tale scenarios, is trapped in the projection of herself within a mythical framework, Selina has liberated herself by establishing a version of this fantastic narrative within reality. After stripping away the mythical and male-dominated qualities of fairy tales and Hollywood cinema, we are left with 'a real' in the shape of a novel which, at 142 pages, is just as slim as the girls themselves (see Chapter 3). Spark offers us a complex meditation on the nature of reality in relationship to gender and on the nature of representation. *The Girls of Slender Means* foregrounds and celebrates the ambiguous rhetorical power of narrative to seduce, and warns against the trappings of myth while making the case for a modified form of reality, and realistic representation.

Although the terms 'realism' and 'naturalism' have always been contested, they attracted a very diverse range of meanings during the long sixties. Critics such as Ian Watt, J. P. Stern, Raymond Williams, Frank Kermode, Malcolm Bradbury, David Lodge and Bernard Bergonzi; French thinkers such as Sartre, Roland Barthes, Alain Robbe-Grillet and Michel Foucault; and British writers such as B. S. Johnson, Margaret Drabble, Rayner Heppenstall and Anthony Burgess all contributed to a feral debate. Some defended realism, and some pronounced the death of the realist tradition of novel writing. In her promotion of experimental artists such as Natalie Sarraute and Eugene Ionesco, Susan Sontag argued against realism, while Watt and Williams were concerned with a certain loss of a shared sense of 'real'. In assessments of literary fiction this caused something of an artificial and overworked split between writers obsessed with the nature of representation within their fiction and self-declared realists. During a BBC radio interview entitled 'Novelists of the Sixties' (1967), Margaret Drabble felt the need to defend the realist tradition: 'I don't want to write an experimental novel to be read by people in fifty years, who will say, ah, well, yes, she foresaw what was coming. I'm just not interested. I'd rather be at the end of a dying tradition, which I admire, than at the beginning of a tradition which I deplore' (quoted in Bergonzi 1970: 65).

This makes it sound as if the sixties were dominated by experimental writing that attempted to crush the British tradition of realism. The opposite is true. The main mode of writing remained naturalistic, but was supplemented by high-profile (and now often out of print) experimental writing (see Chapters 5, 6 and 7 in this book) that contributed to establishing a much wider variety of forms of 'realism'. Malcolm Bradbury has acknowledged that the sixties was particularly valuable in the development of fiction for the emergence of a plurality in representational forms: 'Fiction now ranged from the minimalism of Beckett to the flamboyant play of Fowles, from Lessing's fragmentary notebooks to Iris Murdoch's ornate and baroque forms, from Wilson's mimicry to Spark's black irony. But in all these writers the task of fiction remained that of finding a structure for wisdom, or truth, or experience' (Bradbury 1993: 378). Bergonzi's assessment of changing poetics during the sixties, *The Situation of the Novel* (1970), describes the English cultural and literary tradition as essentially conservative, orientated towards the individual, anti-theoretical and liberal, and the English as 'incapable of radical transformations, as the political and cultural revolutions of the seventeenth century, and the industrial revolution of the nineteenth century indicate [...] may have decided against further total transformations, while still being capable of local ones' (Bergonzi 1970: 60). The nineteenth-century tradition of realist writing remained dominant in sixties fiction, the strength of which lies precisely in its formal plurality.

Over the next chapters, I shall explore some of the different attitudes at work in writers' approach, representation of experience and exploration of consciousness. Whereas Chapters 5, 6 and 7 investigate explicit and radical subversions of the realist genre by *avant-garde*, science fiction and early postmodernist authors, this chapter suggests that what is often written off as a conservative form of realism does allow for a series of subtle and politically astute subversions. In fact, authors writing in the realist tradition almost always appropriate traditional realism to bring to the fore important social, cultural and critical issues and to challenge that status quo on behalf of minority groups. Whereas English culture in the immediate post-war times may have seemed 'a happy enclave of tradition and liberalism, a living fragment of the nineteenth century' (Bergonzi 1970: 62), the 1960s opened pathways to a reinvigorated British literature characterized by an increased multiplicity and a sense of a proliferation of different voices dynamically usurping nineteenth-century poetic preoccupations. It is this vividness and adaptability which has allowed British culture to survive its post-imperial identity crisis by reinventing itself during the post-war period. The sixties can therefore be seen as permitting a loosening up of the established rules of representation to reflect changes in the experience of the contemporary and consciousness of the world beyond the subjective self. This chapter argues that the sixties saw the death of the long realist mode inherited from not only from the Victorian age but from the very start of the novel with the Puritan fiction of Defoe's *Robinson Crusoe* (1719). This is not because its realistic language is unable to communicate any longer but because the very idea of a shared community speaking the same language no longer exists. The legitimacy of realist modes of representation is undermined not because there is intrinsically anything wrong with its aesthetic but because the subject which it traditionally represented – the organic society – is itself transformed beyond recognition.

A short history of 'realism': Realism as revolt

Forms of representation came under intense scrutiny in the sixties because of the increasing socio-cultural complexity and fragmentation of society in the post-war era, the diversification of modes of perception caused by the increased accessibility of then new media such as television and the changing relationship between the individual and the social fabric. These changes triggered debates about the traditional 'function' of the novel, originally associated with the rising bourgeoisie during the heyday of capitalism in the nineteenth century, as a means of keeping together society as a collective and organic whole. Throughout the twentieth century realistic forms of representation have become frowned upon as a conservative vehicle for reinforcing traditional values against anxieties about fragmentation. In many academic circles radical and disturbing literature had become primarily associated with fiction as representation of a new psychological reality, ranging from the high Modernist texts of Joyce's *Finnegan's Wake* (1939), Virginia Woolf's *The Waves* (1931), the poetry of Mina Loy and Djuna Barnes's *Nightwood* (1936) to the high postmodernist fiction of Italo Calvino's *If on a winter's night a traveller* (1981), Salman Rushdie's *The Satanic Verses* (1988), and more recently Tom McCarthy's *C* (2010) and Eimar McBride's *A Girl Is a Half-formed Thing* (2013). The key idea is that in order to disturb the reader both the subject matter as well as the form in which the subject is rendered must be subversive and, some would argue, unnecessarily 'difficult'.

One could argue that this reductive, dismissive attitude towards realism is directed against the origins and very idea of the novel as a form just as complex and diverse as its history, ranging from Cervantes's sprawling metafictional 'novel' *Don Quixote* (1605 and 1615) to epistolary novels such as Samuel Richardson's *Pamela* (1740) and from Jane Austen's work to J. M. Coetzee's subtle reading of realism in *Elizabeth Costello* (2003). Raymond Williams has commented illuminatingly on these issues. In his chapter 'Realism and the Contemporary Novel' in *The Long Revolution* (1961), Williams reminds us that since the Renaissance the traditional function of realism (not to be conflated with the painterly term 'naturalism', a term which has a similarly complex historical evolution often reduced to only a descriptive technique) was as a means of subversion, which, in the eighteenth century, was further underscored by the perception of the term itself:

> A common adjective used with 'realism' was 'startling', and, within the mainstream of 'ordinary, everyday reality' a particular current of attention to the unpleasant, the exposed, the sordid could be distinguished. Realism thus appeared as in part a revolt against the ordinary bourgeois view of the world; the realists were making a further selection of ordinary material which the majority of bourgeois artists preferred to ignore. Thus 'realism', as a watchword, passed over to the progressive and revolutionary movements. (Williams 1971: 301)

It has continued to do so, as Nell Dunn's texts underscore, because minorities that are 'repressed' or written out of the social discourse benefit more from re-inscribing their plight into the social fabric by using a language that is accessible to all, rather than by employing radical poetics that exclude those it aims to represent. Influenced by the 'socialist realism' of artists and critics in the Soviet Union, Williams argues that what is considered realist and non-realist in analyses of representation in the west are in fact connected via their use of 'principled and organized selection' (Williams 1971: 303) in capturing human experience. Williams goes on to argue against claims that representations associated with the nineteenth-century European novel, usually derided as 'realist', have disappeared: the subject matter (contemporary issues), shocking and offensive topics, the traditional intention of realism to investigate psychological states by using realistic description are still the creative dynamos behind late fifties and sixties fiction.

More importantly, Williams goes on to explore the problems of what he considers to be a formal hiatus that prevents the modern novel from being 'the kind of novel which creates and judges the quality of a whole way of life in terms of the qualities of persons' and in which 'neither the society nor the individual, is there as a priority' (Williams 1971: 304). Examples of this balanced connection include Gustave Flaubert's *Madame Bovary* (1857), the work of Charles Dickens, Dostoevsky's *Crime and Punishment* (1866) and George Eliot's *Middlemarch* (1874). Williams claims that this traditional form split into two opposing novel-types in the twentieth century, the social novel (divided up into 'social documentary' and 'social formula') and the personal novel (divided up into 'personal documentary' and 'personal formula').

Williams laments the increasing dominance of, fiction from the 'personal formula' category as a sign that the 'gap between our feelings and social observation is dangerously wide' (Williams 1971: 311). The key question this raises for Williams is whether the personal formula novels evoke a changed reality or 'whether they are they are in fact symptoms of some very deep crisis in experience' (Williams 1971: 312). Williams echoes the Marxist critic Georg Lukács, who in his essay 'The Ideology of Modernism' (1955) vilified the high Modernist writing of Kafka and Joyce for its creation of supposedly anti-Aristotelean worlds based on what he termed 'bad infinity', wherein any notion of objective reality was displaced by an unverifiable subjective experience. As Williams acknowledges, if the very nature of social relationships is changing through an increased individualization at the expense of social cohesion in a new context in which truth itself has become conditional, the traditional social novel becomes an archaic mode of representation.

Williams ultimately wishes to open his criticism up to discovering new forms of realism able to bridge the gap between the personal and the social in a new communicable form: 'It is certain that any effort to achieve a contemporary balance will be complex and difficult, but the effort is necessary, a new realism is necessary, if we are to remain creative' (Williams 1971: 316). Here I would like to start by offering readings of two authors who have usually been described as conservative realists in order to show that they too harnessed the subject matter and form of their work to rethink the inherited realist tradition of the nineteenth-century European novel in the light of a changing social constellation.

Not an alarmist man:
Angus Wilson's *The Old Men at the Zoo* and *Late Call*

Angus Wilson (1913–91) came to writing relatively late, at the age of thirty-three, and made his name in the 1950s as explorer and critic of mythical notions of Englishness. He was the last of six children in an upper middle-class family rapidly tumbling down the social ladder due to his father's reckless investments and expensive tastes. The Wilson family spent two years of his early childhood in Durban, South Africa, and upon the family's return to England they lived a shabby hotel life in London's South Kensington, an experience Wilson was to draw upon extensively for his satirical portrait of middle-class unfortunates in social free fall.

Wilson is a self-declared realist who takes his cue from the great nineteenth-century writers, whose work provided him with a set of representative rules which he used as a form of protection, especially during the nervous breakdown which prompted him to write. In his series of lectures on his own life as a writer, *The Wild Garden* (1963), he states:

> I sought to protect my ignorance by many devious means; for example, I had always been, and still am, addicted to the great Victorian novelists, especially to Charles Dickens. The conflicts of the novels of Dickens and Balzac [...] so frequently clearer on the symbolic under-level than on the surface story level, seem to me to have not only a remarkable social and moral insight but also a cosmic significance [...] I used always to be very impatient of more fastidious critics who took exception to the melodrama or the sentimentality – particularly the sentimentality attaching to childish or childlike innocence; these were such small prices to pay for the intensity, fierceness, of the struggle portrayed. During the time of my mental illness I battled strongly on behalf of this Victorian sentimentality, relishing it rather than making allowance for it as an inadequacy. Reading, as I read then, almost as a drug, had a powerful illusory effect. I have no doubt that I was helping myself preserve my illusions with the assistance of falsities of my chosen reading. (Wilson 1963: 22)

We hear echoes of Nell Dunn, who also noted that she used fiction as a means of returning to a childhood state, but Wilson, writing in the confessional mode, is more self-conscious and critical of the complex intellectual processes at play. Wilson's fiction became a means of finding ways of disrupting the social values that he associated with this supposedly consolatory fiction. One way of doing this was to confront middle-class readers with the poverty-stricken genteel types he had encountered during his upbringing, a dreaded image of what the bourgeoisie could become: 'It is the more peculiar, or, at any rate, unacceptable to respectable middle-class readers, because these raffish characters lay claim to, indeed can claim purely by class, social positions and ranks that the middle-class reader prefers to associate with less vulgar, less meretricious, more disciplined, more "responsible" morality' (Wilson 1963: 38). Although his early works, including his short stories, use a classic model, Wilson was quick to move towards a mode that allowed him to be critical of his own realism.

The Old Men at the Zoo (1961) is a comic, remarkably surreal and strange state of the nation novel for someone often considered a realist writer in the liberal humanist tradition of Dickens, George Eliot and E. M. Forster. It's a move away from the social realism that dominated fiction in the 1950s, when Wilson wrote the short story collection *The Wrong Set* (1949) and novels including *Hemlock and After* (1952) and *Anglo-Saxon Attitudes* (1956). The novel is set in the near future and narrates the story of Simon Carver, a servile secretary at the London Zoo in Green Park, who experiences a crisis after an accident whereby which a young attendant, Filson (in whose name we already hear a self-conscious echo of the author's name), is trampled to death by a giraffe after the animal kicks him in the testicles. Various obstacles precede the story, beginning with a disclaimer by the author: 'The events described here as taking place in 1970–3 are utterly improbable. Our future is possibly brighter, probably much more gloomy. All references to the administration of the London Zoo and to its staff are entirely imaginary' (Wilson 1964: 6). Wilson used this disclaimer to warrant against any libel action by London Zoo but possibly also to pay homage to the comical action of Stella Gibbons's *Cold Comfort Farm* (1932), which presents similar textual obstacles before the novel begins. Wilson also uses and ironizes science fiction and the dystopian novel, which was being appropriated by mainstream literary authors such as Anthony Burgess: just as in Burgess's *The Wanting Seed*, nature is largely gone after 'the final legal abolition of the Green belt zones in 1967' (Wilson 1964: 115).

This temporal conditioning is followed by a Dramatis personæ list of the 'Principal Characters' (Wilson 1964: 7), the theatrical and fictional technique adding to a mechanism whereby the potential realism of the novel itself is further undercut. The opening of Chapter One playfully discusses points of view:

> I opened the large central window of my office room to its full on that fine early May morning. Then I stood for a few moments, breathing in the soft, warm air that was charged with the scent of white lilacs below. The graceful flamingos, shaded from flushed white to a robust tinned salmon, humped and coiled on their long stilts; a Florida pelican picked and nuzzled comically with its orange pouched bill among its drab brownish wing feathers; the herring gulls surprised me, as they did every day, by their size and their viciously hooked beaks. To command one's chosen view of the brute creation was one of the unexpected advantages I had secured by taking on the newly instituted post of administrative secretary of the London Zoo three years before. (Wilson 1964: 9)

Comically mocking the classic trope of the window frame as metaphoric measure of the sense of reality of the fictional world we are peering into, the passage calls to mind E. M. Forster's *A Room with a View* (1908) and Virginia Woolf's *Mrs Dalloway* (1925), which in the opening pages takes the very door out of its frame and plunges us into Lukács's 'bad infinity'. There is a joke here about the position of the novelist, and the 'command' s/he has over worlds created in fiction and the 'brute creation' that is the chaotic 'real': the reader is warned that we are finding ourselves in a comically heightened real that undermines the God-Author. This 'message' is, however, packaged in a beautiful Austenian line redolent in particular of the opening sentence of *Pride and Prejudice* (1813). Wilson's revenge on the seeming chaos and 'inertia bred by a surfeit of crises' (Wilson 1964: 89) produced by rapid social change is thus stemmed by a heightened prose style: the bathetic mode sees sublime prose collapsing into a silly, absurd style.

The first chapter, which narrates the giraffe incident, turns out to be as self-reflective as the title, 'A Tall Story', makes us suspect it will be, when Carver states: 'I could not help saying: "You should mean a short paragraph headed 'A Tall Story'"' (Wilson 1964: 30). This is a self-reflective joke that mocks uses of self-reflexiveness, the first of many reflections on an increasingly mediatized world. The subsequent cover-up of the death leads to questions about animals in captivity and the nature of man's power over other species, triggering a power struggle within the old Victorian establishment, the old men of the title. While the director of the zoo, Edwin Leacock, wants to create 'an open Zoo where the animal are free' (Wilson 1964: 39), his counterpart, the curator Falcon wants to return to the original ideal of the Victorian Zoo. An inspiring 'telescreen' documentary on the giraffe incident results in the Stretton Experiment, a British National Reserve Park at the fictional estate of Stretton on the Welsh border, in which a simulacral version of a pastoral England is created. This reminds us of the Julian Barnes's postmodern state of the nation novel *England, England* (1998), which warns against a regressive denial of English decline when a theme park based on a pastoral England is built on a desert of abandoned coal mines.

The future of human ecology

Throughout sixties fiction we find the zoo as a metaphor that stands for the world itself. In Angela Carter's *Several Perceptions* (1968), the protagonist breaks into a zoo to free a badger. The act of releasing animals resonates on several levels. It should first be read, literally, as criticism of the imprisonment of the (human) animal, counteracting an institution that emerged in the nineteenth century as part of the mission to categorize the world. We find embedded the promise of freedom of the human subject itself, at least in the imagination; for Carter it forms a displaced affirmation of autonomy that chimes in with Sartre's existentialism, while the title connects her novel with David Hume's phenomenological legacy. Secondly, the individual's curious appropriation of animal suffering can be read as a foregrounding the animal's undermined well-being, but also of highlighting the individual's self-importance and self-righteousness. Empathy with animals affirms the centring of the self in more general terms.

In 'Time, Memory and Inner Space' (1963) Ballard uses the zoo to argue for the concept of 'Inner Space':

> In many respects this fusion of past and present experiences, and of such disparate elements as the modern office buildings of central London and an alligator in a Chinese zoo, resembles the mechanisms by which dreams are constructed, and perhaps the great values of fantasy as a literary form is its ability to bring together apparently unconnected and dissimilar ideas. To a large extent all fantasy serves this purpose, but I believe that speculative fantasy, as I prefer to call the more serious fringe of science fiction, is an especially potent method of using one's imagination to construct a paradoxical universe where dream and reality become fused together, each retaining its own distinctive quality and yet in some way assuming the role of its opposite, and where by an undeniable logic black simultaneously becomes white. (Ballard 1996: 200)

Written in 1963, the article pre-empts Michel Foucault's discussion of the heterotopia. Derived from a Borges story, heterotopias are spaces formed of many different orders: they are incongruous, or paradoxical, because they are sites where transgressive acts of many kinds occur, producing many, sometimes contradictory meanings. They may be sites which are uncertain or ambivalent because of the multiplicity of social meanings attached to them. According to Foucault there exist many different forms of heterotopia, but their common value is rooted in their ability to break up the illusion of a seemingly rational and ordered locus originating in a language that produces an unquestioned sense of reality: ideal heterotopias 'contest the very possibility at its source; they dissolve our myths and sterilize the lyricism of our sentences' (Foucault 2002: xix).

At first sight Wilson's writing is a far cry from Foucault, yet he too distances himself from Victorian scientific and sociological methods. When looking out over a group of members of the public, Wilson's Carver comically observes that he is no longer able to categorize people according to their physical characteristics – a jibe at the Victorian obsession with phrenology:

> I didn't believe any more in physiognomy. In any case who can nowadays play such a social-categorizing parlour game? There are only three classes now – the elite with its boasted open end, the great prosperous mass, and the handicapped

or handicapped-prone. Age, arrogance, illness or inefficiency at mental arithmetic alone qualify for descent to this last class. (Wilson 1964: 52)

Wilson's fiction thus observes how the Victorian categorization of society has radically changed, but, even though *Old Men* engages with the changing relationship between man and nature in a comical way, Wilson is worried about our loss of contact with nature. In *The Wild Garden*, written in the run up to *The Old Men*, he writes:

> With the advance of human civilization zoos, or at best natural reserves, may be the only means of preserving wild species for the refreshment, the wonder and the humbling of human spectators; above all, for the instruction of humans in other patterns and rhythms of life, and no less importantly as a recognition and some recompense for our hubris in imposing our will upon the creature world. [...] Zoos and reserves, botanical gardens, even suburban gardens, need administration, the exercise of power, discrimination. Emotionally I can never feel such discrimination in any sphere [...] to be other than a necessary but distorting corrupting duty. [...] And of course, this need at one and the same time for contemplation and social activity, for a secularized form of grace and good works, confronts the humanist as a paradox that can only be imperfectly solved at every level of life. (Wilson 1963: 87–88)

Passages such as these evidence the subtlety of Wilson's thought. That this type of thinking is a traditional literary trope can be shown by the popularity of another important book at the time that helped to rethink the man–nature relationship, Leo Marx's *The Machine in the Garden* (1964), which traces a tradition of eco-critical thinking about the ways in which nature and pastoral tradition were disrupted by new technologies. Examples in American and British literature include the smashing of Huckleberry Finn's raft by a steam boat, D. H. Lawrence's 'The Odour of Chrysanthemums' (1911), in which a horse is startled by a train, and the motor car which kills a cat in E. M. Forster's *Howards End* (1910). Wilson was aware of this ecocritical tradition, as he suggests in his knowing rejection of the prelapsarian world that lies beyond the mythologies of loss:

> The Zoo [...] is trying to present its animals in 'natural conditions', [and] is only a new version of the 'wild garden'. The zoological reserve, aiming to freeze the evolutionary battle at some moment of rich variety and pleasing balance, has affinities with the garden cut out from the wild (but as though this had been frozen at a certain moment of pioneer advance). The solution [...] suggested in these symbols of gardens and wild life reserves is an artificial one, sentimental perhaps, certainly utopian and therefore to some degree absurd. Yet I do not

easily see how a resolution of a dualism so vital to civilized man can be other than artificial. [...] It has [...] been solved for Christians and many other theists by various mythologies of the creation of Eden, but a Lord of Paradise other than man does not convince me. (Wilson 1963: 89)

All these earlier quibbles and musings about power and agency by the 'old men' driven by backward-lookingness turn out to be insignificant when in Chapter Four Britain is invaded by the fascist United Europe movement. The leader of the fascists, Blanchard-White (doubly white) enlists Carver, who unwittingly follows his demonic plans for the zoo, which sinisterly echo the nostalgia of both Falcon and Leacock. Interestingly then, the merits of changes to the social, cultural and ecological landscape in the sixties win out over the mythologizers of loss, equated with the romantic fascist mythologies of *Blut und Boden* and essentialist thinking about nationhood in relationship to individual identity.

Wilson's *Late Call* (1964) is a tamer and less frivolous, and a more subtle work. The novel narrates the story of the hotel manager Sylvia Calvert, who after her retirement moves into the home of her middle-aged and middle-class son's family, together with her pompous husband, the former army Captain Arthur. Her son, Harold, has recently lost his wife, Beth, to cancer and moved to what he considers an ideal environment: a New Town. The infrastructure of the Milton Keynes-like New Town, the fictional Carshall, facilitates 'an experiment in a *new* way of living' (Wilson 2001: 95). A struggle ensues between the traditional English way of life, mediated through Sylvia, and newly emerging innovative impulses, represented by the democratic and egalitarian ideology of Harold. This ideological dialectic between English liberalism and a rather pushy and repressive form of democracy and openness comes to a head during the finale, when Sylvia manages to reinvent herself through a literal and figurative move to a room of her own.

Although now hardly read or taught, Wilson has proven an enduring influence on some of the finest writers of the late twentieth- and twenty-first centuries, including his student Ian McEwan, Monica Ali (whose *Brick Lane* (2003) modelled the awakening of Nazneen on *Late Call*), and his biographer, the novelist Margaret Drabble, whose renegotiation of textual representation of the real will be investigated next. Anthony Burgess too appreciated the subtleties of the novel but also noted that in the refinement of its depiction of human character and the struggle elderly people such as Calvert have in escaping the various ideological and religious conditionings that have shaped their character '*Late Call* takes bigger chances than the other novels: it plunges into a world which Mr. Wilson knows to be heartbreakingly ephemeral, out of which the deracinated Sylvia Calvert chooses some of the rags which clothe the emptiness of her retirement' (Burgess 1981: 34).

Late Call is interesting because it tries to understand the new impact of the new town on community. Its aesthetic, and the fact that its prologue is set in 1911, should remind us of *Howards End* (1910), another analysis of similar social concerns connected to spatial changes. In Forster's novel, the upper middle-class embodiment of humanism and old money, the Schlegel sisters, lose their home in London, where town houses are being carved up and turned into apartments. But the novel's main concern about changing space and social relationship is with the creation of suburbs to the north of London in Hertfordshire, made possible thanks to technological innovations in public transport. The train station in Howards End is described by Forster as follows: 'The station, like the scenery, like Helen's letters, struck an indeterminate note. Into which country will it lead, England or Suburbia? It was new, it had island platforms and a subway, and the superficial comfort exacted by business men. But it held hints of local life, personal intercourse' (Forster 1992: 33). This new England is 'indeterminate', its nature uncertain, and new, yet is able to somehow incorporate the green and pleasant land within it – or, at least within Forster's novel, which tried to create a textual space where such major changes in society could be humanized.

Wilson's new town is described as a 'little microcosm'; Carshall acts not only as a kind of laboratory for understanding the *zeitgeist* but also as a psychogeography for analysing the changing nature of space in relationship to both the human mind and the collective spirit. This new way of constructing the built environment was introduced a year after the Second World War in 1946, an extension of the Garden Cities created in the early twentieth century by Ebenezer Howard, who said that 'Town and Country must be married, and out of this joyous union will spring a new hope, a new life, a new civilisation' (Howard 1985: 11). The thirteen post-war New Towns were highly rationalized places that would be made into civilized, attractive and agreeable places to live through a process of top-down planning. These New Towns, starting with Crawley, were structured with an industrial area separated from residential neighbourhoods, which would all have their own public park, shopping facilities and recreational, schooling and other civic facilities: one of the problems, then, was that there were no unifying sites such as market squares in a town centre, so that a fragmentation and division of the population (in the imagination) took place. Yet the appeal of New Towns was strong: in the decade after 1961 more

than 30 per cent of British population movement was from the principal cities
and towns to New Towns.

Late Call pits different points of view on the New Town against each other.
Harold is a great believer in 'serious social experiment[s] like New Towns'
(Wilson 2001: 94) and sees them as a utopian space where new social values can
be put into practice beyond the rigidity of the English class system. Wilson thus
echoes criticisms of London found in the work of writers such as J. G. Ballard and
Doris Lessing, who argue that the metropolis perpetuates a Victorian ideology
through its very material structure (see Chapter 5). Janice Morphet observes
that 'although Wilson had an underlying sympathy for the New Towns, he also
saw some of their potential disadvantages. He recognized the need for those
with vision, but he also saw the kinds of tension associated with this degree
of change' (Morphet 2003: 56). For Harold, Carshall is a democratizing site
that mirrors the sixties desire for equalizing social hierarchies in a 'rhizomic'
space. But not everyone is convinced. In an echo of Forster, Harold's neighbour,
Muriel Bartlett, notes that '[w]e've helped to make the place, we intend to keep
its character' (Wilson 2001: 95), while another, Chris Milton, notes that 'Some
of us have put a lot of money into this place' (Wilson 2001: 95). And indeed,
Carshall is not the fluid place that seamlessly merges organically with new
structures in post-war society and burgeoning capitalist democracy: 'The New
Town, though it merged into the country, was yet cut off from it by a system of
lanes and roads that turned back on themselves and eventually return to Town
Centre, as inevitably, by contrast, the paths in a maze lead away from its core'
(Wilson 2001: 180). Despite its utopian pretence, the New Town thus forms
a blockage between old and new ideas of community rather than achieving a
Fosterian connection. Sylvia Calvert is confused by these different opinions
as well as the space itself, and retreats into a pastoral idyll which she finds
in the countryside, taking long walks in Goodchild's Meadow and 'Gorman's
Wood, a copse preserved to enrich and soften the lives of those who lived on
the estate' (Wilson 2001: 175). Yet, in the end she is able to liberate herself
from the security of her old values, as does Harold's son, Ray, who comes out
as gay, to which Harold responds in an old-fashioned and dogmatic manner;
his libertarian and progressive viewpoint is surprisingly limited and narrow, as
well as self-serving.

The novel ends with a chapter called 'Harvest', when Sylvia Calvert moves
into her own flat near the old Carshall Town Centre, and experiences a spiritual
renaissance. Her husband dies suddenly, which frees her from the ideology of
this patronizing military man, and her son Harold receives a comeuppance of

sorts. Wilson restores a sense of organicity through the novel's composition, which positions the space of literature as the imaginary site where older forms of community values can be connected with a late-capitalist forms of living. Just as the New Towns are a highly artificial construct, Wilson leaves the sixties with a sense that the novel needs to engage with equally artificial forms in order to do its job – the keeping together of an increasingly fragmented society – properly.

A return to the middle ground: Margaret Drabble

The author whose work was inspired by Angus Wilson, Margaret Drabble, has written works that allow us to investigate the ways in which the sixties sparked a reorganization of the realist aesthetic. Drabble's own interest was in 'a reconsideration and revaluation of the English puritan tradition' strongest in ' "liberal" intellectuals and the northern lower middle class' (Myer 1974: 15). Her early work presents us with the coming of age of intelligent, middle-class 'heroines' confronted with a modern age with shifting social and cultural values. One important traditional institution at stake is marriage and motherhood, which is often depicted as an imprisoning structure whose function is to reaffirm, for better *and* for worse, the order of things.

In her early study of Drabble, *Puritanism and Permissiveness* (1974), Valerie Grosvenor Myer identifies her as a reluctant puritan, noting that she 'is the most contemporary of novelist: a whole generation of women readers identifies with her characters, who they feel represent their own problems' (Myers 1974: 13). Her writing has a representative function: she speaks on behalf of a generation of women who 'were preoccupied with the difficulties of fulfilment and self-definition in a man's world, the conflicting claims of selfhood, wifehood and motherhood, long before the women's lib movement really got going' (Myers 1974: 13).

The values of Margaret Drabbe's heroines – hard work, earnestness, piety, mindfulness, stoicism and asceticism, the negation of instant gratification – run counter to the rebellious ideas at the heart of swinging sixties. Constant self-scrutiny ran strong in the puritan tradition, creating a doubling of self diametrically opposed to the one-dimensional self flattened out by commodification in the capitalist realm. Drabble sends this moralizing Victorian puritanism, which finds its literary equivalent in the Great Tradition of F. R. Leavis, on collision course with a new sensibility and the new social and sexual permissiveness, which itself turned out to be more complex that proponents of libertinism argued. In the last couple of years, there has been a growing recognition that 'permissiveness' is not such a simple concept as it once seemed and that society is now not so permissive as it might have imagined. Margaret Drabble grasped and explored these truths before they became fashionable currency during postmodernity.

In early novels such as *A Summer Bird-Cage* (1962), *The Garrick Year* (1964) and *The Millstone* (1965) Drabble relates her subject matter both with the intentions of realism – by presenting stories that are highly likely to take place in the world 'out there' – and in the language of realism, that is to say, in which there is a clearly unified interior relationship between the signifier and the signified. I investigate two of Drabble's most successful sixties novels, *Jerusalem the Golden* (1967) and *The Waterfall* (1969), in order to illustrate the ways in which this writer, while not directly influenced by French deconstructionists, challenges her own novelistic subject matter and form by means of subtle reinventions of traditional naturalistic techniques and an increasing interest in the potential of metafiction. This is why Lorna Sage took the title of Drabble's novel *The Middle Ground* (1980) as a symbol of what writers such as Iris Murdoch, Edna O'Brien and Drabble were trying to achieve: to inhabit 'the realist territory of the nineteenth century novel tradition' (Sage 1992: 72) while self-consciously exploring 'self-division, the multiplicity of ways to be' (Sage 1992: x). This is a humanist, Fosterian undertaking that tries to connect, and recuperate, the rapid changes in society with the values and moral paradigms afforded by the long history of humanism.

In *Jerusalem the Golden* (1967) naming, as a device for establishing a real world in which the world that is ostensibly evoked without much problems posed by textuality, is probed and renegotiated as means of subversion. The novel narrates the story of a young, educated and middle-class girl from the industrial north, Clara Maugham, who moves to London after winning a scholarship to London University. This provides her with an opportunity to escape the repressive domestic climate shaped by her surly and snobbish mother; when she meets the eccentric and cultured Wilcoxian Denham family of poets and painters, they offer her a window onto a new artistically charged world in which she is able to feature as a character she considers more fictive than real.

Maugham's transformation is determined by a tension between the theatrical and cultured world of London and the down-to-earth reality associated with the north and the stifling domestic climate created by her mother. Although Clara's idea of the world and people are clearly set up as partly based on fictions, they are fictions of a particular kind:

Her experience of life as a child was so narrow that she had no way of telling the possible from the absurd. And even as a child she wanted things to be possible. She read with avidity the endless cosy adventures of wealthy children on farms and in smugglers' caves and country houses, but she found built into them a warning against too much belief. (Drabble 1969: 32–33)

Drabble's narrator sets up a paradox. Clara had an innate desire for things to be possible and probable, in that they would conform to her experience of the world; yet because her northern world is experienced as suffocatingly narrow, she is instinctively aware that the limitedness of experience provided by that world gives her little material for understanding the limits of the real. This in turn triggers an anxiety regarding the imagination, despite her consumption of clearly bourgeois fiction. Drabble's foregrounding of this paradox is a subtle way of thinking about the changing relationship between fiction and reality.

One of the means by which the tradition of the realist novel has aimed to close the gap between the represented world and the language used for representation is by giving characters ordinary, 'real' names. If a writer wants to create a sense of verisimilitude, inconspicuous names are selected. Such names may still draw the reader's attention to the symbolic and literary meanings of a character: names are never neutral nor without any meaning: any act of bestowing a name invests that character with a linguistically produced historical context, and class and geographical associations. Naming thus operates a very complex and subtle system of meaning: even a common name such as Alex in Burgess's *A Clockwork Orange* (1962) has an allegorical significance: 'a-lex' means 'outside the law'. However, in the case of emblematic naming this process is pushed to often satirical or parodical extremes, and in doing so ruptures the rules of realist representation. In Aphra Behn's play *The Rover* (1677) the emblematic caricature names say much about the characters: the cavalier Willmore is driven by his lust for women and drink; Blunt is as thick as his name suggests; and the ironically named Angellica Bianca, the 'white angel', is in fact a courtesan. In more recent times, Martin Amis's *Money* (1982) the name of the protagonist, John Self, forms a highly ironical, parodic sign of self-obsessed times.

Drabble meditates on, and partially questions, traditional realism by foregrounding her use of names in the novel. Clara, whose own name reflects the sober, northern realist context she hails from, ponders on the names of her new friends:

She wondered what her mother would have made of Amelia, Magnus, Gabriel, Clelia and Annunziata, let alone Sebastian and Candida. She hardly knew what she thought of them herself; she could not tell whether they were names exotic to the point of absurdity, or whether they were strange to her alone. She thought it possible, perfectly possible, that many people in the world might hear such names, and be seized not by the faintest impulse to laugh or to admire: and yet on the other hand she had sensed from time to time a certain mockery of the family itself toward itself, and had not Mrs Denham herself expressed a doubt that with Annunziata she might have gone too far? What she could not grasp was the notion that a family might deliberately, and without guilt or irresponsibility, choose for its children names not wholly suitable or conventional, for the sake of a whim or an association, or for the sake of beauty and charm. The use of a singularly beautiful or portentous name had always been derided by her mother; names like Helen, Grace, or Alexander had been known to cause ill-placed mirth. But how, with so fine a sense of distinction and significance, her own mother could have called her Clara, she could neither understand nor forgive. (Drabble 1969: 122–23)

Drabble's passage acknowledges that the author is working in the realist tradition by pointing to the names of the characters, but in the very act of questioning the (meaning of) names Drabble sends the novel into the realm of the self-reflective. Indeed, Clara's reference to the 'possible' destabilizes the conventional stable sense of giving meaning to fictional characters. Clara, whose own name we associate with 'clarity' and transparent representation, understands that the limitedness of her knowledge of the world epistemological uncertainty. Again, sixties fiction moves us from singularity of perception to multiplicity and subjectivity, to potentiality. Clara's new London life is characterized by plurality: whereas in her own home conversation is singular and often silenced by the television, at the Denhams 'there seemed to be no end to current and interesting talk, no possibility of silence, so diverse and rich were the possible permutations, the possible connections: in a room such as theirs, moreover, there could be and frequently were several conversations carried at once' (Drabble 1969: 126). Like Helen Schlegel in *Howards End*, she falls in love with an entire family, yet, whereas the Schlegel sibling falls for a dynamic family of capitalists, Maugham falls for these cultured and civilized humanists.

Confessions of the divided self: *The Waterfall*

Drabble's *The Waterfall* (1969) is an insightful investigation into female psychology undergoing a crisis. It narrates the story of the poet Jane Gray, who begins an affair with the husband of her best friend, James, after the birth of her second child, Bianca. Jane and Malcolm Gray's relationship is described as follows: 'After a year of engagement, Malcolm and I were married. We had known each other for two years, and had never given each other nasty surprises. Safe, one would think: prudent. A responsible marriage, not rashly undertaken' (Drabble 1980: 95). This sensible, rational approach to love is a recipe for disaster and reminds us of a similar investigation in Doris Lessing's short story, 'To Room Nineteen' (1963).

Like Clara in *Jerusalem*, Gray has 'too little grasp on probability' (Drabble 1980: 127); yet the identity crisis that follows her divorce has a much profounder effect on her sense of self, which is split between the sense of herself as a mother and the potential of her own emancipated, agentic self. Jane's split consciousness, which invokes R. D. Laing's *The Divided Self* (1960), is described in the following long passage:

> I could have turned myself into one of those mother women who ignore their husbands and live through their children. But with me, this did not happen; my ability to kiss and care for and feed and amuse a small child merely reinforced my sense of division – I felt split between the anxious intelligent woman and the healthy and efficient mother – or perhaps less split than divided. I felt that I lived on two levels, simultaneously, and there was no contact, no interaction between them: on one level I could operate well, even triumphantly, but on the other I could condemn myself, endlessly, for my inadequacy and my faults. [...] I sound as if I am trying to describe a classic schizoid state, or a state of alienation, but I know that it was not this that I suffered from: it was something less severe, less acute. Less certifiable. I felt, all the time, a possibility of reconciliation; my mind did not reject my body, not my body my mind, and indeed these words ill describe the states of levels on which I lived, for the bodily level was in many ways more profound, more human, more myself. I didn't feel a lack of identity, really. I felt an unacceptable excess. (Drabble 1980: 103–4)

Jane Gray makes a deliberate distinction between 'split' and 'divided' in order to engage with, but also distance herself from, Laing's experimental psychology. *The Divided Self* studies the impact of societal alienation in the modern world, which creates a schizophrenic breakdown when one experiences oneself (or others) as not real. Laing observes that the common position is that: 'A man may have a sense of his presence in the world as a real, alive, whole, and, in a temporary sense, a continuous person' (Laing 1965: 39). However, when what he calls 'ontological insecurity' occurs through depersonalization, the subject may attempt to invent a personality. Laing points to Kafka and Beckett to show that there is a vein of (Modernist) literature that explores the implication of understanding the self as contradictory and non-continuous. Drabble's character distances herself from Laing's male-centred psychopathological discourse by noting that it is not that the content of her identity is experienced as multiple or with hiatuses but that her personality functions on two different levels. What Drabble identifies is not so much a psychological breakdown, as in the case of Lessing, but the clashing roles that the new, 'permissive' society offers to women while not providing the social infrastructure for both identities to be performed simultaneously in equally successful ways.

At the level of form, Jane's confused, contradictory performance of self expresses by a split in the narration, which is divided into a third person account of her affair with James, in which she is referred to as both 'Jane' and 'she', and a first person narrative in which she accounts for, and scrutinizes, her actions.

> I must make an effort to comprehend it. I will take it all to pieces, I will resolve it to its parts, and then I will put it together again, I will reconstitute it in a form that I can accept, a fictitious form: adding a little here, abstracting a little there, moving this arm half an inch that way, abstracting a little there, gently altering the dead angle of the head upon its neck. If I need a morality, I will create one: a new ladder, a new virtue. If I need to understand what I am doing, if I cannot act without my own approbation – and I must act, I have changed, I am no longer capable of inaction – then I will invent a morality that condones me. Though by doing so, I risk condemning all that I have been. (Drabble 1980: 52–53)

Interestingly, the first person narrator has a much broader knowledge base that the third person narrator, which it narrates. Glenda Leeming observes that what 'appears here is a duel narrative approach, which deliberately undermines itself' (Leeming 2006: 37). The result is a highly self-aware narration whereby the first person meta-narration scrutinizes the role of storytelling. This mode is drawn from the self-conscious narrative of the high Modernists, yet, rather than pushing this mode to a postmodernist hyper-self-reflectiveness, Drabble looks back towards the Modernists:

> Lies, lies, it's all lies. A pack of lies. I've even told lies of fact, which I had not meant to do. Oh, I meant to deceive, I meant to draw analogies, but I've done worse than that, I've misrepresented. What have I tried to describe? A passion, a love, an unreal life, a life in limbo, without anxiety, guilt, corpses; no albatross, no sin, no weariness, no aching swollen untouchable breasts, no bleeding womb but the pure flower of love itself, blossoming out of God knows what rottenness, out of decay, from dead men's lives, growing out of my dead belly like a tulip. (Drabble 1980: 84)

Drabble's knowingness is 'deconstructive' without submitting to the theoretical underpinnings provided by Barthes and fellow theorists: this intervention by the first-person Jane Gray exposes the artificial underpinnings of her narrative as both 'fictionalized' and misrepresentative of her own experience. It will not take the most associative of minds to make two connections here. First, to B. S. Johnson, whose *Albert Angelo* (1964), published five years before *The Waterfall*, contains a famous passage in the fourth part ('Disintegration') in which the supposed reality of the story we have been reading breaks down, and the author similarly admits to the reader that the narrative was all a fabrication:

> —Im trying to say something not to tell a story telling stories is telling lies and I want to tell the truth about me about my experience about my truth about my truth to reality about sitting here writing looking out across Claremont Square trying to say something about the writing and nothing being an answer to the loneliness to the lack of loving. (Johnson 2004: 167–8)

Secondly, Drabble's passage reminds us of an at the time much more famous rupture in fictional fabric, published in the same year. Although the reader is happily immersed in the story of the foppish Victorian amateur geologist Charles Smithson and Sarah Woodruff in John Fowles's *The French Lieutenant's Woman* (1969), chapter 13 famously provides a shock when the 'author' steps in:

> I don't know. The story I am telling is all imagination. These characters I create never existed outside my mind. If I have pretended until now to know my characters' minds and innermost thoughts, it is because I am writing in (just as I have assumed some of the vocabulary and 'voice' of) a convention universally accepted at the time of my story: that the novelist stands next to God. He may not know it all, yet he tries to pretend that he does. But I live in the age of Alain Robbe-Grillet and Roland Barthes; if this is a novel, it cannot be a novel in the modern sense of the word. (Fowles 1981: 80)

Fowles's book, and this passage especially, has become the touchstone for thinking about sea-changes in fictional aesthetics and the rethinking of the nature of narration. Yet, Fowles's passage is also so overtly theoretical that there is something alienating about it. What is interesting about Drabble's novel is that it performs that same deconstructive strategy in a less macho fashion: she undermines the authority of fiction in her search for truth, yet feels no need to exclude the reader, as affirmed by the confessional tone. Drabble's aesthetic is much more complex than it at first reads, deconstructing character and behaviour and their societal and linguistic underpinnings to reveal these new uncertainties not by some grand gesture but through a subtle and frank investigation of the consequences of living a life in language.

How easy it is to betray the texture of life

The subtlety and refined engagement with and depiction of human character, emotion and changing behaviour found in Wilson's and Drabble's fiction, although at the time still appreciated, has now been drowned out in a noisy and often macho culture of writers who have felt their privileged position erode – a culture that had its origins in the sixties. One example in particular of this loud, hysterical fiction is Anthony Burgess, who set out to find and shape the texture of the sixties. *Enderby Outside* (1968) contains passages that depict not just change, but continuous change: 'In June both groups were superseded by the Tumers who, intuitively aware of the new shift in the *Zeitgeist*, perhaps wisely reverted to a great simplicity of rhythmical texture' (Burgess 1968: 15). These authors resist jumping on the constant succession of new hypes and styles. As Drabble observes: 'How easy it is to betray the texture of life' (Drabble 1980: 113). What Wilson and Drabble give us, well-constructed line by well-constructed line, is a subtle insight into the human mind: this mode offers the promise that there are artists who have taken it upon themselves to make you feel less alone. They reject the superficial realism of the pulp fiction television that seduces characters such as Sylvia Calvert and ironical, experimental strategies, but embrace a representative form that mediates between a profoundly probing intellect and an unceasing interest in people in order to generate an aesthetics of the human.

3

Women's Skinny Fiction

Fat fictions and skinny prose

As the analysis of the work of Nell Dunn, Maureen Duffy and Muriel Spark in Chapter 1 suggests, power over women is central to our conception of the sixties: legal, scientific, institutional, pedagogic, economic and cultural power, among others. We saw how women appropriated technology to put subversive strategies in place. Yet, according to Deborah Philips, in the sixties, Britain and British fiction were not impacted much by the Women's Liberation Movement. It was beginning to catch up by the end of the sixties and early seventies, with the government introducing equal rights legislation, and the emergence of women's studies at universities, and women's presses, notably Virago, established in 1975. The first Women's Liberation Conference took place only in the 1970s in Oxford (of all places). Philips turns to Lynne Reid Banks's *The L-Shaped Room* and Margaret Drabble's *The Millstone* to suggest that women's writing in the sixties was, on balance, sending out conservative messages.

On the surface, we find a relatively conservative approach by writers who belong to the first wave of feminism, which wanted to create equality between men and women. In order to achieve this, women writers such as Drabble, Iris Murdoch, Doris Lessing and to an extent Maureen Duffy adopt and sometimes modify established rules of representation. They do not on the whole appropriate the provocative, rude language and discourse strategies argued for by Germaine Greer in *The Female Eunuch* (1970) or by Eva Figes in her analysis of the male-dominated historical discourse of the conception of women, *Patriarchal Attitudes* (1970). These writers want to inscribe themselves into the male literary tradition by imitating its modus operandi, resulting in 'fat' novels, that is, books that imitate the heavy materiality of masculine thought at the level of content and form. This discussion reminds of Iain Sinclair's description of Michael Moorcock's writing: 'Julian Barnes's novels are depilated at source, fat-free. Frisking them for a Moorcockian digression, a set of cellulite-heavy parentheses, would be like checking a tub of margarine for a stray pubic hair. Smoothness, the absence of bumps and flaws and evidence of facial baroque, is everything' (Sinclair 2000). Not unlike George Eliot, who was also competing in a context dominated by male writers, Margaret Drabble, Iris Murdoch and Doris Lessing use the realist tradition to neatly package concerns about the sexual revolution and the traditional institution of marriage. Their poetics implicitly align themselves with a patriarchal and phallocentric ideology that comes readily with the history of literary representation, stretching from Aristotle and F. R. Leavis through to James Joyce and D. H. Lawrence. Maureen Duffy's *The Microcosm* consciously harks back to Joyce's *Ulysses*; it is as much an homage as a criticism for keeping the only female protagonist, Molly Bloom, confined to the domestic space. These fat fictions are driven by the quest to find alternative family constellations with Freudian underpinnings. These women writers thought, particularly at the start of the decade, that it was necessary to defend women *as women*, an essentialist mode of thinking part of the first wave of feminism, which forced women writers to harness the revolutionary powers of realistic prose. They argued that identity is rooted in bodily materiality and in sexual difference. This type of writing thought of women's plight in terms of invisible flows of power that impacted itself in very real terms on the mind as well as the materiality of women's bodies.

Simultaneously, another group of women engaged with this tradition through a reversal in strategy: they negated the weight of realism in order to develop a new form of writing that deconstructs the biological materialist traditions of representation in humanism. Their lean, thin novels with skinny prose can be situated within the tradition of 'minor literature' identified by Gilles Deleuze and Félix Guattari. In the second part of this chapter, I will focus on how a new aesthetic 'thinness' emerged, starting with Brigid Brophy's novel *Flesh* (1962), which effects a 'redistribution [...] of weight' (Brophy 1979: 40) at the level of form and content. Muriel Spark's slender novels, Nell Dunn's terse vignettes, Sheena Mackay's *Music Upstairs* (1965) and Angela Carter's *Heroes and Villains* (1969) also contribute to this agenda, as well as two novels published in 1966, Eva Figes's *Equinox* and Jean Rhys's *Wide Sargasso Sea*. These writers undermine and reject what Elaine Showalter called the 'female aesthetic [which] uncannily legitimized all the old stereotypes' (Showalter 1978: 298) and offer a 'new frankness about the body and about topics such as adultery, abortion, lesbianism, and prostitution' (Showalter 1978: 299).

This idea of 'minor literature' comes from Deleuze's and Guattari's book *Kafka: Towards a Minor Literature* (1975). In this tradition, writers are interested in creating their art out of hunger: Kafka features centrally in this tradition, but Beckett too explores an aesthetic of emaciation. The wider work of Deleuze and Guattari is a rich source for rethinking classic literary analyses and conventional perceptions of the world. Their subversive writing aims to destroy traditional ways of understanding society reliant on using reason and is the result of the sixties revolutions. *Anti-Oedipus* (1972) and *A Thousand Plateaus* (1980) are key works, attacking conventional, Freudian psychoanalysis and the culture of therapy which props up the capitalist system that produces schizophrenic subjects. *Kafka* is particularly useful in providing a critical framework which enables a reading of Spark, Rhys, Mackay, Figes, Dunn and Brophy, who subvert the fat house of fiction through what Claire Colebrook calls 'the politics of style' (Colebrook 2006: 117). Minor literature is comprised of short, lean texts that self-consciously foreground any central ideological structures and categories in order to destroy them.

The characteristics of 'minor literature' show why women might be attracted to adopting this aesthetic, beginning with the claim that 'minor literature doesn't come from a minor language; it is rather that which a minority constructs within a major language' (Deleuze and Guattari 1986: 16). Everything about minor literature is political: 'its cramped space forces each individual intrigue to connect immediately to politics. The individual concern thus becomes all the more necessary, indispensable, magnified, because a whole other story is vibrating within it' (Deleuze and Guattari 1986: 17). An important aim of the form is to create a 'language [which is] affected with a high coefficient of deterritorialization', which subverts the hegemonic discourses that enforce rigid categorization, stasis and hierarchy (Deleuze and Guattari 1986: 16). Minoritarian women writers of the sixties go further, by foregrounding their challenge to the house of fiction. They also draw attention to the importance of the relationship between the mouth, body and language, which is an important feature for Deleuze and Guattari:

> Rich or poor, each language always implies a deterritorialisation of the mouth, the tongue, and the teeth. The mouth, tongue, and teeth find their primitive territoriality in food. In giving themselves over to the articulation of sounds, the mouth, tongue, and teeth deterritorialise. Thus, there is a certain disjunction between eating and speaking, and even more, despite all appearances, between eating and writing. (Deleuze and Guattari 1986: 19–20)

All these women writers create an upsetting disjunction between form and content in order to produce work against the weight of realist tradition. Claire Colebrook notes:

Minoritarian and majoritarian are ways of drawing distinctions. A majoritarian mode [...] presents to opposition as already given and based on a privileged and original term. So, 'man' is a majoritarian term; we imagine there is some general being – the human – that then has local variations: such as racial, sexual or cultural variations. The opposition between man and women is majoritarian: we think of woman as other than, or different from, man. A minoritarian mode of difference does not ground the distinction on a privileged term, and does not see the distinction as an already-given order. (Colebrook 2002: 104)

The point is that the power of this minoritarian tradition lies in its denial of the norm and value of majoritarian terminology as valid or as a standard at all. The minor literature of women writers in the sixties enacts this at both the lanky form and subversive content of their work by escaping the male weight of tradition by writing clever novellas.

The weight of realism and masculine materialities

In *Women in the House of Fiction* (1992), Lorna Sage's use of the classic Jamesian structuring trope of the house as a metaphor for fiction aligns writing by women in the post-war period with 'the middle ground'. She appropriates this metaphor from Drabble's allegiance to the realist Victorian novel, and her 1980 novel of the same name. The comfortable, homely metaphor of the house spatializes our thinking about fictional representation in a Freudian way, acting as a neat mental ordering that mediates between society and the composition of the novel. The novel-as-house metaphor has its origins in Henry James, who in the preface to *The Portrait of Lady* (1881) noted that the imaginary architecture of the greatest conceivable work of art would resemble that of a great building. The seductiveness of Freudianizing our conception of space and place, and thus the literary work of art, is evident in books such as Gaston Bachelard's classic *The Poetics of Space* (1958) and Anthony Vidler's *The Architectural Uncanny* (1994). This allows us to 'apply' a (much too) schematic blueprint onto the composition of fiction as well as its characters that 'explains' the psychology of the novelistic enterprise. The classic Gilbert and Gubar thesis on *Jane Eyre* in 'The Madwoman in the Attic' (1979) argues that Rochester's first wife Bertha Mason is locked away in the tower as a symbol of the neurotic part of the human – but especially the female – mind; examples proliferate, from fairy tales to Charlotte Perkins Gilman's 'The Yellow Wallpaper' (1892).

Sage reacts against Roland Barthes, whose *The Pleasure of the Text* (1973) offered a new way of thinking about text, architectures of the imagination, psychology and sexuality. Barthes released the literary text from the restrictions of conventional psychological spatialization and meaning-giving by arguing that texts are atopic, heterocosmic and placeless. This argument was utopian, certainly, but it wrestled literary art away from the constraints of purely historical and social readings, which compromised and contained the aesthetics of literature – as Susan Sontag had already argued in 'Against Interpretation' (1964). For Sage, however, writing 'comes from some place' and 'isn't placeless' (Sage 1992: ix), and for good reasons: she needs to defend women *as* women by using Drabble's middle ground and Murdoch's 'matriarchal realism' (Sage 1992: x). The problem of this need to attribute certain localities to the writing is that the concomitant psychological spatialization is, as Sage well knows, sucked into a Freudian logic that buys into a fantasy of retrieving an organic whole. Germaine Greer argues that if women can liberate themselves from male projectionism in artistic production – which in the sixties we find in the work of Burroughs, Ballard and Burgess (see Chapter 8) – then they will be able to be re-united with what Simone de Beauvoir in *The Second Sex* calls 'the bosom of the Whole' (De Beauvoir 1960: 10).

The middle ground is not as conservative as it sounds: authors such as Drabble, Murdoch, and Lessing were in the business of dismantling crippling mythologies, and their work was 'increasingly ambitious, serious, and open-minded' (Showalter 1978: 307). Whereas the protagonist of Keith Waterhouse's *Billy Liar* (1959) remains trapped in infantile Freudian masculine fantasies and imprisoned geographically in his parents' house in the northern town of his upbringing, his girlfriend, Liz, does escape to London. Many a number of women novelists and characters did also manage to break out of their imprisoning northern towns. This is exemplary of a wider pattern manifesting itself in the sixties whereby women writers, from Sheena Mackay and Margaret Drabble to A. S. Byatt and Angela Carter, escaped from the dead weight of masculine materialities through various forms of emancipation. As Showalter notes of the middle grounders: 'They all use the resources of the modern novel, including exploded chronology, dreams, myth, and stream of consciousness, but they have been profoundly influenced by the nineteenth-century feminine literature, sometimes to the point of rewriting it' (Showalter 1978: 302). Sage's emphasis on place and materiality reminds us that, in the first instance, it was women's bodies as materiality rather than as a discursive construct that was central to the sexual revolution of the period.

The writing of sex

As we saw in Chapter 2, Margaret Drabble's *Jerusalem the Golden* (1967) attempts, not unlike E. M. Forster in his 1910 novel *Howards End*, to find a new aesthetic that marries up a rapidly changing world with a modified form of classic nineteenth century realism: a world in which the real is coded in fictional plotting and literary techniques drawn from the world of the novel, fairy tales and fables with their moral underpinnings. The novel is a relatively skimpy affair, just over 200 pages: yet the prose sits comfortably in the realm of realism, even though the narration is more complex than in Drabble's previous three novels, *A Summer Bird-Cage* (1963), *The Garrick Year* (1964) and *The Millstone* (1965). The use of third person narration allows Drabble more imaginative room than a first person narrative: there is more poetic license and even some manipulation and undermining of perspective that allows the narration to reveal some distance to the protagonist, Clare Maugham (see Rose 1980: 30–31). There is also an increased sexualization of the narrated world: 'most of the girls at the school had managed to infuse a certain erotic passion into their various appeal to the Creators' (Drabble 1969: 31). Drabble's interest in religion, expressed first of all in the title's reference to J. M. Neale's hymn, allows her to appropriate its discourse and to unearth the latent sexuality hidden within it. She impregnates the language of religion and the northern geography with a sensuality. Maugham is unsure of what 'what she had been bred to' and is appalled by the 'random scattering of seeds' (Drabble 1969: 26), yet she uses these term in new ways to upset old conventions rooted in traditional, religion linguistic meaning giving systems. The 'right to flout the weight of tradition' (Drabble 1969: 30) – and we presume this is a male-dominated weight of tradition – then also entails a canny exposure of how Biblical and theological languages have a latent sexuality. This awareness of sexuality already starts early on in school, when the girls are 'titillated by the well-known fact that some of the more daring boys used to watch them through an easily accessible sky light' (Drabble 1969: 48). This youngish male gaze is described as an 'oddly private thrill' (Drabble 1969: 48), which for the precocious Maugham is tied into the discovery of her own awakening sexuality and her gender. Maugham catches 'sight of her own image in the wet tiled floor' and cries 'how weird I look from underneath' (Drabble 1969: 48). In the moment that follows this sexual self-discovery, she experiences herself as someone else:

> She had been truly moved by herself, by her own watery image, by her grotesquely elongated legs, her tapering waist, and above all by the undersides

of her breasts, never seen before. She stood there and stared at herself, seeing herself from that unexpected angle, as though she were another person, as though she were a dim white and blue statue on a tall pillar, a wet statue, a statue in water, a Venus rising from the sea, with veined marble globes for breasts. She had never expected to be beautiful, and she was startled to see how nearly she approached a kind of beauty. (Drabble 1969: 49)

Drabble self-consciously describes this epiphanic moment as a second mirror stage happening ten years after the first one, in a specifically Beauvoirian moment (overtly referred to on page 63) at which Maugham discovers the construction of herself. This moment is also one of awareness that her self-image is created partly by the male objectifying gaze as the knowing reference to Botticelli's *The Birth of Venus* (1468) suggests; it is here that Drabble connects with Angela Carter and her sister, A. S. Byatt, in a rejection of the male gaze. This realization allows Maugham to view herself, her friends and the world 'in a new light' (Drabble 1969: 61), and soon she finds herself in London's strangely seductive commodified spaces, 'a riot of flesh and lights and people and advertisements' (Drabble 1969: 65) and 'Coca-cola' (Drabble 1969: 66), which she dares not order. In this world of surfaces and exteriors, she 'wanted interiors' (Drabble 1969: 63), that is, the depth and weight of intellectual engagement and of history – and thus, implicitly, the humanist tradition. This attitude finds a similarly critical response in Nell Dunn's work.

Entering the household of the eccentric Denham's Maugham falls in love with Gabriel, whose married status adds to the excitement of a potential affair with him. The moment at which she meets Gabriel is telling: 'He was breathtaking: she stood and gaped' (Drabble 1969: 115). The moment recalls a similar one in Jane Austen's *Pride and Prejudice* (1813); Lydia Bennett's gaping has been interpreted not only as a comic rejection of and 'sheer disdain' (Tauchert 2006: 76) for Mr Collins's reading from James Fordyce's *Sermon to Young Women* (1766) but also as a rude latent sexual response whereby the opening of an orifice is connoted with sex. The language in Drabble's novel remains, however, suggestive and tame: 'She thought that she has never seen anyone so sexy off the cinema screen in her life' (Drabble 1969: 115) may sound promising, yet the passionate, potentially sexual encounter remains within the realm of Austen: when the couple kiss, Clare 'return[s] the kiss with ardour' and Gabriel presses 'against her' (Drabble 1969: 138). The scene deflates euphemistically under the certain kind of English embarrassment that Ian McEwan was to imitate and mock in *On Chesil Beach* (2008), with Gabriel suggesting he take the tray of tea and coffee, and Clare the digestive biscuits (Drabble 1969: 138). The first time they have sex, 'with mutual goodwill' (Drabble 1969: 154) under Gabriel's office desk, is described in no less glamorous circumstances, 'amid the smell of polish, and the unswept cigarette ash of the day, and the small round paper punchings from his secretary's filing activities. Clara's hair, shortly, was full of paper punchings, as of confetti' (Drabble 1969: 154). The image of Clara's hair sprinkled with paper punchings suggests a celebratory knowingness about Gabriel and Clara's sexual intercourse as well as Drabble's own literary performance as a writing woman who self-consciously engages with a variety of literary and gendered traditions. Drabble's metafictional passage is highly knowing but not deconstructive as it maintains the emphasis on the materiality of the women's body, and also of paper itself.

Indeed, two interrelated confessions about her character in the afterglow of their love-making say much about Clara's sense of herself as a woman: the phrase 'He lay on the floor, and watched her; she liked to be watched' (Drabble 1969: 155) suggests that, just as when she was a school girl, she is both aware of the male gaze and of her power in relation to it. By inviting and feeding on the gaze, Clara's is able to subtly subvert the traditionally gendered power constellation. This scene is deeply complex, however. After their intercourse, Clara discovers many different pictures hanging over Gabriel's desk (his wife, daughters, some pin-ups and a pop singer) but still does not 'see the point in having [...] those cheaply purchasable photographs' (Drabble 1969: 156), as she puritanically scorns them. She thus becomes aware of a 'stubborn narrow prejudice' (Drabble 1969: 156) – note the wink to Austen's novel of manners – which undermines her powerful estimation of herself in the gazing game of sexual politics. The second admission, that '[s]he liked the unknown, she like to feel familiar with the unknown' (Drabble 1969: 155), thus becomes qualified and ambiguous: the confidence in her ability to be at ease with the unknown is constantly realigned with the knowledge that such ease with the unfamiliar is itself a much more complex issue that Clara estimates. Her attempts to escape from the North are undercut towards the end of the novel, when she reads her hospitalized mother's exercise books, written as a child, in which she expressed her hopes for an agentic life which she never received and understands that she too is unable to escape her past: 'for she was glad to have found her place of birth [...] she felt, for the first time the satisfaction of her true descent' (Drabble 1969: 197). Accidental or not, Clara understands that she has a solid core to her identity, shaped by her upbringing, which is embodied in her mental connection to the place of her childhood. This indeed connects with Lorna Sage's connection of place and psyche to the weighty expressional forms afforded by traditional realism and its concomitant essentialist thinking. In short, the weight of Drabble's prose and the materiality of her books resemble the materiality of the human body, and yet the form of the novel which Drabble uses to shape her body is distinctly masculine and has no qualms about aligning itself with the male tradition of representation. Rather than finding a Woolfian room of her own, Drabble's tactic is, then, to inscribe herself into the male artistic canon, the house of fiction.

The sexual doom of womanhood

Drabble's vision of womanhood is essentially – and 'essentialistically' – humanist, as Jane Gray in *The Waterfall* argues, when thinking of herself, guiltily, as being 'in bondage':

> There didn't seem to be very many female perversions in that book. Perhaps that was because it was old. Perhaps women have developed these things more recently as a result of emancipation. But love is nothing new. Even women have suffered from it, in history. It is a classic malady, and commonly it requires participants of both sexes. Perhaps I'll go mad with guilt, like Sue Bridehead, or drown myself in an effort to reclaim lost renunciations, like Maggie Tulliver. Those fictitious heroines, how they haunt me. [...] In this age, what is to be done? We drown in the first chapter. I worry about the sexual doom of womanhood, its sad inheritance. (Drabble 1980: 153–54)

Drabble's protagonist still takes her cue very knowingly from Hardy's *Jude The Obscure* (1895) and George Eliot's *Mill on the Floss* (1860), paralleled in terms of her sexuality by trying to understand her perverse love affair with James: 'And he had done it: he had made her, in his own image. [...] Her own voice, in the cry of rebirth. A woman delivered. She was his offspring, as he, lying there between her legs, had been hers' (Drabble 1980: 151). James invokes in her a sort of all-consuming desire that she compares to destruction and rebirth: 'It was like death, like birth: an event of the same order. Her cry was the cry of a woman in labour: it broke from her and her body gathered round it with the violence of a final pang. What right had any deity to submit mortality to such obsessive, arbitrary powers' (Drabble 1980: 150). Jane connects her 'sexual salvation' to 'the dreadful, sickening savagery of what [...] one could call human nature' (Drabble 1980: 152). To understand her desire for James she looks up *Studies in the Psychology of Sex* by the Victorian physician and writer Havelock Ellis (1859–1939). Gray compares the mutual sexual desire between her and James to 'bondage' (Drabble 1980: 153), in a form of psychological carceral thinking that thinks of love and (sexual) desire as a perverse form of imprisonment that, for better or for worse, nature makes us want and embrace.

Drabble's articulation of these issues about sexual desire in this third person interior vocalization could not, on a thematic level, be more far removed from that of the experimental author William Burroughs. In the second part of the Nova-trilogy *The Ticket That Exploded* (1962), earth is invaded by The Nova Mob, who set out to create as much chaos as possible through their mind control techniques. The protagonist, Mr Lee, is hired to investigate and counter the alien invaders. His task is to immunize his fellow agents *against* chaos by infecting them *with* chaos. Lee has various weapons that destabilize perception, and is told: 'There is no certainty. Those who need certainty are of no interest to the department. This is in point of fact a *non-organization* the aim of which is to immunize our agents against fear, despair and death. We intend to break the birth-death cycle' (Burroughs 1968: 10). It is perhaps unfair, probably even preposterous, to compare Drabble to the psychotic Burroughs, and yet both writers meditate on the same subject matter – sexual desire as part of an inescapable essentialist thinking about human nature – through the use of diametrically opposed literary forms. My argument is that Burroughs's 'novel' escapes from this apparently causal cycle by reconfiguring thought through a parasitical infection that harnesses the random, repetition and copying in order to explode the eternal return: 'Death *is* orgasm *is* rebirth *is* death *is* their unisanitary Venusian gimmick *is* the whole birth death cycle of action' (Burroughs 1968: 53). Burroughs manages to wake up from the nightmare of repetition of a mindless human sexuality and desire through formal experimentation; Drabble's protagonist, on the other hand, is hopelessly locked into the security of repeating ancient patterns that counter the threat and joy of destabilization. Drabble invokes and promulgates a Freudian logic without questioning his status, at a time when many post- and anti-Freudian thinkers were already lodged into the popular imagination: 'Since Freud, we guess dimly at our own passions, stripped of hope, abandoned forever to that relentless current' (Drabble 1980: 153). This is a kind of natural imperative, as Drabble's support of the organic underscores that it is also part of the deeply moral tradition of English fiction, which occludes the anti-causal arbitrariness of life. As James recounts the car crash that nearly kills him: '*I* respect the organic [...] and if anyone starts using my corpse, even if it's only to recreate the crash I died in, I shan't think much of it. When my body reassembles on the day of Judgement. Because bodies do, you know. They all come together again' (Drabble 1980: 145). Indeed, at the end of the novel, the organicity of life and representation, the mind and human body are merged in an expression of the landscape when Jane and James scale the Goredale Scar in the Pennines: 'It was impressive through not through size, as I have perhaps expected, but through form: a lovely organic balances of shapes and curves, a wildness contained within the bodily limit' (Drabble 1980: 236).

Just as *Jerusalem the Golden* starts with a pubescent girl discovering her body and reproductive parts, Angela Carter's early work shows a much more self-aware and ironical understanding of perception. The opening lines of Angela Carter's *The Magic Toyshop* (1967) make the connection between the materiality of women's bodies and place overt:

> The summer she was fifteen, Melanie discovered she was made of flesh and blood. O, my America, my new found land. She embarked on a tranced voyage, exploring the whole of herself, clambering down her mountain ranges, penetrating the moist richness of her secret valleys, a physiological Cortez, da Gama or Mungo Park. (Carter 1981: 1)

Linden Peach interprets the passages as follows: 'Through her fantasies enacted before the mirror, Melanie begins to explore her different potential identities and the contradictory roles that make up the female subject in art and society' (Peach 2009: 66). The passage is however much more knowing about the materiality of the female body compared with Drabble's comparison of the body and landscape above. Melanie mocks the historical privilege of male explorers and artists who have conquered and claimed the world and appropriates herself through exploration of her pubescent body, in a literary language that is just as bold and adventurous as that of her male counterparts.

A. S. Byatt's *The Game* (1967) contains a similar deconstruction of male representational history and privilege, when Julia Corbett watches a documentary on television: 'The Amazon basin', said the commentator. 'It was first explored in 1500 by Vincent Yañez Pinzon, who referred to it as the Marañón – a name now generally reserved for the Upper Amazon, although geographers differ as to where the Marañón ends and Amazon begins, or whether both names apply, in fact to the same river' (Byatt 1983: 10–11). Byatt argues that television has a new, central representative power, and her novel dismantles not only the male history of geographical exploration but also the male-dominated world of television by focusing on the naming, language, the voice and the camera-work and close-ups within the documentary.

The work of Doris Lessing became central to conceiving women's liberation during the sixties in Britain – against the fantasies that maintain the heteronormative and phallocentric social relationships literally given the meaty weight of realism, various other fictions that no longer seek shelter in the house of fiction but explore a new relationship between physical and imaginative space. As Lessing's sprawling *The Golden Notebook* (1962) points out, the new free women are often Marxists who connect their liberation from men to the class struggle. They have jobs and children and 'lead independent lives; but they are fragmented and helpless lives, still locked into their dependency on men' (Showalter 1978: 301). In a poignant passage at the start of the novel, Richard accuses his ex-wife Molly and Anna of being 'extraordinarily naïve' (Lessing 2013: Loc.676) about people's ability (including and probably especially women) to make up their own mind in the light of business and 'international money' (Lessing 2013: Loc.648). Anna is not impressed by Richard, a powerful business man: 'This has not caused his image to enlarge, for her; rather he had seemed to shrink, against a background in international money' (Lessing 2013: Loc.676). Indeed, it is in the external world of social realities that women are frustrated with, and central to their frustration is the capitalist patriarchy. Eva Figes ends her book *Patriarchal Attitudes* with the clear message that

> the remedy lies in our own hands, and will be found in social change, not on the analyst's couch. That change is one that men should welcome as much as women, because female neurosis and dependence do not make the lives of men any happier either. Now and in the future, patriarchal attitudes will benefit no one, least of all man. (Figes 1970: 185)

The minoritarian response: Fictions of hunger

Besides these formally more conservative works, a different trend starts in the sixties, whereby women writers resist existing heteronormative and phallocentric ideologies. I argue that next to this alignment of women's writing with masculine, humanist, 'majoritarian' tradition, there is an alignment with the minoritarian tradition in writing by Muriel Spark, Jean Rhys, Sheena Mackay, Eva Figes, Nell Dunn and Brigid Brophy.

The most obvious example is Brigid Brophy's comedy *Flesh* (1962), which tells the story of the nervous, lanky Marcus, who falls in love with the strong woman, Nancy, who has an extraordinary transformative effect on him. On the surface, the 124 pages of the novel tell a simple story: Marcus meets Nancy at a party, they fall in love, get engaged, have sex and have a baby. Brophy's novelistic language is one of diegetic brevity that suggests rather than tells mimetically, and the novel can be seen as an extended metafiction that shows how sexual power dynamics changed in the period through an inversion of the male gaze. Marcus is defined by his obsession with Rubens and his paintings of voluptuous, fleshy women, but his gaze in unable to conquer the Jewish Nancy; a reversal of Freudian sexual energies takes place throughout the novel. Marcus starts off as a profoundly Freudian character: his father's death, for instance, causes him to become 'impotent' (Brophy 1997: 55). In an allusion to Spark's *The Prime of Miss Jean Brodie*, which had been published a year before *Flesh* and presented the character of Rose Stanley who 'was famous for sex' (Spark 2000: 7), Nancy has a 'talent […] for sexual intercourse' (Brophy 1997: 42). She is a strong New Woman, who has studied 'domestic science' (Brophy 1997: 28) where she went into 'dietics seriously' (Brophy 1997: 93). When Marcus and Nancy have intercourse, he discovers that he is seduced as much by her body – her vagina is unimaginatively described as 'a magic grotto' (Brophy 1997: 45) – as by her voice:

> When he entered her body, he felt he was following her voice. […] Sensuousness and passion, which his imagination had apprehended to be antithetical, were in Nancy's world plaited together into such a perfect interpenetration of opposites that the one could grow as climax out of the other. […] It was a grotto, a private, underground, enchanted folly, of which neither of them could have enough. It became necessary for Nancy to guide him into it by talking to him – at least with her voice; he became capable of following the complementary of the very pulsations, the hidden constrictions the watery unloosenings, of her body's response to the pleasure his body gave him. (Brophy 1997: 45–46)

The explicitness of such descriptions is remarkable, evidencing the new frankness in attitudes to sexuality, as well as a rejection of Freud's psychology and his emphasis on the polymorphic perverse: 'Nothing is perverse. Nothing at all if you really want to do it' (Brophy 1997: 47), notes Nancy. Marcus's increased sexual appetite expresses itself in his eating habits: his passiveness enacts 'redistribution […] of weight' (Brophy 1997: 40). Important here is Nancy's Jewish heritage, acting as a reminder of the Holocaust in the post-war period in which procreation prompted new questions. They also continue to make love during and after Nancy's pregnancy. Marcus changes from a thin, tall man until at the end he himself has become the subject of the male gaze: 'I've *become* a Rubens women' (Brophy 1997: 124), he notes on the final page of the novel. The form of the novel runs counter to this fattening process: chapters are increasingly shorter, and the prose becomes terse and emaciated.

Muriel Spark's writing has always been terse, making avail of the powers of sparseness. *The Girls of Slender Means* literalizes, but also skews, the relationship between women's body weight and the renegotiation of architectural metaphors and composition of the novel. The novel centres on 'a spacious Victorian house' (Spark 1975: 26) acting as a dormitory for girls; Spark subverts the house of fiction motif. Chapter 3 slices knowingly through the different floors of the house: the third floor houses 'the room of a mad girl, Pauline' (Spark 1975: 29). Although 'very little has been done to change the interior' (Spark 1975: 26) the girls of the May of Teck Club spend most of their time finding ways to escape the house that 'appeared so penitential in tone' (Spark 1975: 27). The girls counterplot their way out of masculine fiction by learning to speak and behave differently, but they also need to slim down in order to fit through the window. Indeed, they escape literally through the window from the house of fiction via Spark's slimmed down, minimalistic prose until at the end of the novel the Victorian house itself is destroyed by a fire. The taut language and tight composition thus enact a rebellion against the male tradition of the novelistic enterprise.

The apotheosis of this tendency comes with *The Driver's Seat* (1970). It tells the story of the psychologically damaged Lise, who works for an accountancy firm in Scandinavia, and flies to an Italian city where she has set up her own murder. In her distanced, zero degree narration of a repressed, curious psychopathology, Spark draws on, but also corrects, Alain Robbe-Grillet's *The Voyeur* (1955) and *Jealousy* (1957), which centred on a white male consciousness. The novella becomes an investigation of how ancient narratives have shaped ideologies and behaviour, presenting a counter-intuitive logic, especially in regards to the complexities of gender and sexual relationships. The conservative Mrs Friedke warns that 'They [men] don't want to be dressed alike anymore. Which is only a move against us. [...] Mr Friedke knew his place as a man' (Spark 1970: 72). Friedke points out that the drive to equality goes both ways: 'All I say is that if God had intended them to be as good as us he wouldn't have made them different from us to the naked eye' (Spark 1970: 72). The counterintuitive assessment of the male body in relationship to their demand for equality is noteworthy because of its diminished representation, which underscored as well by the reversal of the aesthetics of *The Driver's Seat*. Friedke warns that men, in search of equality, will take over traditionally female, domestic roles, which she assesses as a threatening prospect. Spark shows that after the introduction of the pill in 1962, men are having their cake *and* eating it. Lise embodies a disgust and frustration with not simply men but with desire itself: when the stereotypically Italian sex-maniac Carlo tries to talk her into bed, she states: 'I don't want sex with you. I've got other interests and as a matter of fact I've got something on my mind that's got to be done' (Spark 1970: 80).

Lise does, however, appropriate this logic in assuming complete agency through ordering her own murder, a surreal literalization of the sex act, which J. G. Ballard would imitate with *Crash* in 1973. Although we have moved into the realm of the posthuman, bringing with it the threat of nihilism, Spark restores humanism (see Childs 2014: 166) in a cautionary way by referring to 'all those trappings devised to protect them from the indecent exposure of fear and pity, pity and fear' (Spark 1970: 107). We are confronted with a naked condition, stripped of biological and essentialist certainty, in a poetics that reverse the orgiastic teleology of Aristotle and appropriate power over endings.

Sheena Mackay's *Music Upstairs* (1965) is another skinny fiction written in terse prose, which centralizes the female body and various forms of hunger. It tells the story of the young office worker Sidonie O'Neill, who moves from the outskirts of London in Penge with her friend Joyce to a flat in West London's Earls Court. Their landlords, Lenny and Pam Beacon, live a floor above them, with their first born. This social and sexual constellation becomes a closed system, whereby morality and social behaviour are susceptible to the laws of entropy and result in regressive sexual behaviour and increasing chaos. Sidonie becomes the lover of both Lenny and Pam. A latent violent eroticism and transgression charges the pages. Lenny's boorish behaviour expresses itself through linguistic and physically threatening behaviour: ' "You greedy sows didn't leave me much, did you?" His head face voice and trousers, an intrusion into the white evening. He raised the bottle to his mouth, his lips making a thick wet O round the rim, and then wiped them with the back of his hand' (Mackay 1998: 19). When Sidonie and Lenny start an affair, eroticism collapses into perverse, sado-masochistic behaviour; permissiveness and consent are no longer distinguishable:

> Then, with terrible inevitability he started to take her clothes off and she, as if through fog, moved to facilitate it and lay stiff as he organized her arms and legs and she suddenly closed her bursting eyes as she took the next steps in her slow suicide. It didn't last long and then Lenny's head was resting on her and his whole weight pressing on her head as he said, 'It'll be better next time, darlin', I promise. (Mackay 1998: 117)

Such love-making scenes border on rape, but Mackay's novel is illuminating in its frank exploration of Sidonie's attraction to such sexual energies.

Figes's *Patriarchal Attitudes* takes us from Rousseau and Darwin through to Schopenhauer and Freud in order to show how fragility and neurosis are produced by a social situation created by men that asks women to conform to the privileged ideologies that shape society historically. The world of artistic representation is itself complicit as 'the whole hall of mirrors [...] is male-created' (Figes 1970: 18). This analysis, coming in the year that Women's Liberation really broke through in Britain, had already been 'theorised' in fictions by Figes earlier in the sixties. Her novel *Equinox* (1966) traces, like so many fictions of the period, the breakdown of a marriage, in this case between a writer and editor, Liz Winter and her scientist husband, Martin, after the loss of their young child. Traumatized by grief, Liz experiences an inward turn, a diminished sex life, and a lust out of sync with her husband's. The partners rapidly grow alienated; Martin takes a lover and eventually finds a temporary teaching post in the United States. After a disease that hospitalizes her, Liz realizes that she is not acting like a modern woman, freed from old-fashioned notions of fidelity, 'and all that rot' (Figes 1969: 123), and takes various lovers, including the husband of a friend of hers.

Figes creates a kaleidoscopic style that is sometimes a distant, dry observation of both Liz and Martin, while sometimes moving into a heightened, poetic mode and dipping into Liz's stream of consciousness, reminding us of Henry Green's late Modernist *Party-Going* (1939) in its elliptic prose: 'Soft September blurs the edges, the hard bit of winter to come, the skeleton eating into the flesh' (Figes 1969: 7). Figes structures the novel around the month and seasons of the year, yet, rather than finding consolation and resolution in the organic cyclicity, their relationship dies: the novel provokes us into finding new ways of understanding modern life. Indeed, another metaphor is challenged as well when Liz tells Martin 'I hate this house' (Figes 1969: 12), leading later on to a pinpointing of a gap between modern life and art: 'it's just life which is so unfinished and incomplete. We use art as a yard stick because it's full and rounded–life isn't, bits lead nowhere in particular, there's a yawning gap in the middle, as for the beginning and end, they there alright, as birth and death, but they're both more or less arbitrary and accidental' (Figes 1969: 55–56). As the narrative progresses there is a wholesale rejection of Aristotelean poetics:

> The trouble is: we keep trying to plan and replan into the future, plan everything as though it were an organised fugue or a game of chess. Birth, marriage, death, all preordained and made in heaven and leading into each other on Aristotelian principles. A gentle death-bed with great great grand children surrounding the bed, several of them with the same name and one, perhaps, the same image. It can't be like that and if it were you would die prematurely of boredom. If it were like that there would be no sense in it either, simply the extension and repetition of absurdity. (Figes 1969: 101–2)

Besides the reference to the fugue, which will be discussed in Chapter 4, the allusion to the theatre of the absurd here is telling. When at the start of a novel during a dinner party a new Beckett play is mocked by Martin as '[p]retentious rubbish, opium of the intellectuals' (Figes 1969: 30), the last chapter collapses into a Beckettian 'hyper-sane' (Figes 1969: 148) reflection on Liz's disintegrated life worthy of Lucky in *Waiting for Godot* (1953), as affirmed by the final words of the novel 'I know I'm going on' (157), an allusion to *The Unnamable* (1959).

As in Spark, Brophy and Mackay, this Beckettian heritage aligns Figes with a poetics of emaciation and hunger. When Liz makes a casserole in the kitchen she muses:

> There wasn't any excess weight, so puny, the head a hard ball of bone on a thin little neck no strong enough to hold it, not enough muscle on not enough bone to get any leverage and move or hold its own. Skin raw red and wrinkled in large folds on arms and legs. It waved the little sticks very slowly, as though under water, trying to break into life, or out of it. (Figes 1969: 19–20)

And yet Figes's novel does aim to find a new balance, the equinox of the title:

> That was the point of consciousness I reached alone in the dark room under the Bastille. Then it got lighter again and now there is an even balance between day and night. [...] Next month it will be September and after the equinox nights will start to get longer, and I don't know what I shall do then. And it doesn't matter. (Figes 1969: 155)

Jean Rhys's classic *Wide Sargasso Sea* (1966) fits into the *minoritarian* tradition in its dismantling of fantasies about inhabiting the house of fiction. The novel not only corrects the classic, all too neat geometrical spatialization of the human mind as argued for by Gilbert and Gubar but also offers a minoritarian aesthetic that subverts and counters white male (artistic) traditions. It also corrects and scrambles the wonderfully ordered Orientalized representations of the mind in Bronte's novel. The received, postmodern interpretation of Rhys's novel, even forty years later, usually sets out to correct the old power relationships through a reversal of point of view – the marginal becomes central. But it is possible to read the novel not only as an ideological correction of the position of the 'invisible' Black women. Instead, the novel offers a correction at the level of imprisonment in very real, economic and legal terms: the novella depicts both a prison of the mind as well as of the female body and its contextual materialities.

It enacts this deterritorialization through an injection into standard English of the Caribbean English patois of the protagonist Antoinette Cosway, who notes that she is 'glad to be like an English girl' (Rhys 1970: 30) but is not so fully: 'The Jamaican ladies never approved of my mother, "because she pretty like self" Christophine said' (Rhys 1970: 15). In part three, the language increasingly gives way to the orthography of psychopathology, a nightmarish collapse of her mind through a haunted stream of consciousness in which time and place merge, and identity crumbles: 'But it was a dull thought, like a child spelling out the letters of a word which he cannot read, and which if he could would have no meaning or context' (Rhys 1970: 113). The name Cosway itself suggests that slippage takes place between the original and rewriting, again confronting the reader with an unpinpointability. Sometimes called 'Annette', and sometimes called 'Bertha' (Rhys 1970: 155) in part two, even Antoinette's name, and identity, are not safe; slippage between ethnicity, gender, class looms constantly on the liminal space of the island, and forms part of the cause of the purported insanity of Cosway. The point that *Sargasso* makes, of course, is that Cosway is not *insane*: it is the Rochester figure's taking up of gossips and projection of insanity onto her that see her, in a way, institutionalized. As Nancy R. Harrison notes:

> The turned tables are the two configurations or 'complexes' that have been at issue from the beginning of Rochester's narrative and that are at odds throughout the novel. They are the neurotic, misused and distorted versions of the mother- and father texts: the classic Oedipal complex, unresolved, and its correlative, the Olympia complex, which Rhys allows Antoinette to break out of and in which Rochester tries to confine her. [...] Rhys's perspicacity allows her to put the man in the place of the woman, exchanging her text of hysteria, of the terror of immobility, for his text of the legitimacy of manhood (the ruse of reason) and the mobility of action. (Harrison 1988: 222)

Sargasso's strength and originality lie precisely in its refusal to accept the male terms on which liberation would ostensibly take place. We find a metaphor for this in an image of a decimated library which only contains fictions by men:

> There was a crude bookshelf made of three shingles strung together over the desk and I looked at the books, Byron's poems, novels by Sir Walter Scott, *Confessions of an Opium-Eater*, some shabby brown volumes, and on the last shelf, *Life and Letters* ... The rest was eaten away. (Rhys 1970: 63)

The image is important for its attack on Western literary traditions: not only do we only see fictions by men, implying that the literary is part of the ideological underpinnings of the colonial project of submission – one wonders where *Robinson Crusoe* is – but we already see that the Orientalist strategy is sabotaged by the tropical climate itself: it is the very world which imposes different rules, which subvert those of the laws of the west. This passage also foregrounds the importance of consumption in wider terms. Whereas in the Caribbean Cosway has a healthy appetite, when she is imprisoned in Rochester's attic she deliberately shuts her body down as well: 'I told her [Grace Poole] that I wasn't hungry and she didn't try to force me to eat as she sometimes does' (Rhys 1970: 152). This is a sign of self-control, but it also entails an increased shutting away of the outside world: unconscious palliative care for a body which houses a traumatized, amnesiac mind. Indeed, it was Rhys's intention 'to use the motif of the zombi [*sic*] returning to life to transform Brontë's expeditious ejection of Bertha from *Jane Eyre's* story' (Carr 2012: 87); Cosway's image is increasingly that of a starved slave coming to haunt her master. Rhys thought of *Jane Eyre* as a 'fat (and improbable) monster' (Rhys 1984: 147). Through the harnessing of a multiplicity of strategies, Rhys subverts various stigmas that are the result of male projections and aligns herself with a minor tradition of literature, which allows marginal constituencies to inscribes themselves against hegemonic power.

Making matter *matter*

What unites all these works by women writers in the sixties is their ponderous, self-questioning nature and their grim mood of darkness and depression, which stand in stark contrast to the aura of exuberance often associated with the decade. The gloomy atmosphere is heightened by the various contemplations on suicide in, for example, Carter's *Several Perceptions*, Lessing's 'To Room 19' and *The Golden Notebook*, Rhys's *Wide Sargasso Sea* and Mackay's *Music Upstairs*. Figes gives us the 'underground stranglehold of hell, the dark' (Figes 1969: 141); Brophy's sensibility is 'blackened and frost-bitten' (Brophy 1979: 22). This gloom should indeed be directly connected to the desperation of the immobility of women's position. Women's fiction provides a sober assessment of the emancipatory potential of the period, yet ultimately gives way for the quest for the light. Rhys's novel ends with an image of hope: 'I shielded it [the candle flame] with my hand and it burned up again to light me along the dark passage' (Rhys 1968: 156). In Figes, the emphasis on darkness aims at finding a new middle ground as well: 'That was the point of consciousness I reached alone in the dark room under the Bastille. Then it got lighter again and now there was an even balance between day and night' (Figes 1969: 155).

What this chapter has made clear as well is that there sometimes exists a gap between the narratives, as presented to us by historian and sociologists, and fiction. Deborah Philips argued that in early sixties texts by, for instance, Lynne Reid Banks and Margaret Drabble there was no sign of growth in feminist engagement. This chapter shows that Drabble's novels too are pervaded by a questioning of the position and function of women in society, as well as the politics of their bodily materialities. Data by female social scientists such as Myrdal and Klein suggests that there was indeed no significant change to sex and gender attitudes: these texts were written before sex education and the Women's Liberation Movement, which took a long time to find firm footing in Britain. Jane Lewis notes, however, that some of these sociological studies had their own, conservative agenda: 'This may have been correct, but [...] [t]hese studies shared the faith in both the power of social scientific data and rational planning under the Labour government in the 1960s' (Lewis in Moore-Gilbert and Seed 1992: 101–2). What this chapter shows is that such faith in data can blind us to the fact that literature is a tool that allows us a much better, deeper insight into the real 'living experience' at the time: all the texts covered in this chapter have a heightened awareness of the plight of women and politicize their thinking through the self-reflexive knowingness of their narratives.

This discussion and critical framing of this women's writing through this associate series of analogies – realism, the body, materiality, gender, sexuality – come at a moment in the twenty-first century when, after the interest of postmodernism in the weightlessness of discourse and language, materiality is revalued. For Karen Barad, language has been attributed too much power, so that materiality, society and the body could only be seen as narrated and mediated. In 'Constructing the Ballast' (2008), Susan Hekman picks up on Barad's argument by arguing that 'the real' has to be rehabilitated: 'the social world is very real; there are bodies and matter and real consequences of this materiality. If feminists are to understand – and change – that social reality, we must bring the material back in. We must make matter matter, not only in science but in society as well' (Hekman 2008: 116). This reaction is understandable, but the contemporary wholesale rejection of postmodernity's emphasis on construction and language seems silly and overly sweeping: language and discourse form an important constituent in the make-up of our perception and thinking. Women writers in the sixties adumbrated both these movements, and found a new way of addressing these issues, before dismantling became overly jargonized deconstruction. Sixties women writers, before the postmodern revolution and the subsequent radical rejection, seemed to find a fine balance, based on the acknowledgement of materiality through its negation and the middle ground where discourse and ideology are connected to materiality and 'the real world' in intricate ways.

What unites both these groups is that they both explore the way in which women represent themselves in writing before the postmodern emphasis on the (female) body as an ideological and performative construct that could principally be appropriated and liberated through a rewriting in text: one may think of the way in which Nell Dunn's own concerns about the position of the women in society incorporated a more textual approach in *Poor Cow* and Greer's demand in *The Female Eunuch* (1970) for women to reclaim their being back by re-appropriating linguistic power over their bodies through the ironic appropriation of vulgarisms such as 'cunt' and 'bitch'. In the sixties, before the utopian thinking late in the decade that would lead out into the postmodern obsession with the linguistic deconstruction of how power shaped and manipulated the bodily materiality and experience in general, women writers engaged in the hard work of working to liberate their bodies as material objects of a repressive and very real power working its way through every nook and cranny of society and culture. What emerges is a map of new commitment to understanding women, women's bodies, gender and sex, and sexual difference that is grounded in the body yet resists producing a unified thinking about women. Women's writing in the sixties then performs a deconstruction *avant la lettre* without self-aware poststructuralist jargon by denying the validity of the ideological underpinnings of patriarchy, hence negating its power while reclaiming bodily materialities in aesthetic language. Rather than succumbing to overtheorized postmodern thought, these fictions form an array of idiosyncratic texts, always sharp and insightful and more overtly politicized than usually considered.

4

Infinite Londons

Liberated by affluence: The Swinging London myth

As a space of time the British sixties are, in the popular imagination, inextricably bound up with London. Although the city was rivalled, if not emulated, by Liverpool in the production of the most interesting, *avant-garde* culture, Britain's capital became identified with the decade's socio-cultural changes and cultural revolutions and came to be seen as the cultural capital of the world. On 15 April 1966, London was officially declared the world capital of the imagination, when the transatlantic edition of *TIME* magazine published an exciting, full colour version of London consisting wholly of drug-fuelled orgies at endless parties, gambling and strip clubs, boutiques, art galleries and discothèques. 'LONDON: The Swinging City' was a place populated solely by films stars, pop stars and models, hair dressers, fashion designers, entrepreneurs and flocks of shoppers. The city was represented as both the utopian locus where meritocratic values had triumphed and as an Eden where no one had to engage in any laborious activity but that of shopping, dressing up and partying. While in the literary imagination London had been traditionally represented as what Raymond Williams called 'darkest London', grimy, shady metropolis of moral decay, squalor and corruption (see Groes 2009), this Americanized tourist gaze portrayed a city that had cast itself back into a prelapsarian state of timeless innocence:

> In this century, every decade has had its city [...] Today, it is London, a city steeped in tradition, seized by change, liberated by affluence, graced by daffodils and anemones, so green with parks and squares that, as the saying goes, you can walk across it on the grass. In a decade dominated by youth, London has burst into bloom. It swings; it is the scene. (*TIME* 1966: 32)

Exemplary of this representation is *A Swinger's Guide to London* (1967) by the American writer Piri Halasz, who was also responsible for the *TIME* cover story. In *TIME*, Halasz wrote the following about the British capital:

> For all its virtues, which are many, and its faults, which are considerable, London has a large measure of that special quality that was once the hallmark of great cities: civility in the broadest sense. It takes away less of a person's individuality than most big cities, and gives the individual and his rights more tolerance than any. In texture, it has developed into a soft, pleasant place in which to live and work, a city increasing its talents for organizing a modern society without losing the simple humanity that many urban complexes lack. (*TIME* 1966: 33)

It does not take a genius to read this piece in an American magazine adept at producing capitalist Spectacle, generating an idealized image coloured by a rose-tinted outsider's view. Maureen Duffy's novel *The Microcosm* (1966), published in the same year, seems on a surface reading to chime in with *TIME*'s naïve and singular optimism in its description of a nineteen-year-old girl from the north, Cathy, who moves to the capital in search for a job, like so many other female protagonists, from Sheena Mackay's Sidonie O'Neill to Margaret Drabble's Clare Maugham:

> The streets seem friendly and the air alive [...] She turns away from the station [...] and sees across the roar of traffic a wall and above it the moving arms of trees veiled lightly in small green leaves and the suddenness of them in that place maker [*sic*] her more aware of this coming Spring aid its possibilities than she has ever been of any changing season before. (Duffy 1989: 145)

Cathy translates her own newness as an excited *arrivant* in London into a new beginning for the city itself. It is not much later, however, that Cathy discovers that the swinging London constructed by mass media is hard to find:

> Somewhere there must be, they are here I know, there was that article. Never believe all you read in the papers, catchpenny, catch you too if you don't look sharpish [...] All around her were signs, hints, a way of walking of speaking, a style of dress or gesture, the question in the eyes but they were as indecipherable as a tramp's message scratched on a gatepost, understood only by the fraternity. (Duffy 1989: 164)

As we have already seen, the young women in Nell Dunn's *Up the Junction* too find themselves imprisoned rather than liberated by the increased aestheticization of experience and proliferation of signs that dominate the decade: when Joy notes that 'Chelsea sounds good. Catford sounds poxy' (Dunn 1967: 117), she is not saying they *are* but rather that they just *appear* that way. When Anthony Burgess's alter ego Edwin Spindrift returns from Burma with a brain tumour, he states upon his escape from the hospital: 'What an easy world it was to live in, this big innocent trusting London. Back to nature, with food growing everywhere for the plucking. Only a fool, really, would return to the hard graft of teaching linguistics under a Burma sun. Whether he was completely a fool he hadn't decided' (Burgess 1960: 191). This vision of innocence soon makes way for the Dantesque hell populated by London low-life and an imprisoning labyrinth of London accents in which the linguist is caught up.

These examples suggest that literary writers reacted with healthy scepticism against, and a bemused distrust of, such cheap and frivolous flattery by the American magazine. Dunn's fiction had already suggested that the financial boom of the late 1950s had not directly affected those Londoners outside the Kensington-Chelsea-Soho triangle while also questioning American cultural influence. Burgess's *A Clockwork Orange* anticipated the violence and destruction part of the anarchic and urban teenage dominion that resulted in a steep rise of crime on London as the decade progressed. J. G. Ballard in particular set out to destroy the capital in his fiction (see Groes in Baxter 2008). Whereas the capitalist creatives were busy establishing a new London mythology in order to cover up the waning of British Empire, British fiction in the sixties concerned itself with dismantling self-serving mythologies and with understanding the major historical changes the nation was going through. Literary output not only challenged the Swinging London myth but engaged in a wholesale revision of London's politico-economic and socio-cultural history. Writers mistrusted the radical, even apocalyptic nature of recent subversive events and socio-cultural changes, but they bore in mind the long view in which Britain, despite a brief economic upturn in the late fifties that was financing the party atmosphere, had just lost its Empire. They understood this would necessarily have a negative economic impact on the country's sense of selfhood, and thus the capital's tradition representative function.

Sixties London: The critical reception

Before we explore the various strands of London literature, let's look at the existing critical war over how London itself changed during the 1960s. A curious paradox seems to pervade criticism, which wavers between denouncing

Swinging London as a fiction and acknowledging some kind of truth to it. Historian Jerry White notes that it 'was fashionable then and later to decry the myth of Swinging London and, of course, it was a grossly misleading tag: this was the decade, after all, when the plug was pulled on the London economy, when the Brutalist architect had full reign, and when crime and racial antagonism took a turn for the worse' (White 2001: 341). Marwick points out that 'American finance was critical to many British [cultural] achievements after 1964' (Marwick 1998: 16). Sandbrook declares that '[i]n truth, most people remained completely untouched by the swinging "social revolution" that was supposed to be shattering the old boundaries and creating a new class' (Sandbrook 2006: 260–61). In his biography of the city, Peter Ackroyd, usually a liberal and progressive critic of London's life, unleashes a surprisingly fierce attack on the forms of destruction enacted on London's rich cultural and architectural traditions:

> all of London seemed to have changed out of scale and out of recognition. It was a form of vandalism in which the government and civic authorities were happy to acquiesce. Vast swathes of London disappeared in the process [...] What it represented was a deliberate act of erasure, and act of forgetting, not so dissimilar in spirit to the mood and ambience of the 'Swinging Sixties' elsewhere in London. It was as if time, and London's history, had for all practical purposes ceased to exist. In pursuit of profit, and instant gratification, the past had become a foreign country. (Ackroyd 2001: 760)

Ackroyd, whose hyperbolic mode of oration tends to disguise a more complex reality embedded in his grandiloquence, also notes the rise in crime and the loss of industry and docklands trade. His references to the denial of history fit the swinging mythology's discourse of rebirth, a first indication of the complex and contradictory renegotiation of the city and its traditional mythologies. For Ackroyd, the sixties are a time of literal deconstruction, whilst for his nemesis, Iain Sinclair, they represent a fruitful period of poststructuralist, Derridean deconstructive activity whereby the traces of the city so rapidly lost become a mystery which the writer-detective could restore to legibility.

These critics contradict themselves, however. White notes that '[n]one the less extraordinary things happened to London [...] where youth and the new combined so intriguingly with tradition, and where upper-class elements of the London Season seemed to blend effortlessly with working-class talent' (White 2001: 341). Roy Porter finds that 'London's new international cultural trendiness was somewhat fortuitous [...] but the 1960s truly formed a time when special features of the capital interacted to produce creativity and optimism' (Porter 2000: 442). Stephen Inwood does find some merit in *TIME*'s representation of London: 'Weak as its analysis was, the article did something to displace the foggy Dickensian image which had previously dominated international impressions of London, and its emphasis on London's cultural and social vigour was not entirely misplaced' (Inwood 2000: 867). Ackroyd notes that

> 'Swinging London' was not 'new' at all. The city's familiar instincts had never ceased their operation. The commercial imperative of the city's life [...] had identified a 'market' among the newly resurgent youth which could be in turn exploited by intelligent entrepreneurs [...] The phenomenon of the 1960s was essentially theatrical and artificial in nature [...] like so many displays, it glided over the fundamental underlying life in the capital. To see the decade clearly it is important to see it steadily, and as a whole, encompassing all of its realities. (Ackroyd 2001: 759)

Ackroyd's remark is important: in order to understand the Swinging London mythology, he asks us to situate it within a wider London narrative that is both literary and mythological and historical. London, like perhaps no other city, is a structure made up of fictions, stories and myths, as can be seen in the most recent manifestation of the return to craftsmanship and desire for authenticity, the hipster movement of the 2000s.

In a review of the 1960s exploitation film documentary purporting to reveal the truth behind Swinging London, *Primitive London* (Dir. Miller 1965), Iain Sinclair offers his own deconstruction of the myth:

> It used to be thought, back in the 1960s, that there was something noble about cities; living in them, experiencing the squalor (as a non-inhaler, a detached reporter), bearing witness to the end of empire, the acne-encrusted barbarians at the gates. Scars of war were still visible. Overgrown railway tracks like third-world gall-bladder removals. Streets were monochrome, as was human flesh: heavy, powdered, sagging. Complexions of suet made from recycled newsprint. Men lost their heads in clouds of pipe smoke and women protected themselves behind shellac helmets of hair, eyelashes like fly traps. Life was indoors, segregated, peculiar. If you had to travel, you walked fast, seeing nothing: clipclopping like a stripper between engagements. Or one of those City bankers, black as pints of stout, in their school-extension uniforms, photographed by Robert Frank. Beetling between the cracks of sooty buildings. Holding back the terror. One day it will all come down. (Sinclair 2006)

Sinclair's tragi-comic assessment of London in the 1960s depicts a naïve buying into of mediatized images of the new, a relief from the austere climate of post-war rationing. He points out that the world was readily accepting of the Swinging London mythology because it offered them a fantasy that worked against the grim, grey nightmare that the British had been trapped in for a long time. The result is, however, a certain gullibility when it came to those same mediatized images. J. G. Ballard noted that London plays a central role in this process, because after Shanghai 'London in the 1960s has been the second [media city], with the same confusions of image and reality, the same overheating' (Ballard 1991: 197).

This chapter maps and surveys the multifarious reactions to the changes that took place in perceptions of London in the sixties, giving a kaleidoscopic image of literary responses. Many indigenous British writers have written lamenting, conservative visions of the city that caution against the socio-economic and cultural revolutions that they feel undermine a sense of self and nationhood that is such a clear part of the island mentality. Iris Murdoch's London is wholly white, and centres on the classical literary and philosophical traditions that shape it as a place where the pressures of life can be thought through as intellectual problems mapped onto the city. The works of repatriates Anthony Burgess and J. G. Ballard have a predominantly white consciousness, partly shaped by their sheltered experiences in the East. Ballard give us dystopian depictions of London, projecting then current sociological concerns into a nightmarish, Orwellian future; Burgess's dystopian satire *The Wanting Seed* (1962) predicts a vast London covering much of the British Isles where homosexuality is enforced in order to stop overpopulation.

Faced with such concerns, writers responded in different ways. Some sought to bring back London's rich history of mythologies in order to resist the rapid changes ostensibly taking place in the city while embedding these changes is a long tradition of urban evolution and arguing for continuity. There was at the same time an influx of new writing, often from the United Kingdom's colonies, reinvigorating existing literary traditions and representations of the British capital through fresh perspectives. I will also focus on women's perception of London and, in particular, on the way in which Doris Lessing appropriated psychogeography in a way her male counterparts were unable to. Ultimately I offer these Londons as a remedy against the Spectacular heat of the Swinging London myth; these various London writing traditions, taken together, suggest that what we all share in London is, to a varying degree, a certain 'outsiderness'.

'Nigger! Come here, you silly bastard!':
Racism and sixties fiction

Before becoming trendy in the sixties, London became the centre point of a new post-war crisis: to the post-war austerity of the 1950s was added a new generation of Englishmen and women who came on boats from former colonies in the Caribbean. At the fringe of the areas earlier identified as the Swinging Sixties triangle was one of the places that represented the antidote to mythology. In the fifties and sixties, Notting Hill was still derelict. In *Notting Hill in the Sixties* (1991), Mike Phillips notes: 'Now the whole Grove, let's say the square from Portobello Road up to Chepstow Road, coming up Talbot Road, coming back down Westbourne Park Road, and if you want you can sweep up Great Western Road down Tavistock Crescent, down to Portobello Road. That whole area there was total slum' (Phillips 1991: 45). In her foreword to *A Troubled Area: Notes on Notting Hill*, Eileen L. Younghusband states that

> [i]t all began with the Notting Hill race riots of 1958 which brought North Kensington into the limelight as a district where people came to live because they had to and left as soon as possible when they wanted to. [...] The dominant problem of the area is housing, too many people forced into occupying too little space. (Jephcott 1964: 11–12)

Like the East End, Notting Hill has traditionally been a nomadic area for transient populations including gypsies and Irish, Czech, Polish, West Indian and, more recently, Moroccan, immigrants. Tensions grew, with Oswald Mosley's Union Movement and far-right organizations such as the White Defence League stoking hostility towards black families. During the Notting Hill riots of 1958, 400 white people attacked West Indian family homes. Although a few of the rioters were sentenced and the Notting Hill Carnival was first held in 1959, the mood continued to be geared towards exclusion of colonial subjects. The year 1962 saw legislation that made immigration from the ex-colonies more difficult, and 1968 Enoch Powell's 'Rivers of Blood' speech made it feel as if the autochthonous identity was being uprooted from the inside.

Mike Phillips remembers sixties' London as follows:

> Funny thing, history. Since the sixties all sorts of people, moral reformers, rightwingers, leftwingers, politicians, feminists, male chauvinists, law and order campaigners, and censorship freaks of every kind, have invented a straightlaced, well-behaved, public life from which the country somehow strayed with the invention of permissiveness.

But actually the war had changed nothing about the hypocrisy of England's
public morality, which had descended directly from Victorian times. Working-
class poverty and deprivation still, in the sixties, provided the country with
a huge stock of highly visible prostitutes, often patronised by public figures
who at the same time mouthed a rhetoric of puritanical decency. [...] Not
so remarkable. But in the stifling racism of the times, the association which
developed was seen as a demonstration of working-class degeneracy on the part
of women, meeting with the legendary and undiscriminating lust of black men:
and the degenerate tag was extended to characterise any relationship of any sort
between blacks and whites. (Phillips 1991: 50)

From the point of view of ethnicity, Phillips argues against those who blame
'degeneracy' and 'decline in morals' on permissiveness – we saw this with Peter
Hitchins in the Introduction. Phillips claims that the moral standards by which
permissiveness is judged are themselves regressive and hypocritical.

To understand the extent to which this was the case, we may look at
literature, which can tell us much about the self-awareness of such debates
and issues. Let's examine two problematic cases that allow us to pinpoint
two different responses to racism. As I noted in Chapter 1, Deborah Philips
accuses Nell Dunn of racism because the neutral observations of her narrator
don't condemn the racism that exists blatantly in the world that she depicts
(Philips 2008: 51). In *Up the Junction*, for instance, we find characters who utter
such atavistic thoughts as the following: 'You see the blacks have only got half
the brain cells to what we've got. They never had civilization, they never even
invented the wheel – what jerks to go through life without inventing the wheel'
(Dunn 1988: 107). A handyman dated by one of the girls says: 'Sixty per cent
of me calls are black – I'm like the white hunter, at the end of the street you
can practically hear the Tom Tom going "Sandy's back again"' (Dunn 1988:
103). The same man noted: 'Back in the van he says "I've gotta call on a nigger
tomorrow." His wife's a great big Zulu. I think he's trying to pull me. He's got a
big scar down on side of his face – and he'll have a scar down the other if he's
not careful' (Dunn 1988: 106). Interestingly, Dunn is much more sensitive to
race that Phillips suggests. Whereas the tallyman speaks of black people as 'the
Coloureds' (Dunn 1988: 104) and 'darkie[s]' (Dunn 1988: 106), the narrator
speaks of a 'Negro' (Dunn 1988: 107), showing Dunn's awareness of the politics
of language and ethnicity. In *Poor Cow*, institutional racism, misogyny and pure
stupidity are exposed all at once when the gas metre of Joy's neighbour is robbed:
'The police says "I pity you white women in this house with all these coloureds
down the street." They could tell he was coloured from the finger prints' (Dunn

1967: 10). Dunn chooses to not act as divine author-God explicitly judging such thinking, but the brutality of this naked racism itself should shock any reader in understanding the injustice present in early sixties Britain. 'KEEP THE BLACKS OUT FOR A WHITE CHRISTMAS' (Dunn 1988: 105), reads a wall in *Up the Junction*; this graffiti should stir a sense of revulsion at such discrimination in the readers, except for those who are psychopathic or who for whatever reason feel the need to overcompensate.

Anthony Burgess's *The Doctor Is Sick* (1960) provides another, more problematic case. In the opening pages Burgess's alter ego Edwin Spindrift notes '[t]he deep tones of a negro sermon' (Burgess 1960: 3) and observes '[a] Nigerian nurse, her head an exquisite ebony carving' (Burgess 1960: 11). The twin gangsters Leo and Harry Stone, who pester the protagonist Spindrift, have a dog called 'Nigger' (Burgess 1960: 159). In the following example, Leo Stone tries to apologize for 'the hated name' (Burgess 1960: 206):

> 'Nigger! Come here, you silly bastard!'
>
> Edwin saw that three negroes – smart men in raincoats and trilbies – advanced on Leo Stone. They had had enough of the white derision; they had learned that to ignore it was but to fan it. [...] Leo Stone was explaining, genuinely shocked and apologetic, that he'd merely been calling his dog, that was all, named Nigger because of its colour. That didn't go down well. (Burgess 1960: 205)

A few pages down, Burgess repeats the joke: 'Nigger! Nigger! Silly bastard!' Dead on cue a negro appeared in a cap, swaying, throwing the breath of rum before him like flower petals. 'Man', he said, 'you got no right to say what you just said then' (Burgess 1960: 207). Burgess is aware of the problematic integration of blacks in post-imperial Britain and of the history of racial tensions in the East End. However, representation of such problems is difficult: while the emphasis on language is important in connecting ideology with pedagogy, the comedy of the running gag wears off. The Orientalist association of blacks with alcohol (and rum, in particular) is deeply problematic: is the dog-called-nigger-joke a sign of Burgess's underhand stereotyping of black immigrants or is he mocking and ironizing racism? In *The Wanting Seed*, in which procreation has been called to a halt due to overpopulation, such description abound as well: 'Tristram's cell-mate was a massive Nigerian called Charlie Linklater. He was a friendly talkative man, with a mouth so large that it was a wonder he was able to attain any precision in his enunciation of the English vowel sounds' (Burgess 1973: 113). Burgess's sheer obsession with such depictions is suspicious, of course, and, although perhaps we should acknowledge his bravery for writing such provocative jokes about such a sensitive subject, from the current politically correct climate in the 2010s, our verdict on Burgess should probably be much harsher.

There are authors who transcend both neutral and comical approaches. In Jean Rhys's seminal 'Let Them Call It Jazz' (1962), we encounter the half-black half-white immigrant Selina Davis, evicted from her flat by her landlord and his wife: 'She too cunning, and Satan don't lie worse' (Rhys 1968: 47). Ultimately, she is sent to Holloway prison. The reader lives this immigrant experience through the interior monologue of Selina and her Caribbean patois that forces us to imagine her despairing mindset generated by abject poverty and utter loneliness. Rhys exploits the orthography of the immigrant very well, disrupting the readerly process and comfortable access to the world by constantly asking us to imbibe her thinking with her alienating yet intimate voice.

Colin MacInnes's London triptych, consisting of *City of Spades* (1957), *Absolute Beginners* (1959) and *Mr Love & Justice* (1960), gives us an insider's view of teens and immigrants culture in London during the 1950s – the early sixties. Often excluded from overviews of the post-war period, MacInnes was first re-engaged with by Nick Bentley: 'The impulse behind MacInnes's fiction is a desire to represent marginalized voices, as a response to what he considered to be a misrepresentation of youth and black subcultures in the mainstream media' (Bentley 2003–04: 150). MacInnes was a profoundly interesting, conflicted character: bisexual, rude and unconventional but attracted to the establishment, he described himself as an 'insider outsider' (Gould 1986: 108). In *City of Spades*, the Welfare Officer in the Colonial Department, Montgomery Pew, gets involved with an immigrant from Lagos, Johnny Fortune. Written in incredibly short chapters, the novel is fast-paced, anticipating the energies that will erupt with full force in the sixties. The novel is more knowing about racist stereotyping than Dunn or Burgess and dismantles Orientalist and racist attitudes much more decisively, using wit to turn biases against themselves. Here is Pew's friend, the young and naïve Theodora, talking to Johnny Fortune, to whom she is attracted:

> When I returned, I was disconcerted to hear Theodora say: 'This legend of Negro virility everyone believes in. Is there anything in it, would you say?'
>
> 'Lady,' Johnny answered, 'the way to find out is surely by personal experiment.'
>
> 'And is it true,' the rash girl continued, unabashed, 'that coloured men are attracted by white women?'
>
> 'I'd say that often is the case, Miss Pace, and likewise also in the opposite direction.' (MacInnes 1993: 65)

Such knowing, ironical passages are full of witty ambiguities, and the satire is, on the whole, empathetic. MacInnes uses humour to dismantle a cliché about black men and shows how Theodora is trapped in her racist attitude: although she suspects that the association of black people with enhanced sexuality is indeed a 'legend', she in fact hopes it to be true. Indeed, one important element of this context is (sexual) knowledge: it is Theodora who is momentarily led by her desires and irrationality, placing cool Johnny ('He's too intelligent', she notes (MacInnes 1993: 67)) in a comfortable position, from which he is able to use his rationality to seduce her.

At some point, MacInnes representation of this world can be naïve, though, to the point of regression. Pew notes that the influx of immigrants is beneficial because 'they bring an element of joy and fantasy and violence into our cautious, ordered lives' (MacInnes 1993: 66). John McLeod has also noted various other problems, such as Johnny's misogyny and the pervasive representation of the immigrants as naïve about their prospects and in their attitude to the new world they inhabit (McLeod 2004: 46–47). One of the problems critics such as McLeod gloss over is whether this confused, Janus-faced attitude is itself one that MacInnes is trying to represent as present in society at the time. As McLeod, who himself wants to dismiss and celebrate the novel, notes: 'MacInnes remains caught between two contradictory impulses: to assert and critique a regenerative vision of London which rests upon the "overflowing joys" which black immigrants have allegedly brought to the city in the 1950s' (McLeod 2004: 38). The answer again hinges on whether we expect a writer to explicitly place moral verdicts on his characters, whether we understand subtle forms of irony and satire and whether we accept that there is an unwritten contract of knowingness between writer and reader. MacInnes's London triptych is also necessary in ensuring that the writing of the immigrant experience is not confined solely to immigrant writers themselves. In this way, we move away from any kind of essentialism when it comes to claiming the imaginative territory for this important shift in the make-up of Britain's demography and society. The point that the troubled tensions of this insider outsider's novels make is that the inside is 'outsidered' and the outside 'insidered'. London, where one can feel at home without occupying the inside, is the site for testing out such transitions.

Another insider outsider, Maureen Duffy, published the experimental novel *Wounds* (1969), a work concerned with the way in which London's political organs of representation are implicated in the codification of power in London's cityscape and how that power represses those not part of the ideological centre. The wounds of the title are those inflicted on the cityscape and on the psyche of London's marginalized residents, including the lesbian gardener Kingy, the barmaid Maura, and the local mayor, Gliston. Interestingly, the sleeve of the first edition went out of its way to stress that 'these and the many other characters, both Negro and white, illustrate the basic theme of the novel'. The narrative traces the lives of several marginalized south Londoners through five interconnecting storylines, punctuated by one session of intense lovemaking between 'an evidently middle-class, white, heterosexual couple – the very embodiment of the Western ideal' (Brimstone 1990: 31) who rent a *pied à terre* 'just for fucking in' (Duffy 1969: 96). Although this 'ideal' couple embodies the ideological (white, heterosexual) centre, Duffy's marginalization of their story as a mere counterpoint to the main narrative dislodges this supposed centre from its function as a provider of social stability. It is in the south Londoners' lack of acknowledgement that there exists a centre as such that their subversion lies.

In a passage that recalls the use of accents in 'Let Them Call It Jazz', Duffy daringly uses Caribbean patois, or Pidgin English, for her depiction of the inner monologue of the first generation, black immigrant Mrs Fergus. Together with her son she is at a fun fair, supposedly a place of transgression, observing the demure British: 'Even here they enjoy themselves sedately ... No one dance, no one sing only walk about in ones and twos with those blank white faces turning from side to side and the pale eyes taking in, taking in and giving nothing out' (Duffy 1969: 140). By making Mrs Fergus the narrating entity, and the British the Other, this passage acts as an early attempt to break down established conventions and categories. Besides raising questions about the use of accent as a means of representation and the appropriateness for a white writer to use the orthography of the immigrant, this inversion appears to reaffirm the gaps between the autochthonous and immigrant populations, just as in MacInnes. Indeed, the isolated perspective of Mrs Fergus and her use of 'they' indeed suggests a binary division between whites and blacks and a culture of persistent misunderstanding. Do the blacks have a stereotypic image of whites as well, or is Duffy representing valid sentiments that existed in society at the time?

The sheer plurality of marginalized voices are all connected with one another in the novel by the reader making connections (as in the connection between a dancer having her leg amputated and an elderly lady trapped in a high-rise). Thus, this apparent binary opposition gives way to a decentred vision through which every Londoner becomes outsidered, and thereby insidered.

Doris Lessing's female psychogeography
in *The Four-Gated City*

In the same year that Duffy published *Wounds*, Doris Lessing published the fifth, concluding volume of her Children of Violence novel sequence, *The Four-Gated City* (1969). *The Four-Gated City* depicts the private life of Martha Quest against a historical backdrop, beginning with the post-war austerity and Cold War anxieties and their effects on the life of writer Mark Coldridge, whose Communist brother Colin leaves Britain and flees to Russia as a defector. Most of all it chronicles Quest's struggle against separation from her mother and the creative albeit painful way in which she is able to resolve this loss through the adoption of the multifarious identities that London and its residents afford her. The novel also recaptures the sixties *zeitgeist*, from Swinging London to the Campaign for Nuclear Disarmament (CND) and the first Aldermaston March in 1960 (Lessing 1988: 378–80). Over the course of her journey of self-discovery, Quest increasingly becomes attuned to the deepest, hidden parts of her psyche and, aided by her London walks, has utopian visions of London as a New Jerusalem.

At the start of the novel, we find Quest on a long city walk, faced with, like so many other immigrants, a cold, hostile and austere post-war London:

> The dirty sky pressed down over the long street which one way led to South London, and the other to the river and the City. Terraces of two- or three-storey houses, all unpainted since before the war, all brownish, yellowish, greyish, despondent. Damp. Martha stood outside the café where *Joe's Fish and Chips* was outlined by the hearse-dark of black out material. (Lessing 1988: 17)

This description of London as 'a city of darkness, of oppression, of crime and squalor, or reduced humanity' (Williams 1973: 227) comes at the start of a thirty-five-page long depiction of Martha's crossing of the city via the Thames, Queensway, and its 'street of prostitutes' (Lessing 1988: 46), the West End, Notting Hill and Bayswater, 'a climate of money. But the streets, here to the canal, were depressing and lowering: irredeemable by fantasy' (Lessing 1988: 46). Descriptions such as these evidence Lessing's tremendous influence on Iain Sinclair's style. As we walk, the reader follows Quest's inner monologue delivered by a third-person narrator, slowly 'grinding into her day-time consciousness' (Lessing 1988: 49) with her. Indeed, it is during these walks, on her way to the house of her lover, Jack, that Quest discovers how to get in touch with her traumatized self and with the city:

> that somewhere in one's mind was a wave-length: a band where music jigged and niggled, with or without words: it was simply a question of tuning in and

listening. And she had made the discovery, and then forgotten it, that the words, or tunes, were not all that random: they reflected a state or an emotion. (Lessing 1988: 49)

At this moment physicality and materiality dissolve into a metaphysical, even mystical experience that allows Quest to access the deepest part of her (un)consciousness and being. Likewise, Lessing's representation of this London walk aligns her with a long history of urban walking, as she inscribes herself into, and appropriates, a male-dominated tradition of psychogeography.

The Four-Gated City should be seen as part of the history of women city dwellers, which have been put on the map by, on the one hand, Deborah L. Parsons' exploration of the flâneuse in *Streetwalking the Metropolis* (2000), and, more recently, Janet Wolf's 'The Invisible Flaneuse' (2014). What these, and other critics argue, is that, counter to the conventional belief that the flâneur-tradition of Baudelaire signified the male privilege over public, there was a section of (lower-class) women who were always part of the public realm. The theoretical framework of these critics is, however, predominantly sociological and materialist, which has its advantages for thinking about women in concrete historical realities. This rethinking of the city's history in feminist terms is necessary, and I would like to add to this train of thought by arguing that such a rewriting can be supplemented with a focus not only on the historical, physical presence of women in the city but with a look at the metaphysical points of view that women's writing has brought to the city. Indeed, rather than focusing on the flaneur as a figure of contestation, it is the psychogeographer who offers a supplementary, subversive way of rethinking London's history as a psychological construct.

Psychogeography, as we have already seen, is also a male-dominated tradition, from Blake and Dickens to Iain Sinclair and Stewart Home, but women writers too have given their vision of London's psyche. I'm thinking in particular of Clarissa Dalloway's London walks in *Mrs Dalloway* (1925), a major challenge to the masculine, ego-driven psychogeography. However, Elizabeth Bowen's *The Heat of the Day* (1949) and Rose Macaulay's *The World My Wilderness* (1950), which offer descriptions of Blitzed London, and the impact of the city on citizens' minds, serve as precursors to *The Four-Gated City*. Bowen's novel pays particular attention to the city's change in feeling during the Blitz: not only does the possibility of annihilation imbue the city with an increased Thanatos and Eros but the encroaching wildlife in London's bombed sites also brings about a completely different structure of feeling to the metropolis. Bowen's describes the first round of bombings in 1940 as follows: 'No planetary round was to bring that particular conjunction of life and death; that particular psychic London was to be gone forever; more bombs would fall, but not on the same city' (Bowen 1962: 92). Indeed, in the following description, Bowen taps into and makes visible how the radical changes in the material landscape affect people's perception of the city:

> The diversion of traffic out of blocked main thoroughfares into byways, the unstopping phantasmagoric streaming of lorries, buses, vans, drays, taxis past modest windows and quiet doorways set up an overpowering sense of London's organic power – somewhere here was a source from which heavy motion boiled, surged and, not to be damned up, forced for itself new channels.
>
> The very soil of the city at this time seemed to generate more strength: in parks the outsize dahlias, velvet and wine, and the trees one which each vein in each yellow leaf stretched out perfect against the sun blazoned out the idea of the finest hour. (Bowen 1962: 91)

What is interesting about such passages is that they make us understand not what London *looked* like at a particular point in time but how a particular atmosphere *felt*. The detailed description of the phantasmagoric, streaming machinery in the mechanical city is suddenly replaced with, or intruded on by, nature. The listing of vehicles reminds us of Wordsworth's 'Westminster Bridge' (1802), and, although the atmosphere of *The Heat of the Day* is more Gothic and menacing than Wordsworth's celebratory sublime, Bowen too brings back the forces of nature in the city. She adds to this a female element, which lies not so much in the focus on the psyche but in the creation of a lyrical tone of voice that forces the reader into a specific way of seeing and feeling London. Whereas many male responses to the war engaged in material-logistical military descriptions of the war effort, Bowen gives us a counter-narrative about the role women played in the war; in contrast to the objective, materialist depictions of the war by male writers, she also captures the psychology and subjective perception of the Blitz and its aftermath of London's denizens.

A similar example is to be found in Macaulay's *The World My Wilderness*, in which two teenagers run wild in the blitzed yet flowering wasteland of London in the summer of 1945. The novel tells the story of two childhood friends, Barbary Deniston and Raoul Michel, who grow up in rural France during the Second World War. Barbary is the recalcitrant daughter of an upper-class mother, and Raoul the son of a French collaborator, and they both end up in London after the war. Barbary and Raoul are attracted to the wilderness which has sprung up in London's bomb sites, which they roam during the day:

> They got off in Cheapside, and walked up Foste Lane. Having crossed Gresham Street, the road became a lane across a wrecked and flowering wilderness, and was called Noble Street. Beyond Silver Street, it was a still smaller path, leading over still wilder ruins and thicker jungles of greenery, till it came out by the shell of a large church. (Macaulay 1988: 33)

There are many overt references to *The Waste Land* ('this stony rubbish' (Macaulay 1988: 34)) and also precocious existentialist mediations on the meaning of life and the role of religion as a redeemer of modern life. The novel consists of various walks of the City and meetings with figures living on the fringe of society; like Bowen, Macaulay brings back the psychology of London's organic power by focusing on the way in which nature returns, in this mesmeric, lyrical description formed of one 212 word sentence:

> The maze of little streets threading through the wilderness, the broken walls, the great pits with their dense forests of bracken and bramble, golden ragwort and coltsfoot, fennel and foxglove and vetch, and the wild rambling shrubs that spring from the ruin, the vaults and cellars and deep caves, the wrecked guild halls that had belonged to the saddlers, merchant tailors, haberdashers, wax chandlers, barbers, brewers coopers and coachmakers, all the ancient city fraternities, the broken office stairways that spiralled steeply past empty doorways and rubbled closets into the sky, empty shells of churches with their towers still strangely spiring above the wilderness, their empty window arches where the green boughs pushed in, their broken pavement floors – St. Vedast's, St. Alban's, St. Anne's and St. Agnes', St. Giles Cripplegate, its tower high above the rest, the ghosts of churches burnt in an earlier fire, St Olave's and St John Zachary's, haunting the green-flowered churchyards that bore their names, the ghosts of taverns where merchants and clerks had drunk, of restaurants where they had eaten – all this scarred and haunted green and stone and brambled wilderness lying under the August sun, a-hum with insects and astir with secret, darting, burrowing life, received the returned traveller 'into its dwellings with a wrecked, indifferent calm'. (Macaulay 1988: 87–88)

Here, the reader sinks along with the narrator into London's ancient past, beneath everyday, 'fallen' perception, exposed by blowing open physical structures. We find here a constant vying for dominance between spiritual, religious and materialist, economic forces; although the entire novel is heavily influenced by, and full of references to, T. S. Eliot, here spiritual depletion is countered by the Edenic images of greenery.

It is this spiritual trajectory that also lies at the heart of Lessing's *The Four-Gated City*, in a more intense form. Lessing takes the atmosphere of the Second World War and its aftermath as described by Bowen and Macaulay and extends it into the fifties ('Hungary and Suez' (Lessing 1988: 353)) and sixties, which we enter at the end of Part Three with preparations for the Aldermarston to London March of 1960s (Lessing 1988: 460). Quest starts to hear voices and experience visions, and, thinking she is schizophrenic, admits herself to hospital, where she's under the care of Dr Lamb, who explains that there is nothing wrong with her. Her friend Lynda also has various mental breakdowns, and Quest's visions of an ideal city, below London, become increasingly intense, until her earlier vision of London as a deep psychological structure, first emergent in the 1940s, is slowly accessed in more detail. Still walking the streets of London, her mind moves in between Blakean binaries, between hell and heaven; '*All dark or all light*' (Lessing 1988: 567). Through her walks, Quest is able to absorb the multiplicity and diversity of the city and through empathetic identification she is able to replicate the heterotopian nature of London. Just as in Bowen and in Macaulay, it is the Blitz and associated violence, perpetrated mainly by men, that has opened up this new perception of London, for women, even years and years after the war ended, when affluence caused so many changed to the cityscape in the sixties:

> The city had lost its grey shoddiness; that dirty, ruinous war-soaked city [...] it was gone. A fresh soft air moved through it. [...] She walked through this city and that that other one in mind, so that a long street of fashionably built buildings had behind it, or in it, an avenue of nightmare squalor, a darkness and a lightness together. [...] London heaved up and down, houses changed shape, collapsed, whole streets were vanishing into rubble, and arrow shaped of cement reached up into the clouds. [...] It seemed as if the idea of the city or town as something slow-changing, almost permanent, belonged to the past. (Lessing 1988: 278)

Lessing's city is palimpsestic and reminds us of Freud's description of Rome as an unending multi-layered construct in *Civilization and Its Discontents* (1930). London embodies the ability to see through time and space, and to compress and physical manifestations of the city and its people throughout all ages into one four-dimensional image. Although we can connect this idea to a whole raft of male writers, from, for instance, Blake's and Dickens's ability to capture the city's various lives, to T. S. Eliot's 'discovery' of classical structures beneath the surface of the material city, Lessing's London is, according to Christine W. Sizemore, female: 'Because women do not separate out the sense of self as rigid as men do, they are more comfortable with seeing the city as mixed and partial, as districts overlapping one another, rather than as definite precise areas. Perhaps it is also because of this fluid ego boundary that they do not feel threatened by fragmentation' (Sizemore 1984: 178). Given that the lineages of Bowen, Macaulay and Lessing all seem to point to the fact that it is the bombing of London during the war that allows a new perception of the city to emerge, the seeming essentialism of Sizemore's statement becomes more interesting. This new vision, the result of unspeakable male violence, is available to women writers in particular. Indeed, this image of London as a mythical city that contains all of the world and life is also the premise of Maureen Duffy's *Capital* (1975), which would also foreground the image of London as a city made up out of a concentric rings that allows the 'seer' to recreate a model of the world in space and time (Duffy 2001: 93). A certain openness, driven less by an anxiety about fragmentation than the inability to require (and conquer) a whole, seems to link these writers together. It also seems that it is women especially who are able to see, capture and accept the rapid changes in the sixties and that, in many ways, it was during this time that London became theirs.

London has always been an important marker for understanding the psyche of the UK, and England in particular: the capital forms a laboratory in which general problems are tested and taken to extremes. The sixties proved to be a hinge moment in England's recent history, when to the radical economic and material redistribution of the city were added new problems of an ethnic and cultural nature. Marginality has always been a feature of London life, but a new sense of 'outsiderness' has manifested itself since the Notting Hill riots of 1958, when a connection between race and class was forged. The Londons of the 1980s, 1990s and 2000s have all seen race riots tending to be as much a result of dissatisfaction with economic circumstances as with racial discrimination. The London of the 2010s is a city divided, the culmination of a process which accelerated in the 1960s, when the decade's economic boom paved the way for the self-centred aspirational thinking that has since taken hold.

We find a different response in the work of new arrivals, such as Sam Selvon and V. S. Naipaul, which injected a black perspective on the western world that London represented. Indigenous writers who were somehow Other as well, such as Maureen Duffy and Colin MacInnes, also represented the plight of these new Londoners and their representation of black voices moves us away from any essentialism. Doris Lessing provides another strategy, offering a textual London that appropriates the white, male-dominated tradition of psychogeography in order to give a female perspective of London's psyche, something which Maureen Duffy continued in *Capital*. Again, then, the sixties proves to be a space of time when new writers seized the opportunity to appropriate and alter traditions by inscribing themselves within them. Just as the new feminist narratives strengthened a British society and literature which was itself increasingly rudderless, the influx of these new voices gave literature a renewed sense of purpose and direction.

5

English Anti-Novels

A vortex swarm of myriad intention:
The endgame of the anti-novel

We killed him there on the pavement outside the shops, together we all
crushed the life out of him, lying there expecting help. That is how I see it,
and since I was the closest, since it was my lips, my knee, my forearm, you
should see something in the way I see it ... I was the one you all made kiss
him as he died there under my face, and I was the one who kissed him,
though I had no choice. We all had choice and no choice that morning.

(McEwan 1975: 62)

Thus starts one of Ian McEwan first short stories, 'Intersection' (1975), which
shows through a seemingly random eruption of violence how the quotidian lives
of ordinary citizens in a British town are connected. A young boy (John Fisher),
a woman whose car won't start (Mrs Radcliffe) and the nameless narrator are
all drawn together in the killing of an innocent victim, an office worker called
Blygh. Separated by white lines, the story rotates four different blocks of narrative
chronicling the seemingly ordinary mornings of these characters, which come
together at the titular intersection on a High Street, where the narrator beats
Blygh to death, encouraged by the surrounding crowd. Rather than calling an
ambulance, they move in closer and closer to gaze at the body, until they all
crush the narrator and Blygh. McEwan's experiment throws all grammatical
rules out of the window, and the individual interior monologues merge into a
collective point of view and voice with a chorus-like function.

This particular twenty-page-long 'experiment' would not be collected
in McEwan's first two major publications, the short story collections *First
Love, Last Rites* (1975) and *In Between the Sheets* (1978). 'Intersection' offers
a twenty-two line sentence, which dips into the consciousness of individual

characters via the stream-of-consciousness technique; and the use of ellipsis is reminiscent of Natalie Sarraute's 'The Planetarium' (1959). These narrative techniques are aimed at formally capturing 'movement sinuous and bobbing, a vortex swarm of myriad intention' (McEwan 1975: 85). What does the story mean? In a way reminiscent of Ballard's surreal literalization of the sex-as-crash metaphor in *Crash*, McEwan explores through this violent encounter how human relationships have evolved in the post-war West. Blygh is killed by a violent, Spectacular gesture, that is, through a metaphorical ritual that enacts Debordian hyper-mediation whereby the gaze of the multitude converges on a random scapegoat, and their centripetal force rents their victim apart. This sacrifice seems to protest against the atomization of a society of individuals mediated by state and media, which is temporarily re-united into an organic, countercultural mass. Central to the narrative is McEwan's questioning of ordinary causality, morality and the responsibility of citizens in modern society: 'there was a will here, not the sum of its parts' [...] an intention which no single person could claim' (McEwan 1975: 64). The McEwan story is also the endgame of the sixties revolution: the mob's disillusionment and frustration with their impotence and inability to implement change at grassroots' level spills over into ugly violence that is turned against the people: the dream of innocence is over.

The story shows how much British writers were influenced by continental literary experimental forms, in particular the high Modernists and also the late Modernism of Beckett. One of the characters in the short story is called 'Mr. Ball', recalling Beckett's Watt, but in many ways the trajectory of the experimentalist revival in the sixties was in decline. In an interview, McEwan remembers this period as follows:

> I had lost faith in writing. I had been tied to a restricted aesthetic of the novel that I now find quite puzzling. It was the existential trap, the novel cleansed of all reference to place or recognizable public spaces, with no connection to time or historical context. This mode of writing didn't permit itself the luxury of describing inner states; it was all down to what someone said or did. This was my home-grown version of Kafka. (Groes 2013: 152)

The formal heritage of 'Intersection' comes directly from the *nouveau roman* experiments of Alain Robbe-Grillet, Natalie Sarraute, Michel Butor, and Claude Simon, and theorization by Robbe-Grillet, Sarraute, Maurice Blanchot, Roland Barthes, E. M. Cioran and Michel Foucault. McEwan's story is interested in achieving a profoundly forensic mode, the emptying out of narratorial feeling through observational distance and obsessive, neutral descriptions of the minutest detail:

> The sunlight fall on his knuckles, his page, his pen, ceasing at the wrist, at the tunnel of his black coat, this sun through the company office window, showed his knuckles less distinct than their shadows.... He pulls them into the shade on this, *his side* of the desk at the precise moment he stands, scraping back the chair. (McEwan 1975: 64)

McEwan would come to regard this posthumanist line of enquiry as a dead-end. Indeed, the English exponents of the 'anti-novel' investigated here, including B. S. Johnson, Eva Tucker, Ann Quin, Brigid Brophy, Alan Burns, R. C. Kenedy and Rayner Heppenstall, seem to have rejected exactly what the novel form is good at: the exploration of consciousness using language. This view of the novel form is often seen as embodied in the Modernist novel. However, the fiction that I will be discussing looks back not to this Anglo-American strand of Modernism but to the more surreal and defamiliarizing European Modernism. This European line of Modernism operates an aesthetics of dissociation: it divorces thought from feeling, presents us with a hyper-critical introspection producing expressionist mindscapes separated from bodily and material situations; it is obsessed with time, memory and consciousness, exploding the borders between the internal and external worlds in a quest for intersubjective modes of narration. This alternative Modernism begins with *Don Quixote* and *Tristram Shandy*, and then proceeds via Dostoevsky through Kafka, Bergson, Proust, Joyce through to Beckett, Camus, Sarraute and Robbe-Grillet. In the sixties it resurfaces in writers such as Maureen Duffy, Christine Brooke-Rose, Anthony Burgess, J. G. Ballard and B. S. Johnson, and, more recently, in writers such as J. M. Coetzee, Kazuo Ishiguro, Paul Auster, Tom McCarthy and Eimear McBride. This chapter investigates the influence of the Modernist poetics on the work of sixties writers such as Duffy, Quin and Johnson. In reading sixties fiction in terms of its continuation of this alternative Modernist legacy, I will explore how sixties writers sought an escape from the confinement of the traditional composition of the novel form, and in doing so created new forms and structures that anticipate the twenty-first century's renegotiation of consciousness and the mind. This chapter explores the different manifestations of the English anti-novel, arguing for a rich, challenging series of experiments that together contributed to opening up British literary conventions. They also challenge the English parochial spirit through an engagement with the intellectual challenges put forward by their continental colleagues and finding new ways of internationalizing the English consciousness.

Reality, et cetera

McEwan's disappointment and frustration with prose fiction around this period parallels a complaint made by Susan Sontag in an essay published in *Against Interpretation*. In 'Natalie Sarraute and the Novel', Sontag suggests that fiction is lagging behind other art forms in terms of its development. Literature lacks the 'technical revolutions' which have taken place in music and painting; the novel 'remains intransigently *arrière-garde*' (Sontag 2009: 101), that is, backward rather than forward-looking:

> The novel is (along with opera) the archetypal art form of the nineteenth century, perfectly expressing that period's wholly mundane conception of reality, its lack of really ambitious spirituality, its discovery of the "interesting" (that is, of the commonplace, the inessential, the accidental, the minute, the transient), its affirmation of what E. M. Cioran calls "destiny in lower case". The novel, as all the critics who praise it never tire of reminding us and upbraiding contemporary writers who deviate, is about man-in-society; it brings alive a chunk of the world and sets its "characters" within that world. (Sontag 2009: 101)

Sontag's viewpoint is diametrically opposed to the arguments for realism as voiced by, for instance, Raymond Williams (see Chapter 2). Her attack is aimed not so much at representation per se but at society's conception of the world itself. She points to the writing and theory of Natalie Sarraute as a way forward for the novel. In her essay 'The Age of Suspicion' (1950), Sarraute sets out a manifesto for suspicion of realistic literature:

> The sense of life to which [...] all art harks back [...] has deserted these erstwhile promising forms and betaken itself elsewhere. By virtue of the ceaseless movement which tends to bring it ever nearer to the mobile point where, at a given moment, experiment and the peak of effort meet, it has broken through the earlier novel form and forsaken, one by one, all the old, useless accessories. Today, warts and waistcoats, character and plots, may offer the most infinite variety without revealing anything other than a reality, the slightest particle of which we are familiar with already, from having been over and over it, in every direction. Instead of inciting the reader, as in Balzac's time, to attain a truth whose conquest denotes hard-won struggle, all these accessories now appear

to him to constitute but a dangerous concession to his inclination towards laziness – as well as to that of the author – or to his fear of change. The swiftest glance about him, the most fleeting contact, tells him more than all these external appearances, the sole aim of which is to give a semblance of likelihood to the characters. (Sarraute 1963: 87)

Sarraute's essay was published in 1950, but it adumbrates Roland Barthes's renegotiation of writerly authority in 'The Death of the Author' (1967):

To begin with, today's reader is suspicious of what the author's imagination has to offer him. [...] Indeed, the whole problem is here: to dispossess the reader and entice him, at all cost, into the author's territory. To achieve this, the device that consists in referring to the leading character as 'I' constitutes a means that is both efficacious and simple and, doubtless for this reason, is frequently employed. Suddenly the reader is on the inside, exactly where the author is, at a death where nothing remains of the convenient landmarks with which he constructs his characters. He is immersed and held under the surface until the end, in a substance as anonymous as blood, a magma without name and contours. If he succeeds in finding his way, it is thanks to the stakes that the author has planted for his purposes of his own orientation. No reminiscences of the reader's world, no conventional concern for cohesion and likelihood, distract his attention or curb his effort. Like the author, the only barriers he encounters are those that are either inherent in all the experiment of this kind, or are peculiar to the author's vision. (Sarraute 1963: 85, 93–94)

Although Barthes's essay is much more famous for renegotiating the power structure in which the author-God, reader and text are involved, Sarraute shares some of his key concerns, such as the demand for a more active reader, a distrust of realist trickery, and a wholesale rethinking of representation of the real.

Although Sontag is exhilarated by Sarraute's polemic, she does question Sarraute's thinking on the necessity for the 'multiplication of realities' as well as a tendentious definition of 'reality' (Sontag 2009: 109). Sarraute wants a vision of, and connection with, reality not incarcerated by lazy, ready-made conceptions of the real. Sontag finds that Sarraute's very invocation of 'reality' undermines her argument: by railing against 'this rather vacuous notion of reality (a reality lying in the depth rather than the surface)' (Sontag 2009: 110) she buys into various false binaries, such as the objective versus subjective, and original versus preconceived ideas. Sontag:

It really is science, or better yet, sport, that Sarraute has in mind for the novel. The final justification for the novelist's quest as Sarraute characterizes is – what for her frees the novel from all moral and social purposes – is that the novelist is after truth (or a fragment of it), like the scientists, and after a functional exercise, like the athlete. And there is nothing, in principle, so objectionable about these models, except their meaning to her. For all the basic soundness of Sarraute's critique of the old-fashioned novel, she still has the novelists chasing after "truth" and "reality". (Sontag 2009: 110)

The state, and status, of the novel as form of art and its ability to represent human experience was central to intellectual debates. The English anti-novel forms a force field of imagination where this conversation would be taken to its extremes.

The microscopic eye: Materiality, psychology and vision in the *Nouveau Roman*

The English anti-novel was mainly published by John Calder. Calder not only published literary classics from around the world since 1949 but became increasingly politicized when he published American authors censored by McCarthyites in the 1950s. Calder then published the late Modernist work of Samuel Beckett, the French *nouveau roman*, and the Theatre of the Absurd, all of which fed into the English version of the anti-novel.

The English anti-novel as produced by Christine Brooke-Rose, Rayner Heppelstall, Ann Quin, among others, contains some of the minutest observation of detail in literature. In an essay, 'Serious Noticing', James Wood explores how writers use detail in fiction. He notes of Chekhov's use of detail:

Details are not, of course, just *bits of life*: they represent that magical fusion, wherein the maximum amount of literary artifice (the writer's genius for selection and imaginative creation) produces a simulacrum of the maximum amount of non-literary or actual life, a process whereby artifice is then *converted into (fictional, which is to say, new) life*. Details are not lifelike but irreducible: things-in-themselves, what I would call lifeness itself. (Wood 2015: 36)

For Wood, the genius writer is able to capture life through detail, and bring it to life again by making the reader look at it in a specific way: in a defamiliarizing way that makes the world come alive. Wood refers to John Berger's *Ways of Seeing* (1972), which makes the distinction between 'seeing' and 'looking': ordinary people see, and artists and writer look.

The *nouveau romanciers* were obsessed with pushing 'looking' to the extreme. Susan Sontag on Nathalie Sarraute:

The use of the psychological microscope must not be intermittent, a device merely in the furthering of the plot. This means a radical recasting of the novel. Not only must the novelists not tell a story; he must not distract the reader with gross events like a murder or a great love. The more minute, the less sensational the event the better. (Sontag 2009: 107)

The British anti-novels that followed in the sixties push this art across a particular boundary. Brigid Brophy's *Flesh* (1962) has various 'microscopic' (Brophy 1997: 37) observations, and Eva Figes's *Equinox* (1966) has many passage of 'microscopic attention' (Figes 1969: 25):

Air, not moving much, the odd current through an open doorway, and odd fly sending tight little vibrations of angry atmosphere. Doesn't go far. Silence. Words wandering round my head, one or two at the time, without direction. The sun is warm on my arm. b blood warm. t tree. b blue. Bones and blood blossom. I. Eye. It. Them. You. U. Even rock is mainly empty space, a field of force. Families sleep five, eight to a room a few miles away and I am alone in all this air and brick. Even the bricks are large pockets of air. (Figes 1969: 145)

Figes gives us detailed observation packed in a stream of consciousness, yet more is happening than in a Modernist narrative: minute observations of the world but also bodily sensations and mediations on physics, which together create a new state of consciousness, fully concentrated on existence, on pure Being. Although fragmentation takes place, such moments of focus seem to instigate a process of dematerialization, inflected by linguistic defamiliarization. We have moved into a utopian, idealistic mindset in which cognition is expanded, encompassing the physical world completely.

Let's have a look at some anti-novels in which the act of looking itself is defamiliarized, sometimes to the extent that it becomes inhuman. In Rayner Heppenstall's *The Connecting Door* (1962), an unnamed protagonist, a journalist working for a paper called 'The Examiner', finds himself in an unnamed city (which is in fact Strasbourg) to report on negotiations on the future of the Rhine, itself symbolic of Europe after the Second World War. It is 1949. Nothing happens, and the narrator is more interested in observing various young people flirting and dating. The 'novel' has a very peculiar way of narrating, by finishing observations with a staccato, factual remark about a detail. For instance: 'At the station entrance stood a young man who looked a bit like the Austrian film actor, Anton Walbrook. This was Joseph from the hotel. He wore no cap' (14). Here, the remark about the hotel employee wearing not the usual head gear is important because through this absence it says something about the employee and the hotel, about status and social conventions. Another instance: 'I went downstairs [...]. Without a special key, you cannot, from an upper floor, call the lift up. Unless somebody has left it with the open gates on your floor, you walk down. The stair-carpet is red' (15). This passage was picked up on by a *TLS* reviewer, who noted that this moves us away from the symbolic content of description in the realist novel, where details (about the curtains) say something about the world of the characters (that they are bourgeois, or poor, etc.). Here, the focus on carpet seems to have no real function: it is emptied out of symbolic content, but it is also disconnected from the world of which it is supposed to be a seamless part. Heppenstall's mode of narration is thus interested showing how forensic, clinical observations have a defamiliarizing strategy on the world – it points out the strangeness of the material thing-in-itself when unused by humans. This strategy is supposed to bring out the wider thematics of disconnection within the post-war world, a world in which people are losing touch with one another. This effect also has its repercussions for the reader, whose smooth observations of the world within the book is constantly challenged and subverted; it also has an alienating effect to the extent that it seems to want to exclude the reader entirely.

Christine Brooke-Rose's experimental novels of the 1960s most readily defy the reductive question of defining what a novel is 'about': the novels are interested primarily in the relationship between language and metaphor. According to Sarah Birch, *Out, Such* and *Between* explore 'the construction of personal identity' by 'employing one discourse as a metaphor for another' in situations in which a protagonist is alienated psychologically, socially and culturally (Birch 1994: 13). I would like to show, however, that the process described by Brooke-Rose's fiction is actually interested not only in the individual, subjective consciousness. As the protagonist is a metaphor through which we read the wider social constellation, the novel forms a commentary on how society itself is changing in the sixties.

The 'novel' *Out* (1964) is set in a futuristic, dystopian world following a mysterious, apocalyptic event called 'the displacement'. The narrative seems to be set in a fictional country in Africa, where previous race relationships have been reversed; it adumbrates Maggie Gee's *The Ice People* (1998), which also thinks about how race relations might be inverted when Africa has a temperate climate due to the effects of climate change. The narrative starts with a few fictional entries in the files of the nameless male protagonist, who has fled a fictional country called 'Ukay' – a phonetic spelling of UK. The reader is plunged into an opening scene that minutely observes two flies copulating (Brooke-Rose

2006: 13). We slowly come to understand that the narration is driven by various tools and technologies for understanding the world, some real and some made up. Here are some examples:

> A microscope might perhaps reveal the animal ecstasy in its innumerable eyes, but only to the human mind behind the microscope, and, besides, the fetching and rigging of the microscope would interrupt the flies. (Brooke-Rose 2006: 11)

> A microscope might perhaps reveal animal ecstasy among the innumerable white globules in the circle of gruel, but only to the human mind behind the microscope. And besides, the fetching and rigging of the microscope, if one were available, would interrupt the globules. (Brooke-Rose 2006: 15)

> A telescope might perhaps reveal a plant off course, a satellite out of orbit. (Brooke-Rose 2006: 18)

> A bronchoscope might perhaps reveal – (Brooke-Rose 2006: 20)

> A telemetre might perhaps reveal the distance to be three and a half metres, of four. (Brooke-Rose 2006: 20)

> A periscope might perhaps reveal a scene of pastoral non-habitation. (Brooke-Rose 2006: 21)

The repetition of 'might perhaps' introduces a tautological phraseology that foregrounds the conditionality of knowledge about the world, despite the ostensible security that technologies of observation seem to provide. Even more important is Brooke-Rose's invention of fictional tools which measure 'biograms': if a person's mind-body relationship is out of balance, then 'psychoscopy' is recommended, a New Age term associated with psychic readings. Sontag's complaint about Sarraute's ideal for her poetics being science and sport because they are rationally and calculably observable falls to shreds at this point: the act of measurement leads to uncertainty, and the act of observing influences the observed object so that the assumption of a forensic gaze, which is assumed to be at the centre of the *nouveau roman*, is undermined. In this sense, Brooke-Rose both corrects and complicates the ways of looking in, for instance, Robbe-Grillet and Sarraute; she seems to agree with Sontag that observation, both through science and fictional narrative, cannot ever lead to a fundamental fixation of reality.

What Brooke-Rose's novel rescues, then, is the *human* eye, and vision, but in doing so it pushes the Modernist obsession with the crisis in perception even further. Brooke-Rose's narrative plays with physical attributes of materiality, and mobility and speed versus stillness in particular. If we want to observe an object without it succumbing to Heisenberg's uncertainty principle, one has to take out speed of the equation:

> The squint, very wide and very blue, hovers in the doorway, a planet off course, a satellite out of orbit. The skin around the eyes, both the mobile eye and the static eye, is waxy. There is no reproach in the mobile eye. The emotion expresses in nearer to concern. The static eye expresses only off-ness, since it is static, and it is this off-ness which emphasises whatever emotion the mobile eye is expressing. (Brooke-Rose 2006: 23–24)

In the light of this wholesale scientific approach, the Enlightenment legacy is mocked and exposed as being merely a projection of human sentiment and emotion on the world of phenomena. This undercutting of supposedly rational structures operates from the miniscule to the societal, and ultimately becomes an attack on racist attitudes in Western society. In the following discussion of science in Ukay, the scientific discussion bleeds out into a verdict on ethnic tensions in contemporary society:

> The left foot is inside another adenine molecule, the right foot having blotted out one of the energy-rich phosphate bonds East of ribose. The energy-rich bonds cannot be directly used for biological work of any kind, unless transferred to adenosine diphosphate so as to generate new triphosphate molecules. The phosphate radicals –
> – I'm afraid that once a triphosphate molecule has shed its terminal phosphate radical its life as an energy-donor is at an end. In my country –
> – In your country men were lazy. That is why they lost the battle for survival. It is an article of faith.
> – This dialogue is out of place, he's nice, he likes you.
> – They're conceited, lazy, unreliable.
> – We don't bother with them here, they're a typically temperate flower, you know. Mrs. Mgulu says that chrysanthemums remind her of damp December funerals in the North. (Brooke-Rose 2006: 37)

The pun on 'conceited' provides a metafictional reflection on the modus operandi here. The racist attack on the protagonist, which is supposed to diminish the status of his knowledge, should not only be read as a rude intrusion but also as a metaphor whereby the different discourses are read in term of one another. The passage starts off as a meditation on plants and flowers – on organic matter but moves on to thinking about the role of chemistry in creating fertilizer in this post-apocalyptic world. This transposition is then also used in terms of culture, namely, Orientalist thinking often associated the Other with the infinitely fertile soil and procreation, which becomes ironized and reversed, here. The fertile soil of the North is now associated with death, and stereotypes and mythologies are cancelled out. At a more blunt level, this inversion of racism takes place in the dismissal of the Ukayan's 'lazy, unreliable' characteristics, which would normally be aimed at colonial subjects.

Vision is problematized differently in A. S. Byatt's quieter but brilliant *The Game* (1967), where the television too has usurped human vision. The novel tells the story of two sisters, one an Oxford don (Cassandra Corbett), and the other a best-selling novelist (Julia Corbett), locked in an old rivalry. Both are aware of how mass media, and the television in particular, skew the relationship between reality and representation. When Julia Corbett watches a wildlife documentary presented by her former neighbour Simon, she awakens to the idea that the human eye is being increasingly replaced by new forms of vision. She wonders if she'll be invited to appear on television:

> In her mind her own voice echoed, lively, stimulating. She would meet new people. Hopefully, ready to see it as a new world to be entered, she turned on the television. The screen flickered. Julia had a momentary, jumping vision of a huge sheet of water in a haze of heat, and then, superimposed on this, the rounded, superlatively normal face of a girl whose cultured vice about her cultured pearls quavered, came into being and continued. (Byatt 1983: 10)

Watching a TV programme, she awakens to the nonhuman vision encroaching on modern life:

> Only, as the camera made plain, they were not rows, there was no pattern, they were a mass. Julia's eye was bewildered by a series of changes in focus – close-ups of knots of creepers or areas of powdery bark, vistas into the depth of externally extended, haphazardly cluttered cathedrals, between whose pillars the sub occasionally burst in long, white, hissing stars which rested not on the leaves – a phenomenon a camera can hold, as the eye cannot. It was alien and enveloping, in no pretty way. (Byatt 1983: 11)

This is in contrast to the more masculine, positivist attitude of Simon: 'And the scientist with a camera', he said, 'can, as it were, rediscover innocence. The innocent eye, not ignorant, but trained, detached, seeing everything for itself, for what it is, with no apprehensions and very fluid preconceptions' (Byatt 1983: 21). Mariadele Boccardi notes: '*The Game* dissects the ways in which any form of representation inevitably distorts, but at the same time poses uncomfortable questions about the power of the imagination to create reality, thus reversing the intuitive order between the two' (Boccardi 2013: 39). Mid-way through the novel, 'Cassandra's Journal' traces this new crisis of representation, which has much in common with Miles' Notebook of Particulars, in Iris Murdoch's *Bruno's Dream*, which appeared two years later:

> Tyranny of objects. There is a point beyond which the apparent antagonism of certain chairs, or paper-weights, if dwelt on, ceases to be ludicrous. As though they might crush or crowd out. This may also be true of human beings. [...] It could be argued that I resent the simply idea of reality conveyed in the solid presence of chairs and paper-weight. I am particularly disturbed by glass objects [...] because they contain, being transparent, the suggestion they are not simply solid. [...] let it be remembered that these objects have weight, as well as transparency. Not only surface, and heaven beyond the surface, but ponderous weight. There are degrees of reality to be apprehended in all objects, at any given time, and degrees of capacity, in ourselves, to apprehend them. (Byatt 1983: 137)

On one level, this 'glass' refers to the television, which ostensibly creates a sense of a transparent window onto the world through an immersive experience, but it also harks back to a long philosophical and literary tradition that struggles with glass as a metaphor of representation: glass that is solid but transparent – present, and not present. Boccardi notes of Byatt's protagonist that 'in her own life the imagination has taken over reality to such an extent that she finds herself fighting the real, immovable objects in her room, which appear to possess independent existence and are therefore threatening' (Boccardi 2013: 39). Television introduces a new dimension to this problem. The external world and the world of television are mediated, or fused, seamlessly, by her subjective perception, decentring the subject, and placing it in new, complex relationship to the world beyond the subjective self.

The English anti-novel's experiments in cognitive states

One striking feature of sixties experimental fiction is its exploitation of the book as a material object. We might think of writer Marc Saporta's and illustrator Salvador Plascencia's *Composition No. 1* (1962), Tom Phillips's *A Humument* (work in progress since 1966), or of B.S. Johnson's *Albert Angelo* (1963), which has a hole in a page that allows the reader to literally see into the future, and also various 'found' bits and pieces, such as an advertisement for paranormal mind reading. John Fowles's use of epigraphs is also a constant reminder of the fact that the book we are reading is just that, a book, a linguistic and material construct.

We can frame such experiments in twenty-first century explorations of cognition in literature. Alison Gibbons's *Multimodality, Cognition, and Experimental Literature* (2012) explores what she terms a 'multimodal cognitive poetics' (Gibbons 2012: 5) through readings of novels that include interventions such as:

(1) Unusual textual layouts and page design.
(2) Varied typography.
(3) Use of colour in both type and imagistic content.
(4) Concrete realization of text to create images, as in concrete poetry.
(5) Devices that draw attention to the text's materiality, including metafictive writing.
(6) Footnotes and self-interrogative critical voices.
(7) Flipbook sections.
(8) Mixing of genres, both in literary terms, such as horror, and in terms of visual effect, such as newspaper clippings and play dialogue. (Gibbons 2012: 2)

These types of authorial intervention are important for our understanding of sixties experimental fiction in allowing us to pinpoint the precise nature of the shift in consciousness during the period. Indeed, interventions such as graphic deformations have a long history, from Sterne's *Tristram Shandy* (1759) through to Zadie Smith's *White Teeth* (2000). Yet, the density of adventures in materialism during the sixties is conspicuous, and points to writers' interest in playfully engaging with the changing psychological climate. Gibbons notes that 'Cognition is what happens when the body interacts with the physical/cultural world. Minds are not internal to the human body but exist as webs encompassing brain, bodies and world ... "embodiment" refers to the dynamical interactions between the brain, the body, and the psychical/cultural environment' (Gibbons 2012: 66–67). We must see these sixties experiments as a series of interconnected commentaries on the altering psyches of individuals, and of society itself.

Johnson, for instance, continued his experimentation with materiality in the book-in-a-box *The Unfortunates* (1974), which consists of 27 loose chapters, 25 of which can be read in any order. This permutation allows for 15,511,21 0,043,330,985,984,000,000 different readings, exploiting chance to an extreme extent and putting the onus on the reader's frame of reference. David Hucklesby (2014) has written on Johnson's thinking about new media. Hucklesby invokes N. Katherine Hayles's reading of Danielewski's *House of Leaves* (2000) but doesn't explore the implications for reading Johnson's work. Mark Hooper wrote an article about the Johnson experiments as suitable for the digital age, and e-readers, and Jessica Norledge explored the cognitive play in Johnson's work, foregrounding the work's interactivity: 'by overtly presenting the materiality of the book Johnson positions his readers at an emotional distance, only allowing them to fully engage with the novel externally, through the interaction with form' (Norledge 2011: 11). *The Unfortunates* is in many ways analogous to the internet because of its non-linear ordering sections, 'which are governed by the choices of the reader' (Norledge 2011–12), thus behaves like a hypertext, whereby the reader and text are moving into a symbiotic relationship with one another.

Indeed, a more important concept for understanding *The Unfortunates*'s cognitive play is Hayles's notion of 'technotext', formulated in *Writing Machines* (2002), whereby the product carries traces of its production process. All these material traces made by technology lend themselves to forms of reading and interpretation, and the most interesting work will often acknowledge, and challenge, that inscription by technology that it is being produced by, in which case 'it mobilizes reflective loops between its imaginative world and the material apparatus embodying that creation as a physical presence' (Hayles 2002: 25). B. S. Johnson's work in particular, then, combines the creation of cognitive circuits and loops between book and reader with an astounding degree of contingency, which frees up the possibility of interpretation. More so than in a 'common' book, the reader is not only aware that the interpretation is much more dependent upon her frame of reference but that it also builds in and produces a self-critical awareness of the randomness that is at the heart of her reading, and of life. Johnson can be linked with play with mathematics in novels such as Italo Calvino's *Invisible Cities* (1972), as well as with postmodern, hypertextual explorations of change and randomness, such as Shelley Jackson's *Patchwork Girl* (1995). Johnson unsettles the reader by making her not only aware of her own increased role in the readerly interpretation of the book but simultaneously that the infinity of interpretations is an inexhaustive process that destroys conventional meaning as it dwarfs the individual human being: the 'empty', immaterial mathematical way of thinking usurped the physical materiality of humans, and in this sense one might claim that Johnson is already confronting us with new, twenty-first century developments such as Big Data and the digital revolution.

In Brooke-Rose's *Out* we also find unorthodox uses of the book page: the novel starts, for instance, with a series of 'official' documents about individuals and institutions in the fictional state of Ukay. There are details of resettlement camps, labour exchanges and State Hospitals, with details of 'Psychoscopy' performed by doctors on Ukayan subjects. These bewildering documents appear 'real' – there are even crossed out and corrected sections – but contain unknown words and concepts. What is the effect of these authorial interventions? Whereas in Johnson's *Albert Angelo* and in Smith's *White Teeth* graphic deformations have a comical effect, Brooke-Rose employs a different strategy, placing these boxes with mysterious information at the start of the novel, triggering in the reader a desire to understand their context.

Indeed, by foregrounding the materiality of the writer's medium, these writers point out that writing and thinking do not happen in a vacuum but that they have very real and profoundly material implications in society. As we saw earlier in Chapter 2, where women exploited the materiality of the book as comment on women's bodies, writers such as Johnson and Brooke-Rose remind us that the (literary) book has a very important and direct relationship to 'the real', which it shapes and makes in the continuous cognitive loops that make up the human experience.

'A whirling world of words': The Modernist style

As we have seen thus far, British fiction of the 1960s can be characterized as a fragmented and disparate, yet in effect perhaps unconsciously concerted and forceful effort to test our understanding of 'the real' via the upsetting of conventional literary rules of representation in order to challenge conservative literary critics and criticism. It is not surprising then that Patricia Waugh's *Harvest of the Sixties* connects these aesthetic reconsiderations to the postmodern literary production that followed it; published in 1995, the work was heavily influenced by the postmodernist context. Twenty years later, with postmodernism scapegoated for the decline of English Studies because of its centralizing of high theory, we have seen a return to Modernism in many different works of fiction, from Kazuo Ishiguro's *The Unconsoled* (1995), Ian McEwan's *Saturday* (2005) and Ali Smith's *The Accidental* (2005) to Tom McCarthy's *C* (2010) and Eimear McBride's *A Girl Is a Half-Formed Thing* (2014). This raises important questions about the relationship between Modernism and postmodernism, which cannot be discussed here, although it should suffice to say that Modernism was never entirely rejected by the postmodernists; Rushdie's allusions to James Joyce in *The Satanic Verses* (1988), for instance, continued to pay homage to the great innovator.

Anthony Burgess is perhaps the most obvious sixties writer not shy about his allegiance to Modernism. His interest in Joyce has been investigated by numerous critics, from Ákos I. Farkas to Alan Roughley. In the decades that followed Modernism, there was a notable return to modified forms of realism: the politically engaged writing of Isherwood, Auden, Orwell in the 1930s and 40s and the 1950s were dominated by the angry young men and The Movement. Although friends with Kingsley Amis, Burgess distanced himself from the writers of The Movement that came to fame in the 1950s. Burgess satirizes the writers grouped together under the name the Movement: in *A Clockwork Orange*, a street is named after Amis, and in *Enderby Outside* (1968), Hogg has never heard of the poets 'Wunn, Gain, Lamis, Harkin' (Burgess 1968: 7). Burgess's creative word play suggests, indeed, where his literary affections lay. As a linguist lecturing on phonetics, it is no wonder that Burgess is obsessed with the Modernist interest in the creative possibilities of separating the signifier from the signified. The influence of Ferdinand de Saussure can be felt everywhere, for instance in an early novel, *The Doctor Is Sick* (1960), where Burgess's alter ego Edwin Spindrift, professor of linguistics, mediates on the relationship between language and the world beyond the subjective self:

> Words, he realised, words, words, words. He had lived too much with words and not what the words stood for. James Joyce had been such another, with his deliberate choice of a sweetheart from a sweetshop, his refusal to correct a visitor who had called a painting a photograph, because 'photograph' was such a lovely word. [...] A world of words, thought Edwin, saying it aloud and liking the sound of it. 'A whirling world of words.' Apart from its accidents of sound, etymology and lexical definition, did he really know the meaning of one word? [...] Let him loose in the real world, where words are glued to things, and see what he did: stole, swore, lied, committed acts of violence on things and people. He had never been sufficiently interested in words, that was the trouble. [...] He'd treated words as things, things to be analysed and classified, and not as part of the warm current of life. (Burgess 1960: 152–53)

I'd like to claim that the obsession with Modernism in the work of sixties writers is not a form of 'late' Modernism nor a postmodern pastiche but that it acts as a key hinge moment that passes on the Modernist legacy in modified ways to our twenty-first century times.

In 1957, Doris Lessing had lived in Britain for nearly a decade and complained about the insularity and parochialism of British writers and intellectuals, commenting sardonically that the proclaimed New Left's idea of 'thinking internationally means choosing a particular shade of half-envious, half-patronizing emotion to feel about the United States; or collecting money for

Hungary, or taking little holidays in Europe, or liking French and Italian films' (see Waugh 2011: 13). According to Patricia Waugh, there was little substantial change until 1980, when the explosion of 'internationalist' writers such as Rushdie, Amis the Younger, Timothy Mo broke through, accompanied by writers such as Ian McEwan and Kazuo Ishiguro – a group who together broke open the intellectual and geographical horizon of English culture (Waugh 2011: 13).

My first argument is that sixties literature was in search of, and found, an international, cosmopolitan spirit by looking outward to, and connecting with, European and American writing and culture. The 1960s should be viewed as a writerly attempt to prise open the perceived narrow-mindedness and provincialism of the austere post-war English consciousness, through various modes of writing. The first wave of postcolonial writing took place, and the sixties drew its literary energy from repatriates such as J. G. Ballard and Anthony Burgess. At the level of form the conspicuous harnessing of Modernist strategies created an internationalist atmosphere. The sixties saw not only the birth of postmodernism with its celebration of surfaces and mediation but also an ambiguous investigation of the effects of cultural and economic globalization occasioned by the 1957 economic boom and mass marketing of culture and identity that caused homogenization and erasure of cultural and social difference.

My second argument follows from this interest in the European intellectual tradition, which stretches beyond Modernism and connects with liberal humanist philosophy. At University College London (UCL), Frank Kermode introduced the high theory of French poststructuralists, which siphoned through in writers such as Christine Brooke-Rose, John Fowles, Muriel Spark and A. S. Byatt. British writers were also influenced by new forms of culture rising in the United States, including the Beats, resulting in Alexander Trocchi's provocative work and Iain Sinclair's earliest publication *The Kodak Mantra Diaries* (1970). Many writers were influenced by the radical psychology of the Scotsman R. D. Laing, including the new sf movement spearheaded by Michael Moorcock and J. G. Ballard in 'New Worlds' magazine.

A mosaic style: Maureen Duffy's queering of Joyce

Born in 1933, Maureen Duffy is an extraordinary author who published her first novel *That's How It Was* in 1962, and has gone on to publish seven collections of poetry, nineteen novels, seventeen plays and seven works of non-fiction; she published her most recent novel, *In Times Like These* in 2013. Her work is characterized by generic eclecticism, formal experimentation and political progressiveness, and covers uncomfortable topics such as terrorism, homosexuality, the rights of animals and censorship. *That's How It Was* is to Duffy what *A Portrait of the Artist* is to Joyce: an analysis of how one's personal history relates to a wider, national history, an exploration of how the status quo can be rewritten by exploring and exploiting mythologies, and a rewriting of one's home city in terms of personal and historical myth. The novel, like Joyce's *Portrait*, is a *Künstlerroman*, which sees the transformation of an adolescent into an artist. This fictional autobiography portrays Duffy's upbringing during the war and her early life in a linear manner, using the language of realism: the book is a dutiful rendition of her youth, where any experimental pretence would betray the loving relationship with her mother.

After the chronological realism of *That's How It Was* Duffy's fiction turns to anti-Aristotelian experimentation. Duffy's 1966 novel *The Microcosm* is a key example of how sixties writing brings back Modernism on its own terms. The novel has its origins in a series of interviews Duffy did with lesbians in the early sixties (see Chapter 1), and although this modus operandi is comparable with Dunn's *Up the Junction*, Duffy reimagines her original source material into a multiplicity of perspectives, resulting in a polyphonic, complexly stratified novel. *The Microcosm* is set in a lesbian bar in Swinging London called The House of Shades – the microcosm of the title, a place consciously harking back to Radclyffe Hall's descriptions of lesbian bars and salons in *The Well of Loneliness* (1928). We follow the story of a multiplicity of seemingly disparate characters, Judy, the gym teacher Steve, the factory workers Jonny and Sadie, the woman gardener Bill, Marie Pacey, Cathy and Matt, who features as a vocalizer of the disparate lives that meet at The House of Shades. All of them are, in their own way, outsiders; in different ways they are all traumatized by a mainstream society from which they are excluded. The novel becomes an investigation of what Duffy calls 'all the symptoms of the outcast' (Duffy 1989: 58).

Joyce's importance is acknowledged in an Afterword to *The Microcosm* (1966):

> I wanted to use a language for fiction that was capable of rising to poetry, and that had all the sinewy vigour and flexibility of the London demotic I had been brought up on [...] I wanted a structure in which the parts would take their meaning from being juxtaposed to each other rather than chronologically consequent on each other. I wanted a novel that could put on any dress not just a sober suit ... I invented for what I wanted to do the term 'a mosaic style' that would break the tyranny of linear narrative, and that consciously harked back to Joyce. (Duffy 1989: 290)

Duffy's engagement with Joyce is important for a number of reasons. She acknowledges Joyce's mastery but appropriates his formal innovations to queer him: rather than having the white heterosexual male determining the rules of representation, here both form and content are used for representing marginalized subjects.

Duffy cuts the novel up into discrete sections, superimposing distinct rules of representation onto each section. Where *Ulysses* used this modus operandi in a very rigid manner, Duffy operates within a much looser framework. Like the Nighttown chapter, the opening section of *The Microcosm* is dominated by the recording of dialogues between various disembodied voices, creating a ghostly cacophony in which the reader is lost. These sections centre on 'Matt', whose gender the reader is unsure of. The formal arrangement supports and amplifies the identity struggle of these outcasts. The next section, focusing on the young gym teacher Steve, makes use of interior monologue to test (sexual) morality when she starts an affair with a French teacher. This is followed by a picaresque historical narrative about the misfortunes of a member of the gentry, Charlotte, who cross-dresses as 'Charles'. This section is written by a fictional woman novelist who already in 1755 'lives by her pen' (Duffy 1989: 97), recorded in a fictional encyclopaedia of women dramatists in 1812.

Duffy is also finely attuned to the distinctly Joycean speech and sound patterns at sentence level. Here is passage that describes Matt and his lover Rae sitting in a car at night:

> Blades of light scythe through the dark air mowing down the night in swathes that fall blackly from the lamp-path, lying thick in the gutter and at the roadside. Inside the car is warm and drowsy with the scent of her body. She puts a light hand on his thigh and he is conscious of them both rushing under the dark branches, cut off from the rest of the world by a thin skin of glass and painted metal, hurried along together in its soft upholstered belly. (Duffy 1989: 134)

The cadence of these sublime sentences invoke the seductive rhetoric of Joyce's aesthetic, which is so intricately intertwined with his ability to invoke epiphanic experiences.

Another technique Duffy borrows from *Ulysses*'s Penelope section is the destruction of conventional forms of punctuation in the interior monologue of a young lesbian woman, Marie Pacey, who in order to please her parents denies her feelings for Matt, and marries a man who gives her a baby, and beats and rapes her:

> he beat me with a big stick i never knew it was so big it frightened me. and there was only once just once early in the morning when i was still half asleep and

i didn't understand what was happening and id been dreaming about her and there we were on holiday like it always is in dreams lying on the warm sand side by side listening to the water eyes closed and voices drifting from a long way off and she took my hand but she never did it wasnt true and I started to wake up and was saying there that didn't hurt did it theres a good little princess and the back of my legs all wet and sticky and he put his hand round in front and touched me there and i felt. (Duffy 1989: 107)

Here is the orthography of a profoundly traumatized mind, a nightmare from which Pacey is trying to wake up. Marie has a mental breakdown and is unable to teach any more: 'sick o I am sick indeep' (Duffy 1989: 99). Her trauma is depicted through a breakdown in orthography, syntax, capitalization, punctuation, grammar and typography. The graphical deformation of the syntax stands for the woman's damaged sense of self: the lower case 'i' instead of and upper case suggests a diminished identity, and her inability to work through her trauma and admit her true sexual identity. This is in marked contrast to Stephen's overconfident 'I, I, I, I' repetition in *Ulysses*. The loss of punctuation suggests that Marie is unable to control life in more general terms, and her lack of use of the apostrophe suggest that there is a nasty politics of possession and ownership playing itself out: Marie lacks possession of herself as she is unable to escape her brutal husband but also because she is unwilling to acknowledge her homosexual identity. In more general terms, Marie is unable to withstand society's rules and pressures. She meditates on the authority of doctors, who wield (male) power over her body, on the tensions between modern women and men, who no longer understand women today, and her inability to connect with her mother: 'i hate my mother. i am pushing her into a washtub of bubbling sulphuric acid. the flesh strips from her bones clean bones bleached' (Duffy 1989: 102). The reader's ability to inhabit this trauma expressed at the level of language is thus one way of understanding and empathizing with a section of people whose exclusion from mainstream society resulted in mental breakdown.

A last stylistic feature of *The Microcosm* is a typically Duffy-esque 'queer' orthography in the historical narrative about the cross-dressing character Charlotte/Charles. In this section we encounter sentences such as the following:

Here he stayed for some months chearfully and agreeably .... (Duffy 1989: 80)

Ten of the best hands in town compleated his band of musick ... (Duffy 1989: 80)

...he was absolutely changed to a driv'ling ideot nor was there the least consistency in one single syllable he uttered (Duffy 1989: 81)

These misspellings form a pastiche of archaic spelling, signalling to the reader that these are deliberately falsified versions of these words, suggesting that this 'historical' section is counterfeit and the novel exposes the constructedness and artifice of heteronormative identities in modernity, and the role that language has in underpinning the self. Harking back to *Finnegan's Wake*, the artists is a forger and a 'sham'.

For Duffy, Joyce is the pre-eminent figure of authority to aspire to but also to write back to, and to write against. Duffy admires Joyce for his the sensuousness and the frank depiction of sexuality, but, like Freud, Joyce acts as a Father, and needs to be challenged, and corrected. One correction of Joyce's 'fatherhood' takes place in relation to his heteronormative politics: Joyce is queered. In *The Microcosm*, the gender confusion surrounding Matt is a key element: Matt works in a garage, and is referred by through the book by masculine pronouns. In Christophe Bode's words: 'The subject matter may be the trials and tribulations of a group of people who are systematically discriminated against because of their sexual orientation and preference – the formal, narrative presentation of this, however, is a constant questioning of our habits of perception, classification, conceptualization and construction of identities. It is the reader who in constantly on trial' (Bode 1997: 44).

Yet, despite the radical experimentalism of *The Microcosm*, the novel is an attempt to express the sixties experience in new forms while connecting past traditions with new conditions and contexts. *The Microcosm* ends with a clear message about the value of humanism, and of some kind of organic wholeness, both at the level of the individual and for society. For Duffy, Joyce is not just a Modernist innovator but also part of the European tradition of humanism. When Matt decides to leave the safety of the refuge that is the House of Shades, the isolated shelter that houses the marginals, he takes his 'whole personality' to the world outside in order to see what will happen. She says:

> There's no such thing as a microcosm. [...] Society isn't a simple organism with one nucleus and a fringe of little feet, it's an infinitely complex living structure and if you try to suppress any part of it [...] you diminish, you mutilate the whole. [...] Not only can you say that the microcosm doesn't exist but it shouldn't exist because it's an idea that springs from the fragmentation of experience and knowledge. [...] But somehow we ought to be able to keep the idea of the totality of experience and knowledge at the back of our minds. (Duffy 1989: 287)

Duffy acknowledges the vastness and complexity of the modern world, and yet she wants us to keep the *idea* of a total knowledge which is Joyce's project. What we have here is a rejection of the binary opposition of the centre versus margins concept of society, so deeply ingrained in twentieth-century thinking. Matt rejects easy compartmentalization and labelling, as a form of self-ghettoization, of self-exile – another point where Duffy deviates from Joyce. This takes place at the level of the subject matter but also in the form of the novel, which prefers no particular style or mode of narration: Duffy's project is then a key part of the new realisms generated by the sixties, a modified form of narration and representation that is inclusive and which, unlike Christine Brooke-Rose's rejection of realism, gives us change and transformation.

Ann Quin's *Berg*

Ann Quin's *Berg* (1964) is a compelling, unrelenting narrative that demands new forms of critical inquiry. After a troubled life suffering from mental breakdowns, Quin committed suicide at the age of 37 in the same year as B. S. Johnson, 1973; unlike Johnson there has not been a major revival of interest in her work, despite Quin's fine writing style. After producing two unpublished novels, her third attempt, *Berg* (1964) was published by John Calder, who had by then the monopoly on publishing experimental writing, from Trocchi to Burroughs. The novel was followed by *Three* (1966), *Passages* (1969), which was written after extensive travel across Europe, and *Tripticks* (1972), a novel that mocks the modern family in the consumer society that emerged in the sixties.

Berg consists of a series of chapterized hyper-solipsistic monologues by a young man, Alistair Berg, who has returned to his home town of Brighton to murder his despised father, Nathanial Berg, a washed out purveyor of hair treatment products. Alistair has reversed his late name to 'Greb' – a telling inversion. Alistair stakes out his father's flat, where he lives with his mistress Judith, after his mother Edith has been abandoned; Alistair is in constant dialogue, however, hearing her voice, and talking to her and writing messages on postcards. Alistair's wish is to see his father suffer rather than die, and, rather than going through with the patricide immediately, he first procrastinates and hesitates, fuelled by perverse fantasies that result in various, increasingly complex and preposterous, imaginative scenarios. Nathanial is only truly able to connect emotionally to a budgerigar, Bertie, and Alistair fantasizes about killing the bird. He then decides to seduce Judith – second in line for Nathanial's affections – but he realizes this would turn him a surrogate of the father. After producing a dummy of Nathaniel, he kills and discard the 'corpse'. These imagined killings are merely symbolic, of course, and Quin leads to an uncomfortable finale in which Alistair dresses up in Judith's old clothes, and wearing a wig and make-up, is raped by his father. Impotence wins out: Alistair is unable to free himself of the anger towards his father, which, rather than being a source of power acts as a form of entrapment.

Various intertextual lines intersect in *Berg*, woven into a complex, experimental web of literary and psychological influences. Working from a set of classical themes, Alistair reminds us of Odysseus, who comes home after a long voyage for retribution of his Penelope, in this case his mother Edith. The myth of Oedipus is also of central importance, although the novel gives us a modern variation on the myth, voiced through Freud's work. The nightmarish atmosphere is created partly through allusions to Dante's hell: 'Berg sat on the bed, kneed sliding together, tracing concentric circles in the eiderdown' (Quin 1989: 90). The bed, place of copulation and procreation, is hell for Greb. *Berg* is also a variation on *Hamlet*: leading to a heavy intertextual import of Hamlet's existential meditations, and, just as Hamlet stalks Elsinore and Stephen Dedalus roams Dublin's beachside, Alistair haunts Brighton's beach front: 'Slowly across the park; I a ghost who walks abroad, a Cheshire smile that grows and grows, and giant hands which will squash everything that refuses to hold the rules and regulations I may assign' (Quin 1989: 60). We hear watery echoes of *The Tempest* too throughout the novel, continuing the allusions to death and suicide: 'Your hair's like seaweed' (Quin 1989: 158), is one example and we also feel in passages such as the following: 'Like entering the sea. The sea alone. Alone by the sea. By the sea. Alone. By yourself. Oh it's nice to do that, do it again, oh it's lovely' (Quin 1989: 146). Much of these texts are filtered through Joyce's engagement with the classics; Greb's interior monologue can be viewed as an extended nightmare version of Joyce's 'Nighttown' chapter in *Ulysses*.

On the surface the novel is profoundly, perhaps annoyingly self-reflexive, creating an atmosphere where nothing is authentic but always mediated and bracketed by various forms of mediation: of language, social barriers and power, gender, and bodily materialities. The traumatized protagonist, Alistair Berg, experiences the world as composed out of surfaces: 'As he approached the house everything appeared almost without concrete formation; the dance hall, churches and houses all flat shapes' (Quin 1989: 31). This technique resembles Marcel Duchamp's painting 'Nude Descending a Staircase' (1912), which, for Sontag, the point 'is not so much to represent anything, much less a nude, descending a staircase, as to teach a lesson on how natural forms may be broken into a series of kinetic planes' (Sontag 2009: 100–1). The point is that

Quin is attempting to take out all materiality out of lived experience, or, at least try to show how Alistair's own psychologically traumatized vision has reduced the physical world to an abstract set of representations, devoid of content but manageable and inhabitable.

Quin's language is remarkably effective in creating a restless, meandering mind whose rage is directed against the Father; it is easy to see why existing criticism has taken a Freudian line of enquiry. Whereas Burgess's Spindrift is lost in his whirling world of words, Alistair's existential crisis and metaphysical speculations brings back his need for authenticity, materiality and 'the real':

> But I have to feel certain, absolutely sure I have everything under control, that nothing is intruding. How his head ached this morning, as through many fingers poked amongst the tissue, blood and bones. I must recall the present circumstances, when nothing at all from outside interfered, not even thoughts of time past, present, or time future, when doubt of my own reality have dwindled away. Isn't there a moment caught between two moods, that space within, separated from life, as well as death, when the sun is face without blinking, when eternity lies inside; no division whatsoever, simply a series of circular motivations? But these hands with their veins from a leaf, there is no separation, only a distasteful similarity. Why though search for proof? Surely I'm no philosopher to analyse the value of reality as opposed to idea, and what is gained by delving into such linguistic labyrinths? Definitely the supreme action is to dispose of the mind, bring reality into something vital, felt, seen, even smelt. (Quin 1989: 22–23)

However, the questioning of the value of delving into the linguistic labyrinths of Joyce is important as it sets out boundaries and markers for Quin's experiment. Quin is interested in interior states and investigating the operations of cognitive processes, but, just like Maureen Duffy, ultimately she is in search of some form of wholeness, of human identity, and life and society itself. Indeed, the novel is full of broken connections, between family members, so that the only things left are artificial performances of such previous realities. In this sense, *Berg* feels more Beckettian than Joycean, and Alistair's condition resembled that of Hamm and Clov in *Endgame* (1957), where the past can only exist as fictional performance. What is more striking, however, is that the novel seems to be an experiment in fluctuating cognitive states. In this sense it is, through its reworking of Joycean techniques and of the *nouveau roman*, an attempt at textualizing consciousness in its various facets.

The difficulty of *Berg* is enjoyable precisely because its rules of representation are so very different, creating a cognitive flux that represents a particular kind of trauma of psychological imbalance. To understand mode of Quin's writing of consciousness, it is useful to first quote neuroscientist Stanlislas Dehaene, here, who helpfully conceptualized approaches to consciousness:

> The word *consciousness* [...] is loaded with fuzzy meanings, covering a broad range of complex phenomena. [...] the contemporary science of consciousness distinguishes a minimum of three concepts: vigilance – the state of wakefulness, which varies when we fall asleep or wake up; attention – the focus on our mental resources into a specific piece of information; and conscious access- the fact that some attended information eventually enters our awareness and becomes reportable to others. (Dehaene 2014: 8–9)

Berg attempts to represent all of these three different phenomena: Alistair zones in and out of different forms of alertness and his attentiveness fluctuates, rendering an image of that human mind that is deeply unstable. And consciousness is often blocked: Alistair is, like Hamlet, locked into a mind which has trouble connecting with the outside world.

However, even more interesting in its representation of the human mind is Quin's attempt to understand how experience is made up of consciousness as well as the Freudian unconscious processes and the cognitive nonconscious, that is, the non-attentive working of the mind. When Alistair walks along the beachfront of Brighton, a scene that imitates Joyce's beach scene in *Ulysses*, he mediates on the nature of consciousness: 'Fallen into ways where no one in a conscious state would dare to thread; gone astray in a slender thread. There must be some clue, hasn't there been a recognition, a little subjugation from all this' (Quin 1989: 99). This passage is important because it explicitly moves us away from the notion of the Freudian unconscious, and aligns itself with a *non*conscious state. We are moving away from a psychological line of argument to a cognitive perspective, which can be elucidated by looking at what in neuroscience is called the 'default mode network', which has only been mapped in the late noughties. This default mode network is essentially the activity of the brain when it is in a resting state, and people start 'mind-wandering into their own thoughts' (Dehaene 2014: 187). Another idea is that the base state of humans is not vigilant and alert: consciousness is a tool that we develop in order to protect ourselves from the phenomenological impact of stimuli in the outside world. Interesting is *Berg*'s close attention to and analysis of dreaming:

> A desire to know everything about her, the colour of her hair before touching it up, the way she might sit up suddenly, or slowly stretch out in bed, in the

mornings the curve of her back, her dream murmurs. Surely an idle dream, where the point of reality? (Quin 1989: 112)

We certainly hear Shakespearean tones here, but Quin's novel adds another critical layer by constantly being on the verge of slipping into different cognitive states. The resulting inability to tell the difference between the 'real' and dream result in the loss of fixed epistemological parameters that anchor our understanding of reality. This idea of the distributed base state of the human mind is helpful because it again allows us to invoke a number of key ideas which the sixties explored. Not only is there the anti-Freudian drive that we find in psychologists such as R. D. Laing, but again we see how *Berg* acts out an extended fugue, or mind-wandering, in its protagonist's nomadic wanderings through Brighton.

Mind-reading with Eva Tucker

Eva Tucker's two fine novels published by John Calder in the sixties, *Contact* (1966) and *Drowning* (1969) are out of print. Both are brilliantly written, and, like *Berg*, present us with cognitive experiments that draw much on the Modernist legacy of thinking about consciousness, while also going beyond Modernist techniques to think about how theory of mind works in the novel. *Contact* is composed of loosely connected episodes, divided up by three asterisks. It narrates a story of a 'week-end house-party in England' (Tucker 1966: 112) organized by the writer Richard and Sarah Mason, who live in the countryside with their two children, and a cat called Caliban. They invite a sundry group of people, including the bookseller Toby, who has his shop on London's Tottenham Court Road, his lover Jeanie, the 'cyberneticist' (Tucker 1966: 52) George Denton, the university lecturer Jessica Allford, and her friends Jessica, Max and Simon and the married couple Vera and Arnold. Richard's and Sarah's marriage is in crisis, as Richard has lost physical attraction to Sarah, and the novel centres on the restoration of their relationship. During the dinner party, the company have high-minded conversations about existentialism, but in the meantime Eros rages. Richard is interested in Jeanie, while Sarah wants to sleep with Toby, and is sexually no longer interested in Richard: 'I want to enjoy it. I love him. I want him to want me. Why can't I?' (Tucker 1966: 9). These questions, about marriage and infidelity, are found in many different sixties novels, but Tucker's refined writing and experimental modus has an aesthetic that adds a fine formal layer.

Although the novel has a clear telos, geared towards either a divorce or renewal of Richard's and Sarah's love, the novel is really an experiment in understanding psychological states, and in tracing how communication works – or doesn't. The novel is full of broken connections, human and technological. When Sarah rings up to invite George Denton, of the company Cybernetics Laboratory, she mocks him for working very late: 'George Denton, your circuits need rewiring' (Tucker 1966: 29). Denton notes that he is too busy, and thinks: 'A whole weekend off? Impossible. And yet.... Absent-mindedly he mended the broken connection on his translation machine' (Tucker 1966: 30). When Toby rings a telephone number, the phrase 'Toby is waiting to be connected' (Tucker 1996: 34) is not just referring to the operators. The voices coming down the line are uncanny: 'Jeanie laughed. The laugh distorted and magnified down the telephone sent shivers down Toby's spine' (Tucker 1966: 34).

The novel begins with Richard being told that Toby is a 'good man' by Sarah, prompting the following response:

> Richard opened the window and smelt autumn. Sun, wildly orange, beginning to set. Sky, intensely blue, thinned to jade where it touched purple mountains. Every crevice, ever clump of heather, every thread of smoke, quite clear in the incandescent light. Smooth sea: oystercatcher beating shell against pebble. Two herring gulls shrieked on a rock; parting the waters, a cormorant emerged, spreading heraldic wings. Richard turned away, bored. Life is other people. Other people.
>
> He put his head out again and closed his eyes. London. Roar of red buses. Petrol fumes. Hot overused air blowing up from underground. Plate shop fronts, dirty posters peeling off walls. Small spots of warm rain from grey sky; smell of beer from pubs, smell of scent of women; loud and garish music, brass and silver, blind man, box for disabled in the war; mottled barks of plane trees in quiet squares, quiet but not dead; quiet people with faces; small untidy bookshops full of quiet books; smell of old and dusty books. He drew his head in and shut the window with a bang. (Tucker 1966: 5)

The reader is not sure what is going on and will only later realize the wider implication of this meditation, which sets up, in remarkably beautiful language, the various divisions in the novel. We have two Joycean lists battling it out over what is the best form of living: nature or the city. We also learn that Richard, the writer, has some problem connecting with his wife: her phrase a 'good man' puzzles him, and he has to look up the meaning of the word good in the dictionary.

Tucker is adept at exploiting the interior monologue of the various characters and showing how despite their ostensible psychological and physical/sexual separateness, they are in many ways similar. The novel also explores some very intricate forms of cognitive logic, and Tucker is adept at exploring theory of mind in particular. Theory of mind, a concept stemming from evolutionary psychology, is basically the ability to imagine what others are thinking about something else: I think you think I'm angry. Human beings 'are far more sophisticated than any other creature' (Ridley in Groes 2014: ix) and much better able than animals to 'describe our ability to explain people's behaviour in terms of their thoughts, feelings, beliefs, and desires' (Zunshine 2006: Loc.189). People are able to handle fourth-order or even fifth-order intentionality: 'I think that you think that he thinks she thinks I am angry'. This is hard to get your head around in the form of an artificial experiment, but this layering of intension is the driving force behind political fictions such as the *West Wing*, or any clever detective thriller. Lisa Zunshine's *Why We Read Fiction* (2006) explores how novels exploit theory of mind. One of the finest practitioners of using 'mind-reading' (Zunshine 2006: Loc. 189) in the novel is Virginia Woolf, for Zunshine, as she can both represent and invite the reader to engage in fourth- and fifth-order intentionality.

Tucker is an expert at writing mind-reading as well and at inviting the reader to engage in theory of mind. At the start of the book, we are moving into the mind of Toby, and he is shamefully thinking: 'Kissing Sarah's breasts was a sentence that hardly made sense, yet as he thought it, Toby went red, not with sudden desire but because surely, well, certainly, Richard had done this, still and often would again, kiss his wife's breasts' (Tucker 1966: 21). A transition from third- to fourth-order intentionality takes place, here: we move from 'Toby thinks lustfully of Sarah and this makes him ashamed' to 'Toby thinks of Richard thinking of Toby thinking lustfully of his wife, Sarah'. However, we must also include the reader and then we arrive at fifth-order intentionality: 'I [the reader] see Toby becoming aware of Richard being aware of Toby's lustful thoughts about his wife, Sarah'. Needless to say this is just a thought experiment on Toby's part, but we can see how human empathy is part of a very complex psychological structure that in this case provides a kind of moral surveillance within this circle of friends. The reader is involved in this as well, in complex ways: although we may not necessarily subscribe to Toby's Puritan conscience, we are subtly drawn into a contract with this character, whose deeply private thoughts we are able to read.

Tucker complicates these ideas even further later on in the narrative. During the weekend at their house, Richard is increasingly aware that he desires Toby's lover Jeanie: 'He looked at Jeanie's breasts. Why don't I touch them? She wouldn't mind. He put out his hand, but it landed on the table, like a spastic's, a good six inches short of its goal' (Tucker 1966: 110). We find here the same psychological layering of intentions, with added irony: because we already know that Toby is attracted to Richard's wife, Richard's lust has another meaning, namely, that they are bound by the same desire for their friend's wives – that is, that they are operating with the same psychological defects, an inability to understand theory of mind, or empathy. The point is, of course, as the novel's title points out ironically, that the characters do not realize this. Just as Lessing's women in *The Four-Gated City* become increasingly telepathic as a sign of their openness toward other minds and tools outside their corporeality, Sarah too is frustrated about men's inability to be more empathetic:

> She looked angrily at him, willing him to open his eyes. But he was never a good subject for intended telepathy – only when her thoughts would have been better uncommunicated did Richard uncannily divine them. As when, for instance, the shadowiest image of a desirable man flitted across her mental image screen and caused him immediately to turn away from her in bed. (Tucker 1966: 33–34)

Miscommunication abounds in the novel. At the start of the novel Toby thinks he should say he'll marry Jeanie but doesn't do it, and Richard states later: 'Again he [Toby] could have said – I'm going to marry her – but he didn't' (Tucker 1996: 37). The reason for this miscommunication is, just as in Lessing's 'To Room 19', a failure of (too much masculine) rationality. At the dinner party in *Contact*, 'Simon was saying "Even if all humans were destroyed, rationality would remain a predicate of all human nature"' (Tucker 1996: 56). However, towards the end we find that *peripetia* and the various disconnected characters are making spiritual and bodily connections:

> She held out her hand. He shook it.
>
>   Monk's hand.   Wife's hand.
>
> Hand. Hand.   Thank you. Thank you. (Tucker 1996: 127)

And although Toby is uncertain about a long-term relationship with Jeanie ('marrying her will entail such a drastic cauterisation' (Tucker 1996: 130)), he does seduce her. Vera's husband Arnold, who is a distant father to their daughter, Sarah, finally manages to make contact: 'Arnold dared not move forward. He was dying to kiss Sarah. Then he lunged forward and seized hold of his daughter. They kissed firmly. Infinitesimal second of love. Father/daughter love, Sarah/Arnold love, this/that love, x/y love' (Tucker 1966: 144). These moments of connection build towards a finale in which, ridden with self-doubt and pangs of morality, Sarah makes her choice. This moment coincides with Richard's realization that any commitment to other people will require a form of giving up, to a certain degree, freedom, as is explained in the heavily Sartrean revelation: 'It occurred to him that the blankness he had just experienced was what freedom amounts to, if freedom was stripped of its trappings with which the *mauvais foi* [bad faith] of its protagonists embellished it; freedom essentially contentless. Being free equals being nothing' (Tucker 1966: 154). Sarah returns to the countryside, and the narration flits back and forth between their two perceptions of one another, and until Richard realizes, in the final line of the novel: 'She's back. I'm back' (Tucker 1966: 158).

Alan Burns: Towards the 'Extreme Sixties'

With Tucker's work we are moving to the idea that is explored in Chapter 6, namely the idea of the 'Extreme Sixties', which involves texts which present us with radical subject matter executed with equally radical formal rules of representation and logic, which often take precedence over the content. One of these extreme writers is Alan Burns, who, like J. G. Ballard, is interested in taking a specific situation and pushing it into extreme circumstances, or following a particular logic to its end. Whereas his first novel, *Buster* (1961) seemed to fit the aesthetic of the Angry Young Men, *Europe after the Rain* (1965) is a complete rejection of any kind of realist poetics. It shares with Heppenstall's *The Connecting Door* its setting, Europe just after war, and, as the opening lines suggest, the Rhine as a symbolic site of contestation about the ruined continent's future: 'We were approaching the river. The modern bridge had been demolished, a wooden one constructed' (Burns 1965: 5).

The mode of narration is blissfully radical. From the start, very short, repetitive sentences that observe, clinically:

'We knocked. We said we could not stay. We went to two cinemas. Someone called for her. She discussed her plans.'
'As a matter of fact I have not got any plan.'
'You have her name and addresses.'
'I am probably standing on a dead body.'
She bought two and a half pounds of sweets. Everyone did a little buying and selling. Loot. Casual labour received high wages. She did private work in the evenings. Quality work. One house was famous. The owner sang those songs. She sang the one we heard in the street. (Burns 1965: 9)

Where are we? When are we? Who is narrating? We only have these staccato, military, factual observations that render a disjointed content. We move, ghostly, from neutral observation to neutral observation, coolly distant. In contrast to Heppenstall, Burns' prose has a relentless rhythm, formed of short, staccato sentences:

> All bridges were broken. The front wheels were over a trench in the road. We got help, with concrete blocks we build a way across the trench. It was dark. We clambered out of the hooded wagon. We quarrelled. It was not clear what it was all about. We fought. She did not want to be forced. There was silence. I needed help. (Burns 1965: 18)

This formal narrative drive is also present at the level of plot; much is happening and everything is moving forwards, although the meaning of these narrative movements are totally obscure: we seem to deal with a group of fugitive nomads. We see, constantly, a breakdown in communication:

> The girls sang as a choir, the boys played instruments. They broke off to gaze at me. A hurried talk, then three of them formed themselves in a row, and three stood behind them. By keeping close they made a compact group, their bodies rigid, they kept time with the sharp marionette movements of hand and head. It was effective, even menacing, but I could not interpret it. I knew it portrayed something powerful and perhaps reckless. (Burns 1965: 15)

This creates an increasingly indeterminate text, whereby interpretation is thwarted, a technique we will also see employed by J. G. Ballard's *The Atrocity Exhibition*. What this Burns novel shares with J. G. Ballard is its interest in Surrealist art. Its title refers to Max Ernst's painting 'Europe after the Rain II' (1941), which the Calder edition contains as frontispiece. The painting depicts an abstract landscape, an apocalyptic vision of post-war Europe. For the painting, Ernst used a collage technique called 'decalcomania', in which gouache is pressed onto a canvas using paper; this creates a multi-layered effect, which Burns tries to imitate textually in his novel.

Like Joseph K. in *The Castle*, the narrator needs a 'travel permit' (Burns 1966: 55). The novel is full of vague, unnamed characters: 'This fellow is a foreigner' (Burns 1966: 52). It seems then, that post-war Europe has become the Kafkaesque nightmare. At one point the narrator states: 'You know that I am trying to trace a girl. Have you any information as to where she might be?' The reply is, again, disturbingly and frustratingly indecisive: ' "She's in a room." He was joking' (Burns 1966: 41). There is a constant emphasis on food, described as 'scarce' and 'a constant theme' (Burns 1966: 61), which is not just a metaphor that allows us to relate it to the Deleuzian minor tradition (see Chapter 3), but is presented as a very real, material issue which has its textual effects on the emaciated, starved prose. The novel ends with a four-page-long paragraph.

Conclusion: A literary form of suicide?

The young Ian McEwan, as we saw at the start of this chapter, was influenced by the 'difficult', theoretical writing of the high Modernist, *nouveau roman* and the writers of anti-novels, including Alan Burns, whom he met at the University of East Anglia in the early 1970s:

> In the summer, Alan Burns, the lawyer turned novelist, was the university's first writer-in-residence. After reading my stories he told me to read Beckett's trilogy because I appeared to be 'unconsciously influenced'. I took his advice, and immediately understood what he meant. Such are the tricks of memory that when I think back on those times the people I knew appear in perpetual good moods, their voices unusually loud, their gestures wildly exaggerated. The city [Norwich] itself was in a good mood. By 1971 the Sixties had spread up across the fens to take the town. I still have a hand-out inviting the citizenry to attend a smoke-in in Chapelfield Park where, it was comfortably predicted, clouds of cannabis smoke would envelop and confound the 'fascist pigs'. (McEwan 1995)

McEwan's rejection of the anti-novel's recalcitrance is telling. The problem with all these minute observations is that they work, as the term 'anti-novel' suggests, against the very idea of the novel. The anti-novel does not just destroy character and plot, but it also moves away from that which the novel form is good at, namely, the representation of consciousness and interiority, of history, or community. The postmodern novel left plot intact: Fowles's *French Lieutenant* and Spark's *The Driver's Seat* present new intellectual challenges to the reader, but they keep teleology, that is, narrative drive. The anti-novel cancels out interiority causing much concern for the anonymous reviewer of Heppenstall's *The Connecting Door*:

> Movement, direction, a relationship of parts are unavoidable even in anti-novels, and however desperately the characters may try to escape they are still caught in the ancient web of words, still the prisoner of human motive and action. What the new school tries for appears more like vivisection or specimen-hunting; it wants its flies in amber, or impaled on moments of time. The final danger is not obscurity but paralysis. It may be the way, or one way, that writers have to go,

but will they take their readers with them? At best, to will to read on is strained. At worst, the anti-novel may breed the anti-reader and turn itself into a literary form of suicide. (*TLS* 1962: 162)

Of course, we can tell the psychology of the characters in the way they observe (and interpret, if this is the case), but literature goes beyond psychology and sociology because it is able to somehow represent the texture of the human mind, which uses language though is not exclusive to other forms of thinking that make up our mind (visual representations, etc.). Yet, the novel which takes out character and plot seems very rare after the sixties anti-novel and literary experimentation has hardly recovered. We only find it in more stylized form in recent works such as Tom McCarthy's *Satin Island* (2015). The sixties anti-novel is important in relation to a wider context of literary experimentation in terms of a simultaneous sense of both ongoing development and radical discontinuity. These writers sought out to create their own forms, faithful to experience and insight if not convention. If, in doing so, they went so far as to write fictions unrecognizable as novels, this is all the more to show their commitment to literature as an embodiment of the mind. These writers acknowledge and draw on Joyce's early twentieth century renegotiation of subjectivity and consciousness, reclaiming the same spirit of the formal innovations of the Modernists, who were also exploring the changing texture of contemporary cognition and consciousness. In the early twenty-first century, when advances in cognitive science, new forms of mediated experience and new technologies once again challenge cultural models of selfhood, these anti-novels remind us that the novel form often assumes its role as the exploration of consciousness through language but also by questioning the very novel form itself.

6

The Extreme Sixties

'Operating formulae, for a doomsday weapon': *The Atrocity Exhibition*'s subversive aesthetic

J. G. Ballard is one of the most provocative and disturbing writers to work in post-war Britain, and his most experimental, extreme 'novel', *The Atrocity Exhibition* (1970), offers itself up as an interpretative puzzle impossible to solve by even the most experienced and knowledgeable of readers. Jeannette Baxter notes that *The Atrocity Exhibition* 'has acquired a reputation for being the most difficult and the most inaccessible' Ballard text (Baxter 2009: 59). It should be contextualized with other extreme texts that use randomness and contingency, such as William Burroughs's series of vignettes *Naked Lunch* (1959) and his subsequent use of cut-up in the 1960s in novels including *The Soft Machine* (1961), and B. S. Johnson's *The Unfortunates* (1969). *Atrocity* plunges the reader into a curious and confusing series of fifteen texts in which we are able to discern recurring and echoing elements, objects, characters, themes and situations reconfigured according to the kaleidoscopic, shifting point of view within every 'chapter'. Each chapter forms an associatively and seemingly randomly constructed narrative, headed by a title in bold font which (sometimes) forms part of a sentence that comments on the chapter in question. Ballard's overall text defies summary; the texts have undergone a process of 'condensation', leaving 'nothing more than a three-dimensional geographic model' (Ballard 2006: 150). *The Atrocity Exhibition*, I argue, explores the shift from the analogue period to the digital age and, through its presentation of constant permutations, combinations and series of possibilities focalized via an intersubjective, non-human perspective, anticipates the database logic that we in the twenty-first century are immersed in. *Atrocity* is a fundamentally posthuman text, exploring what happens when the dominant ideology is no longer a humanist one, but an algorithmic, 'dividual' database in which the individual human is peripheral.

Atrocity is the apotheosis of sixties literature and embodies the 'Extreme Sixties', which violently breaks down the realist novel in favour of an experimental aesthetics that stretches the rules of novelistic representation to its very limits. What characterizes *Atrocity* formally is its refusal to subscribe to any single narratological structure or artistic technique. It makes use of or references surrealism, pop-art collage, James Joyce's exploration of parallax vision in *Ulysses* (1922), *détournement* and the stream-of-consciousness technique made famous by Joyce and Virginia Woolf. The novel places all these experimental modes in a cumulative continuum with a view to establishing a form of defamiliarization that destroys any certainty of origin, unitary *telos* and organic organization. Ballard's point is to make us aware of the limits, and, perhaps, the very impossibility, of knowledge within the modern experience.

We might consider Forster's *Howards End* if we want to think about how fiction's increased interest in randomness related to the negation of artistic structure, defined by Aristotle in *Poetics*. 'One might as well begin with' foregrounds randomness as central to the attempt at chronological ordering of life and the world in the novel; various sixties writers let go of linearity, introducing even more complex narratological structures. One can enter *The Atrocity Exhibition* at any point; this is even truer of Ballard's novel than of Johnson's *The Unfortunates*. As a way in, we will look at the twelfth 'chapter', 'CRASH!', which formed the basis of Ballard's seminal postmodern novel *Crash* (1973). Together with Spark's *The Driver's Seat*, also published in 1973, *Crash* forms the endgame of the Long Sixties. It starts with a passage on the curious relationship between celebrity culture, violent death and 'perverse' sexuality:

> **Each afternoon in the deserted cinema**
> The latent sexual content of the automobile crash. Numerous studies have been conducted to assess the latent sexual appeal of public figures who have achieved subsequent notoriety as auto-crash fatalities, e.g. James Dean, Jayne Mansfield, Albert Camus. Simulated newsreels of politicians, film stars and TV celebrities were shown to panels of (a) suburban housewives, (b) terminal paretics, (c) filling station personnel. Sequences showing auto-crash victims brought about a marked acceleration of pulse and respiratory rates. Many volunteers became convinced that the fatalities were still living, and later used one or other of the crash victims as a private focus of arousal during intercourse with the domestic partner. (Ballard 2006: 153)

This passage contains some of the key obsessions that make up the distinctly Ballardian mythology of modernity. It depicts an Americanized and celebrity-obsessed consciousness in which the motor car, as key signifier of twentieth-century technological innovation, is turned into an ambiguous aphrodisiac that equates sex with death, and vice versa, through what Ballard calls 'extreme' metaphor. We find a Borgesian joke about the supposed rationality of listings, which playfully alludes to Foucault's heterotopia in the Introduction to *The Order of Things* (1966). The passage becomes a criticism of scientific positivism, which is undermined through the random entries that suggest the exhaustion of traditional western logos.

We encounter similar and related yet slightly different and deviating entries throughout the text. Earlier we were presented with a meditation on the car crash's latent sexual content as 'a fertilizing rather than destructive event – a liberation of sexual energy'; with an exhibition of crashed cars; and with an entry called 'Autogeddon' and later we encounter a reimagining of John F. Kennedy's assassination as a car race (Ballard 2006: 26; 28; 41; 171–72). We appear to have entered the hall of mirrors of an exemplary postmodern text that explores the power of the heterotopia, but I would argue that to read the novel in this way is to lose the sense that Ballard has his origins in the radical intellectual and cultural movements of the first three decades of the twentieth century. Ballard is a central figure to the literary sixties, a hinge thinker who, together with Maureen Duffy, B. S. Johnson, Christine Brooke-Rose and the sf writers of *New Worlds* magazine (including Brian Aldiss, John Baxter and editor Michael Moorcock), communicates Modernism's radicalisms to the late twentieth- and early twenty-first-century 'minor' traditions of writers such as Will Self, Zadie Smith, Tom McCarthy and Will Wiles, to name but a few of the authors influenced by Ballard's set of 'operating formulae, for a doomsday weapon' (Ballard 2006: 31).

One strand of Ballard's writing is informed by the Modernism of the equally curiously positioned writer Joseph Conrad, as *The Drowned World*'s Kurtzian homage Strangman evidences. Ballard's *Crash* (1973) takes *Howards End*'s treatment of the motor car into extreme circumstances: whereas Forster's novel shows human's lack of control over the car, killing animals in the countryside, in Ballard's postmodern world human and machine have merged into a hybrid entity. What makes *The Atrocity Exhibition* the apotheosis of the literary sixties is that it looks back to Modernism, while its critique is not yet formalized in overt metafictional jargonized theory, which postmodernist texts wear on their sleeves. The tropes and metaphors, the Freudian connection, the surrealist influence and various transliterations as well as the extreme aesthetic at work in *Atrocity* make it a late Modernist text. *The Atrocity Exhibition* is in many ways just as symbolic as T. S. Eliot's seminal *The Waste Land* (1922), for its capturing of the violent, fragmenting and traumatizing impact of new and rapidly changing politico-economic forces, ideologies and technologies on modern consciousness and experience.

One of the narrating entities, sometimes a doctor and sometimes a patient at a hospital, tries to resolve a number of traumas after surviving a car or plane crash, an effort hampered by a post-natural world that suffers from total mediatization. This narrator is variously called Talbert, Talbot, Travis, Traven, Trabert, Travers; Roger Luckhurst calls him 'T-Cell' (Luckhurst 1997: 86) and Michel Delville calls him 'a kind of portmanteau entity' (Delville 1998: 23). Our experience of the post-war world is, in Ballard's words, 'mimetised', that is, made 'real' through representation; the narration constantly shifts between different narrative levels and points of view. Sometimes it is Travers, sometimes Dr Nathan, sometimes the intersubjective, nonhuman space in between these characters that forms the narrating consciousness. This produces what Ballard has famously called the 'death of affect' (Ballard 2006: 108–9) – the imagining of a non-human point of view, devoid of feeling and emotion, and as such captured in an anti-humanistic language. In short, the text irrevocably destroys traditional notions of both plot and character, and asks us to inhabit a posthuman perspective and consciousness. Indeed, this chapter argues that Ballard, ahead of his time in many respects, has anticipated the struggle of individual in the digital age of Big Data and algorithmic patterning.

Traditional critical response has engaged itself with the text's hermeneutic uncertainties. Roger Luckhurst has framed it in the history and theory of the *avant-garde*; Michel Delville has read the novel as part of the New Wave science fiction movement; Andrzej Gasiorek and Jake Huntley employ a fragmented methodology that mirrors the text's eclecticism, while Jeannette Baxter reads the text through the intellectual history of surrealism. Yet there always lurks the temptation to impose order onto this most disorderly of texts, and to restore the intelligibility of the text by engaging in what Frank Kermode describes as a 'display of hermeneutic scrupulosity' (Kermode 1980: 6), inadvertently working against the subversive nature of the project's aim to thwart conventional interpretative strategies. Luckhurst appears to slip into a discourse of restoration when he notes that 'to unpack the compacted space of this disquieting text or set of texts will require counteracting expansiveness' (Luckhurst 1997: 73). Delville speaks of a 'central figure' and 'protagonist' (Delville 1998: 23–23), and Huntley also refers to the 'central figure' (Huntley 2008: 25), which reframes the jackets, music is distinctly pre-Beatles, and, although the girls, are aware of the fashion revolution taking place across the river in moneyed, swinging Chelsea, they are forced to make do with hand-me-downs and the 'Pay-as-You-Wear shop' (Dunn 1988: 23). The most obvious example is the episode 'The Gold Blouse', in which the girls cut the sleeves off a blouse to make it fashionable: 'There you are love, all set for the Jazz Band Ball' (Dunn 1988: 30). Prime Minister Harold Macmillan's 1957 pronouncement that 'most of our people have never had it so good' certainly does not include them. The girls are part of the generation of working-class youngsters who do not benefit substantially from the brief economic boom at the end of the fifties, and are unable to inscribe themselves into modernity. While the protagonist of Sheena Mackay's novel *Music Upstairs* (1965) is employed as a secretary, and Iris Murdoch's work features Westminster-based blue collar workers, Dunn's girls work in a sweet factory or pull pints in pubs. And yet, these texts could also be read as an attempt to capture the energy of the changing social dynamic that inscribes women into the public, male-dominated realm.

Dunn's work is primarily preoccupied with exploring gender in relation to class, and most existing scholarship has focused on this. The typically British obsession with class is also exemplified by Dunn's other writing, such as the interview book *Talking to Women* (1965), which includes conversations with fellow women writers such as Edna O'Brien and Ann Quin. In the play that reignited Dunn's career in 1981, *Steaming*, a run-down Public Baths erases the class difference in disparate group of women (see Groes 2007 for more detail). Because of its focus on these two themes, the reception of Dunn's early work was, and remains, divided. Critics have paid particular attention to the relationship between the representation of the girls and their ostensible lack of morality, as well as to Dunn's authorial presence within the representative processes. As the daughter of the wealthy industrialist Sir Philip Dunn, she grew up comfortably in an upper-class environment and was educated at a convent school, which she abandoned at the age of fourteen. After marrying the writer Jeremy Sandford in 1956, she moved from Chelsea to a small house they had bought in Battersea. They started a collection of newspaper articles, interviews and research on the local South London residents they had befriended, resulting in *Up the Junction*. Although Dunn and Sandford divorced and Dunn brought up their child by herself, the critical reception of the work was driven by a suspicion of this upper-middle-class woman living among the plebs – a case of class tourism.

One core trope that holds together Dunn's sketches is the 'heart' (Dunn 1967: 108 (twice); 112): she notes that she explores 'matters of the heart' in art, which raises the question of whether Dunn's books attempt a realistic portrayal of these women or whether she offers a sentimentalized view. Indeed, there is a tension between these two poles in her work: women's lives are constantly under threat of collapsing back into stereotypes produced by the patriarchal society, which is subverted by the anti-romantic brutal imagery and a growing self-consciousness. At one of the low points in Joy's life towards the end of *Poor Cow*, when she has become reduced to a housewife by husband Tom, she states: 'If yer heart's in yer home it's all right, otherwise it's useless' (Dunn 1967: 111). The devastating irony of this woman's consciousness debased to an apathetic state of bourgeois mindlessness works against critics' claims that Dunn's work is guilty of misrepresentation.

As authentic as a tape recorder: The ethics of realism

Dunn's work engages with the same problematic questions of 'authenticity' as many sixties authors, among whom B. S. Johnson, who struggled with them until his untimely death by suicide in 1973. Early reviewers had concerns about the mode of narration. An unsigned review in the *TLS* accused the author of being non-committal: 'the thing about this kind of poker-faced writing is that you can read into it any emotion or lack of emotion you like. Miss Dunn sounds as authentic as a tape recorder' (*TLS* 1963: 941). Interestingly, the review spends two paragraphs on Dunn, one on David Storey and half a paragraph on Hackney; Dunn's work clearly offended the imagined moral superiority of the reviewer. Indeed, the hidden complaint here is not so much about Dunn's potential misrepresentation of her subjects, nor a lack of artfulness, but the inability of the reader to discern a clear moral position of the narrator: implicit in the tone of the reviewer is the failure of Dunn to judge her subjects, to assert the hierarchical social position with which the Author had been associated for so long. Accusations of reducing the artfulness of the work at the expense of 'realism' continued with the publication of *Poor Cow*, which was criticized for being written without personal commitment: 'The basic flaw is [...] the absence of the author [...] it would be good if she were to move from the self-deceiving "I-am-a–camera" angle and find some way of to bring herself into her fiction' (*TLS* 1967: 373). Besides warning us against the naïve and erroneous urge to use 'novels as "documentary" sources for illustrating the contemporary scene' (Bergonzi 1970: 7), these reviewers alert us to the ethical problems of representation within Dunn's work, which linguistically unstable Travers character in unitary terms. Gasiorek's language captures the tension of approaching this text in conventional literary terms:

> The protagonist's passage through the text in some way holds its multiple themes together, since so much of it is filtered through his consciousness, but he is a metamorphic figure whose name-changes in each chapter provide a number of variations on his character, which not only signal its radical instability but also track the path of his psychosis. A doctor who is haunted by his experiences as an air-force pilot and the death of his wife, Traven is on a doomed quest for meaning. (Gasiorek 2005: 60–61)

This split discourse is in danger of translating the experiment back into conventional terms, and the assertion that Travis is engaging in a 'series of ever more bizarre conceptual experiments in an attempt to reintegrate self' (Gasiorek 2005: 61) is also a potential danger of the critic's enterprise. Jeannette Baxter notes that *The Atrocity Exhibition* 'has acquired a reputation for being the most difficult and the most inaccessible', and offers *the* 'key to reading the complex narrative forms of *The Atrocity Exhibition*', lying 'in the historiography of Ballard's experiment' (Baxter 2009: 59).

Attempts at teleological explication, and at making this mysterious text make sense, run several risks. Once the work of careful recontextualization has been done, once re-inscription of the characters and stories into our 'real' world has been achieved and the 'proper' spatio-temporal coordinates have been identified, there is a danger that the Barthesian *jouissance* that is so important to the project's interest in 'affects' will be diminished, if not cancelled out completely. In general, such a process of reordering tends towards to a closed, reductive reading and a re-establishing of a teleological framework negating the text's anticlimactic, cyclical structure. Once the heart of the work has been exposed – short of excavating more and more historical subject matter and materialist teleology – the work of the critic has been terminated. The aim of this chapter is to map out the rules of representation that make reading *The Atrocity Exhibition* such a confusing experience, while avoiding the Aristotelian pull of placing the text within the conventional epistemological frameworks and discourses that it in fact tries to undermine. *The Atrocity Exhibition* is a profoundly anti-Aristotelian project, which aims to destroy organic plotting, narrative linearity and centralizing forces in order to convey epistemological uncertainty characteristic of this specific, closing sixties moment.

In order to demonstrate this, I invoke the work of Gilles Deleuze and Félix Guattari. Much of their critical writing, and *Anti-Oedipus* (1972) in particular, originates in reaction to one of the fathers of modern thought, Freud, while their literary focal points are representatives of the radical, Continental strand of Modernism: Kafka and Joyce – both of whom Ballard has acknowledged as an influence (Ballard 1996: 349) – as well as Marcel Proust and Beckett. Ballard shares with these Continental Modernists an obsessive interest in representing the modern consciousness, within which the unconscious plays an important part. He is also exploring the slippage of identity occasioned by the divorce of the signifier and the signified due to new practices in the post-war world of commerce and mass media. What Ballard's text explores, criticizes but also celebrates are the possibilities of an intensely commercialized and sexualized world, emerging in the fifties and sixties, in which the proliferation of sign systems obscures the possibility of retrieving any sense of 'the real', and questions the very act of interpretation. On the other hand, the text goes beyond this framework, plunging us into a digital age in which individuals are logged and surveilled in great data banks, and the self is no longer the humanist, single identity, but what Deleuze calls a 'dividual'. *Atrocity* is one of the first texts to explore what the posthuman condition means: not just in the sense of investigating what would be left behind if humanist ideology were to disappear as a major framework underpinning the west, but also as the irrevocable reimagination of the very idea of what people are.

The image maze

The Atrocity Exhibition is the product of a schizoid subject, who is (mis) reading and reproducing experience of the world at the level of signs. The 'central figure' has become an unstable projection of linguistic play performed by a patient at a mental institution. This is Travis's condition, summed up by Captain Webster's observation that 'You can see he's trying to build bridges between things', while Karen Novotny is also 'conscious of the continuing dissociation of events around her' (Ballard 2006: 29). Travis is not attempting to reconnect meanings to objects, but trying to connect signifiers to other signifiers, knitting them into a decentred network of surface readings, which produces a continuous, infinite flux. Luckhurst's T-cell derives from Beckett's Trilogy novels (*Molloy* (1950), *Malone Dies* (1951) and *The Unnamable* (1952)), in which protagonists and antagonists become increasingly indistinguishable from one another, their names all starting with the letter M – Molloy, Moran, Malone, Moll, Mollose, Mellose and Macmann. In contrast to T. S. Eliot's use of Tiresias as a central narrating entity through which *The Waste Land* is voiced, we find an attempt at an intersubjective form of representation: the 'thin thread' (Woolf 1992: 123) that Lady Bruton imagines existing between people in *Mrs Dalloway* (1925), in which the narrating consciousness is located not in one but in many points of view that destroy any claim towards autonomy of the subject.

The episodic form of the text, for instance, suggests that we have lost Aristotle's *entelechy*, or complete reality, a whole world ordered by a rational system of causes and effects. No longer are we in the realm of necessity held together by a balance between potentiality and actuality. Aristotle, as Stephen reminds us in *Ulysses* (1922), sees reality as 'an actuality of the possible as possible' (Joyce 1992: 30); Joyce maintains the connection between actuality and potentiality, but reverses the priority of the relationship by having many possibilities lead to an actuality. Ballard's text, however, opens up a space containing all possibilities, all of which are valid. As Ballard notes in 'Notes from Nowhere' (1966), some of these ideas can be seen in his four recent 'novels'. 'The linear elements have been eliminated, the reality of the narratives is relativistic. Therefore place on the events only perspectives of a given instant, a given set of images and relationships' (Ballard 1966: 149). Reading *The Atrocity Exhibition* is therefore akin to reading Joyce's *Finnegan's Wake* (1939), which first coined the idea of the 'dividual' as the breakdown of the coherent self in modernity, an experience aptly described by Stephen Heath: 'The writing opens out onto a multiplicity of fragments of sense, of possibilities, which are traced and retraced, colliding and breaking ceaselessly in the play of this text that resists any homogenization' (Heath 1984: 31–32). This Joycean influence is affirmed when Talbert looks at the projection of a film actress on a bedroom wall, in which he sees the resemblance to the planetarium he visited earlier: 'Soon the parallax would close, establishing the equivalent geometry of the sexual act with the junctions of this wall and ceiling' (Ballard 2006: 83). Another important Modernist writer for Ballard is Kafka, whose work is renegotiated in an excerpt at the deserted exhibition hall, where Talbot steps into 'a maze from photographic billboards' in which images from the Vietnam War and himself are displayed:

> **The Image Maze** [...] The pilot stepped through a doorway cut into an image of Talbot's face. He looked up at the photograph of himself, snapped with a lapel camera during his last seminar. Over the exhausted eyes presided the invisible hierarchies of quasars. Reading the maze, Talbot made his way among the corridors. (Ballard 2006: 22)

Kafka's surrealism is at work here. In his work, real-life situations are transliterated into metaphors, metaphors are transliterated into real situations and ideas are turned into concrete situations. Unconsciously, Gregor Samsa feels that the machinery of his middle-class existence reduces him to an animal consciousness, and so wakes up transformed into literally a giant bug in 'The Metamorphosis' (1914); Joseph K. is literally lost in a labyrinth of bureaucratic machinery in *The Trial* (1925). The post-war world for Travers feels like a labyrinth of images, so it is presented literally as such.

In order to understand why Ballard engages in this radical form of anti-Aristotelian representation, we should situate him within a critical context appropriate to the time at which he was writing. Among the key interests emerging in the mid-fifties was the idea that society was undergoing 'subliminal' manipulation though the association of feelings and ideas with particular objects operated by politicians and advertising companies that employed psychoanalysts. Vance Packard's *The Hidden Persuaders* (1957) argues that the use of mass psychoanalysis by polling-driven and focus-group-based marketing, commercial enterprise and politics results in a mass persuasion of the population in the west through the mobilization of collective desires by tapping into the unconscious. These 'depth manipulators' and 'subconscious salesmen' attempt to achieve, according to Packard, a 'new-dimensional perspective' (Packard 1960: 45; 27):

> many of us are being influenced and manipulated – far more than we realize – in the patterns of our everyday lives. Large-scale efforts are being made, often with impressive success, to channel our unthinking habits, our purchasing decisions, and our thought processes by the use of insights gleaned from psychiatry and the social sciences. Typically these efforts take place beneath our level of awareness; so that the appeals which move us are often, in a sense, 'hidden'. (Packard 1960: 11)

Packard mentions research by depth merchandisers into the traditional signifier of masculinity, the beard, which inhibited the sales of razors and shaping preparations because 'the daily act of cutting off this symbol of manliness is a kind of daily castration' (Packard 1960: 80). The sales of cigars peaked in 1955 at six billion because a Chicago ad company targeted 'men who are basically weak and small. A cigar helps the little guy feel big' (Packard 1960: 80–81). Ballard's earliest work dramatizes such analyses, arguing that these processes are produced by new forms of consumerism which demand that we invest emotional and sexual energy in a variety of objects and a complex matrix of social relationships, resulting in a confusing sexualization and commercialization of the private and public realms. Ballard's short story 'Subliminal Man' (1963) is exemplary of an interest in the potential of this process, whereby these new and dangerous modes of commerce can be used as a means to explore and understand man's unconscious life. The story is set in a future world long *after* the banning of subliminal advertising sees the renewed erection of gigantic roadside signs, which worry Hathaway, the psychiatric patient of the protagonist, Dr. Franklin:

> Forget it, Doctor, there are more important things happening now. They've started to build the first big signs! Over a hundred feet high, on the traffic islands just outside town. They'll soon have all the approach roads covered. When they do we might as well stop thinking.
>
> 'Your trouble is that you're thinking too much', Franklin told him. 'You've been rambling about these signs for weeks now. Tell me, have you actually seen one signalling?'
>
> Hathaway tore a handful of leaves from the hedge, exasperated by this irrelevancy. 'Of course I haven't, that's the whole point, Doctor'. (Ballard 1963: 110)

The schizophrenic Hathaway argues that these signs are transmitting subliminal commands, and, despite his warning, it is not long before all citizens are enslaved to a new system of persuasion. As the sixties, and Ballard's analysis, advance, towards the end of the decade his work appears to take a new stance towards these developments, suggesting that the manipulation of man's subliminal life has created an epistemological break within contemporary experience. Ballard's thinking is closely aligned to that of one of the founding members of the Situationist International, Guy Debord, whose *The Society of the Spectacle* (1967) formulated the principles upon which the post-war experience was founded:

> 2. Images detached from every aspect of life merge into a common stream, and the former unity of life is lost forever. Apprehended in a *partial* way, reality unfolds in a new generality as a pseudo-world apart, solely as an object of contemplation. The tendency towards the specialization of images-of-the-world finds its highest expression in the world of autonomous image, where deceit deceives itself. The spectacle in its generality is a concrete inversion of life, and, as such, the autonomous movement of non-life. [...]
>
> 4. The spectacle is not a collection of images; rather, it is a social relationship between people that is mediated by images. (Debord 1994: 12)

These are just some of the keys to *The Atrocity Exhibition*, which pushes Debord's logic further by projecting the intense bombardment by mass media during the sixties onto extremely traumatic circumstances. Luckhurst notes that

> *Atrocity* concerns the explosion of the 'media landscape'. Televisions, film festivals and billboards project images from Vietnam. The Zapruder film of Kennedy's assassination endlessly replays. The content of these images suddenly matches the violence that had been so long accorded to the form of the media channels of mass culture. [...] The media have released irresolvable traumatic material which can only induce repetition of the trauma, in a futile attempt at mastery. This is the media as the embodiment of the death drive, the compulsion to repeat. (Luckhurst 1997: 95)

Luckhurst's connection of the novel's content with the form of mass media is important; due to the overwhelming commercialization of these spheres, there is an increasingly overwhelming flow of sign systems, causing a structuring desire that is partly uncontrollable due to the translation of different sign system in terms of one another. This process of translation simultaneously foregrounds difference as well as sameness: the car or washing powder or a cigar may be different objects, but the relatively crude marketing and advertising processes that generate desire are essentially the same, so that the wires may be accidentally crossed, with unintended consequences. Indeed, once the signifier–signified relationship is severed, meaning becomes uncontrollable due to the proliferation of 'translations', despite those 'professionals' who attempt to manipulate consumer patterns and desire.

'Faciality': Algorithms, database, posthumanism

Atrocity is not, however, simply an investigation into the effects of modern culture on the psyche. It is also an incisive investigation into the way in which scientific innovation and new technology have a corrosive effect on human identity and cognition, and on humanist ideology, which came under attack during the sixties. Ballard uses various narratological strategies, but he also harnesses 'extreme metaphor' again. In this case, the human is eroded through the disjointing of the face–landscape vehicle–tenor relationship. First, we find the classical, humanist metaphorical relationship between the face and landscape as two surface structures that can be substituted for one another:

The Geometry of Her Face. In the perspectives of the plaza, the junctions of the underpass and embankment, Talbot at last recognized a modulus that could be multiplied into the landscape of *his consciousness*. The descending triangle of the plaza was repeated in the facial geometry of the young woman. (Ballard 2006: 26. My emphasis)

Ballard uses the idea of extreme metaphor whereby ostensibly disparate clusters of thought or materiality can be placed into a continuum. The car crash can be translated into an arousing form of sex: the violent uniting of materiality merges sign systems that create an (illusory) wholeness, at least in the imagination. Through a similar process of metaphoric expansion, architecture may be construed as a human body because the same interpretative act is taking place: both fuse in the mind, as 'his consciousness' suggest, and become interchangeable. Self and world become cognitive extensions of one another. In this sense, Ballard's work anticipates 'extended mind theory', championed by philosophers Andy Clark and David Chalmers (Clark and Chalmers 2011). They argue that consciousness is not just a phenomenon generated by the brain, but that technologies and objects outside the body are used by the mind to augment cognitive processes. Our thinking relies increasingly heavily on such tools, and I have elsewhere termed the hybrid cognition between humans and technology 'The Prosthetic God' (Groes 2014). This context presents us with fascinating new ambiguities and ethical dilemmas, as well as a sense of a diminished agency for human beings.

Yet, as the face becomes mass reproduced through cinematic representation, and is brought into the domestic realm by the increased affordability of televisions, a new set of problems are evoked. The entry 'How Garbo Died' was provocatively written when Greta Garbo was still alive (she died in 1990 but was professionally deceased after the Second World War). It shows Webster leading Catherine Austin into a basement cinema along 'a series of plaster casts of film stars and politicians in bizarre poses' which 'seem to have been cast from the living models, LBJ and Mrs Johnson, Burton and the Taylor actress, there's even one of Garbo dying' (Ballard 2006: 11). Ballard's reference to Garbo, a star whose name was made in the interbellum, is significant; the image evokes Roland Barthes's piece 'The Face of Garbo', from his collection of essays *Mythologies* (1957), in which the 'admirable face-object' of Garbo's deified face reconciles two different iconographies. On the one hand, we find a classic Platonic ideal, the sexually undefined face created by a plaster mask of make-up making visible some essence of her bodily person. On the other hand, Garbo's classic, androgynous singularity as icon of early cinema 'represents this fragile moment when cinema is about to draw an existential from an essential beauty, when the archetype leans towards fascination of mortal faces, when the clarity of the flesh as essence yields its place to a lyricism of Woman' (Barthes 2000a: 57). The face of Garbo straddles these two ages, on the brink of being turned into 'an infinite complexity of morphological functions' (Barthes 2000a: 57), which Barthes associates with Audrey Hepburn: 'The face of Garbo is an Idea, that of Hepburn, an Event' (Barthes 2000a: 57). Whereas Garbo remains inaccessible to the mortal, fallen spectator, Hepburn becomes a collective experience that connects us by producing a shared structure of feeling and group cognition.

It is in the shift to this second iconographical age, which implies a move to a more complex and dangerous matrix of connections involving a dissolution of the subject–object binary, that we should situate Ballard's thinking about film stars and their faces. Garbo's death is the death of a humanist intellectual legacy in which the face as a system of coordinates signals the spectator, but is now unable to reconnect to other sign systems as the modern experience entails a break in signification and meaning-making processes. In Ballard's writing, this shift to the Hepburn-Event function is attributed to Elizabeth Taylor, who has a major significance within Ballard's work. Consider the following excerpt:

> **The Enormous Face**. Dr Nathan limped along the drainage culvert, peering at the huge figure of a dark-haired woman painted on the sloping walls of the blockhouse. The magnification was enormous. The wall on his right, the size of a tennis court, contained little more than the right eye and cheekbone. He recognized that woman from the billboards he had seen near the hospital – the screen actress, Elizabeth Taylor. Yet these designs were more than enormous replicas. They were equations that embodied the identity of the film actress and the audiences who were distant reflections of her. The planes of their lives interlocked at oblique angles, fragments of personal myth fusing with the commercial cosmologies. The presiding deity of their lives the film actress provided a set of operating formulae for their passage through consciousness. (Ballard 2006: 12–13)

Magnification as an aesthetic belongs to the sixties, with films such as Michelangelo Antonioni's *Blow-Up* (1966) exploring the problems of experiencing the world through the camera lens, but Ballard aims to make visible not so much the perils of the male gaze as the connecting thread between individual, private lives and the imagined, public ones of Hollywood icons. There is a manipulative psychology at work here: the close-up as used in

Hollywood films creates an intimate moment which we only experience in two other circumstances: first, when as babies, we suckle the mother's breast, and, second, when we kiss our lover. The close-up of cinema exploits this moment of intimacy, immediately establishing this irresistible intimate relationship between us and the Hollywood star (see Bloom 2011: 80).

Whereas Ballard underscores the commonplace interpretation which suggests that ordinary citizens start imagining themselves through the fantasies portrayed by their icons, Ballard also notes that the imagination sparked by Taylor fuses with private fantasies into a collective jumble of perceptions, underlined by the face's enactment of a strange form of surveillance. Here, the psychoanalytic theory of Jean Laplanche is useful, because it reconfigures Freudian Oedipal theory in relation to seduction. What we receive when being adored by the face is not any specific content or message; instead, we are enticed by the seductive and seducing gaze of the face, who appears to sees us as a wholeness, an image of the face's own lost, formerly whole self. We experience this gaze as the desire and fantasy of an Other that is fragmented and not fully present, and we unwittingly submit to a position in which we are trapped in the act of interpreting the other's desire (Laplanche 1999: 169–200). Rather than Freud's personalizing of desire and his reduction of desire to a familial model with, at its centre, the subject trapped in fantasies of power over an enclosed world, Ballard suggests that desire is organized impersonally and collectively.

Claire Colebrook notes that for Deleuze '[d]esire begins impersonally and collectively, and from a multiplicity of investments which traverse persons. Body-parts are invested *before* persons' (Colebrook 2002: 141). Deleuze and Guattari also point out the correlations between the face and landscape, pointing to Christian education in which face and landscape were both employed as manuals of pedagogy, and to architecture as the creation of a face within a wider landscape. Yet, due to the magnification of the advertised face, it becomes disembodied, which also ruptures the traditional metaphorical relationship between the face and landscape. Deleuze and Guattari help us think about the difference between the head, which belongs to the body as volume-cavity system, and the face, which is a self-contained system:

> The face is surface; facial traits, lines, wrinkles; long face, square face, triangular face; the face is a map, even when it is applied to and wraps a volume, even when it surrounds and borders cavities that are now no more than holes. [...] The face is produced only when the head ceases to be a part of the body, when it ceases to be coded by the body [...] when the body, head included, has been

decoded and has to be *overcoded* by something we shall call the Face. (Deleuze
2000: 170)

After severing the relationship between the body and head, and the head and
the face, deterritorialization manifests itself: both systems (body–face) are
freed to establish connections with other systems of signification. The face is
an interesting system to explore because its deterritorialization is a slower but
intense and absolute form: 'it is no longer relative because it removes the head
from the stratum of the organism, human or animal, and connects it to other
strata, such as significance and subjectification' (Deleuze and Guattari 2002:
172). Indeed, 'even a use-object may become facialized; you might say that a
house, utensil or, object, etc. is *watching me*, not because it resembles a face, but
because it is taken up in the white wall/black hole process, because it connects
to the abstract machine of facialization' (Deleuze and Guattari 2002: 175). The
idea of the facialization of the world, operated through the proliferation of
icons and images into a multiplicity of surfaces, provides us with a sense of how
the public realm and the private self connect and becomes extensions of one
another.

The other effect established by Ballard's text, however, is that we are
confronted with the idea that we as individuals are no longer ourselves: the
face as intricately caught up in this system no longer belongs to itself, but to
a massive database, which is the world. Contemporary, twenty-first-century
digital culture is determined by databases, from which continuously new
selections are made, and new narratives constructed, in an infinite series, which
is suggested by the open-endedness of *Atrocity*. The database is now a dominant
form in organizing and shaping our culture and thinking, and the infinite
storage and retrieval possibilities of digital technology are foreseen by Ballard's
text. *Atrocity* explicitly embodies an infinite series of orderings, permutations
and reworkings of the original source materials: it explores seemingly infinite
combinations, serialization and infinite re-splicing together of the past and the
present from the future. Added to this is a non-humanistic narratorial point of
view, a kind of intersubjective and constantly shifting perspective, which indeed
may be called properly kaleidoscopic. It is not the different individual images
offered by this technique, but the creation of a sense of constant movement
between individuals, space and time.

The kaleidoscopic splicing of the individual into an endless series of
combinations is a frightening one, to be sure, but it is also liberating. *Atrocity*
explores the logic of an endless process of cross-referencing and recombining

of possibilities so that images of different spheres – say, the Vietnam War, the assassination of JFK, car commercials and washing powders – start to swirl within the same realm, and are experienced as existing at the same level; this ironical process of transliteralization has several, often conflicting, effects. The 'final', fifteenth chapter of *The Atrocity Exhibition* demonstrates this kaleidoscopic effect very well. This chapter, 'The Assassination of John Fitzgerald Kennedy Considered as a Downhill Motor Race', cognitively reconfigures the titular event – one of the key mediatized events in modernity – by dis- and reassembling the different images to tragicomic effect:

Oswald was the starter.

From his window above the track he opened the race by firing the starting gun. It is believed that the first shot was not properly heard by all the drivers. In the following confusion Oswald fired the gun two more times, but the race was already under way. [...]

The course ran downhill from the Book Depository, below an overpass, then on to the Parkland Hospital and from there to Love Air Field. It is one of the most hazardous courses in downhill motor racing, second only to the Sarajevo track discontinued in 1914.

Kennedy went downhill rapidly. After the damage to the governor the car shot forward at high speed. An alarmed track official attempted to mount the car, which continued on its way, cornering on two wheels.

Turns. Kennedy was disqualified at the hospital, after taking a turn for the worse. Johnson now continued the race in the lead, which he maintained to the finish.

The flag. To signify the participation of the President in the race Old Glory was used in place of the usual chequered square. Photographs of Johnson receiving his prize after winning the race reveal that he had decided to make the flag a memento of his victory. (Ballard 2006: 171–72)

Here Ballard appropriates some of the images of Kennedy's assassination in Dallas, and translates them into the codes of a car race, the world of sports and mass media entertainment. The chaos and ensuing uncertainty of the event are restored by injecting it with teleology and the climax of reaching the finish line, a fake deterritorialization that suggests that there is no sense or truth to be retrieve, only sinister play. Once again, death is expressed through the language of sex, with orgasm as a strategy to 'deal with', to put it in therapy-speak, collective trauma. This rhetorical process turns tragedy into something that generates laughter, while suggesting that in the media age epistemological certainty is both increased and obscured, as the note on the remaining 'puzzling aspects of the race' (such as the presence of Jackie Kennedy in the car and the Warren Commission's controversial report) underscore (Ballard 2006: 173). This attempted restoration is doomed to fail because the process of mediation has severed the possibility of 'the real' at the outset: sense and truth are perpetually postponed in the Zapruderization of the world, but also offers us the evolution from analogue media to digital ones.

Atrocity thus anticipates what happens to identity and the human in the digital age of coding, Big Data and algorithmic pattering. Gilles Deleuze forms a link between the theorization of the schizoid individual and the understanding of the effect of the digital age upon human beings and society. Deleuze claims that, subject to the 'the digital language of control', 'individuals become "*dividuals*"' (Deleuze 2002: 319). Rather than persisting in outdated conceptions of the individual, our best response to these changes may be to assert that such new formations of the subject can be understood and negotiated through a recognition of their presence in the past. N. Katherine Hayles has written of the transformations of the digital age as creating 'a highly heterogeneous and fissured space in which discursive formations based on pattern and randomness jostle and compete with formations based on presence and absence' (Hayles 1999: 27). *Atrocity* is thus one of the first texts to explore the emergent 'database logic', a term coined by Lev Manovich, and the new posthuman subjectivities that belong to the twenty-first century (Manovich 2001).

Texts that radically explore randomness and intersubjectivity, such as Burroughs's work and B. S. Johnson's *The Unfortunates*, foresaw the shift from the analogue period into the digital age. *Atrocity* belongs to this select group of extreme writings that manage to make the sixties a space that could be experienced as a hinge moment that saw various cognitive shifts, and new imaginative challenges for human beings. Reading *The Atrocity Exhibition* remains a problem, but a profoundly blissful and visceral one. This text is a profoundly anti-Aristotelian project, which is both a reflection and criticism of dangerous developments in post-war politics and mass media. Ballard's text dismantles the binary oppositions between the possibility of knowledge and the lack thereof, between doctor and patient, between institution and the institutionalized, between science and art, between sexual innocence and experience and between consciousness and the unconscious. It shows that the modern world we experience is not wholly our own, and that it can never be so because we are immersed in a process in which all relations are mediated. The reader of the text is confronted with a choice, either to refuse this conclusion and revert to an artificial state of innocence or to accept this situation of powerlessness and to revel in the contingency and transgression. This is the dangerous proposition put to us. In Ballard, representation has moved beyond the individual to a form of intersubjectivity while the psychological deep structures have been exploded across the surface. Like Travers, the post-war reader is lost in cognitive uncertainty. *The Atrocity Exhibition* does not present us with a fixed image of experience nor with a singular interpreting subject, but it brings to the fore the problematic nature of reading in the post-war period itself. Ballard stretches the novel form to its representative limits, and asks us to consider the very end of interpretation itself – of human, and by humans.

7

Pornotopia

The delta of life's possibilities: Introducing the ending

Julian Barnes's fine contribution to what we now designate as postmodern literature, *Flaubert's Parrot* (1984), provides a way into the next chapter, which investigates why British writers in the sixties foreground questions about the endings of the novel. The narrator, amateur Flaubert scholar Geoffrey Braithwaite, is meditating with an irony characteristic of his favourite author on the ways in which the novel form is able to represent the complexity of modern life:

> if novelists truly wanted to simulate the delta of life's possibilities, this is what they'd do. At the back of the book would be a set of sealed envelopes in various colours. Each would be clearly marked on the outside: Traditional Happy Ending; Traditional Unhappy Ending; Traditional Half-and-Half Ending; Deus ex Machina; Modernist Arbitrary Ending; End of the World Ending; Cliffhanger Ending; Dream Ending; Opaque Ending; Surrealist Ending. You would only be allowed one, and would have to destroy the envelopes you didn't select. *That's* what I call offering the reader a choice of endings; but you may find me quite unreasonably literal-minded. (Barnes 2002: 99–100)

The faux naïve Braithwaite not only is unreasonably literal-minded, as he well knows, but also protests overtly against Jean-Paul Sartre's, Albert Camus's and Roland Barthes's redefinition of the novel just before and after the Second World War. These French writers had all attempted to emphasize the act of reading as a subjective, actively cognitive process of the reader bringing meaning to texts rather than passive consumption of stories in which the meaning was determined by the all-controlling Author-God. One of the ironies of Barnes's novel is that he unwittingly engages with Flaubert, the supposed textbook example of nineteenth-century omnisciently authored realism, in a distinctly Barthesian manner: the more Braithwaite tries to find Flaubert the Author-God, the more he slips away in contradictory textual sources, absent information and his own subjective and limited interpretations. By the end of *Flaubert's Parrot* the narrator leaves the reader full of speculation and uncertainty about his object of interest, with a 'perhaps': defeated by the overwhelming unknowability of history and the inaccessibility of the past, he is unable to achieve the meaningful narrative closure he desires. The only author he has exposed in the process of writing is himself.

Barnes is different from most contemporary British authors because he is also interested in European, rather than Anglo-American, culture, and French culture in particular. His work reminds us of British fiction's long-standing engagement with continental and French culture and philosophy. As we have seen, experimental sixties fiction in particular was heavily influenced by French novelists and thinkers such as Sartre, Camus, Barthes and Alain Robbe-Grillet, whose innovative ideas about writing character, plotting, style and endings filtered through into the innovative branches of sixties writing and literary criticism. In the sixties, more than in any decade, we find a variety of endings much wider than Braithwaite's encyclopaedia encompasses. After Molly Bloom's ecstatic, orgiastic 'Yes' on the final page of Joyce's *Ulysses* (1922) and the sudden, mid-sentence break of his circular novel *Finnegan's Wake* (1939) – which Braithwaite would term the 'Modernist Arbitrary Ending' – perhaps an equally famous ending of a novel is that of John Fowles's *The French Lieutenant's Woman* (1969), which contains a double, or perhaps even triple, ending. In the same year, B. S. Johnson published *The Unfortunates*, a 'novel' consisting of twenty-seven sections of which, although the opening and final sections were predetermined, the reader was to arrange the order randomly. Anthony Burgess's *The Doctor Is Sick* (1960) ends with the line 'The end, that's what's it', and is reinforced for a second time to the reader by inserting the traditional ending with 'The End' (Burgess 1960: 178). Just so we know it.

This chapter asks questions about the obsession with the endings of sixties fictions, arguing that writers in subtle ways foregrounded the idea that the sixties were a period with a great variety of endings, and new beginnings. Centuries of patriarchy and Victorian morality are replaced by a new gender balance; television allowed for a new, increasingly international perception of the world, although this exacerbated a perceived loss of authentic connection to the world; Victorian architecture was demolished and replaced by Modernist buildings; and so on. New technologies such as the pill had a major impact on social relationship and sexuality, and new legislation equally restricted the way in which society operated, often, but not always, in more liberal ways. Its revolutionary sheen makes it seem that the decade is composed of an endless series of endings, rejected by people such as Peter Hitchens (see the Introduction).

This chapter looks into how and why they foregrounded narrative structure and created an exceptional awareness of the importance of the ending. Within this general assumption, I argue that new attitudes to sexuality, desire and the body were expressed through new and highly self-conscious narrative strategies. I will put forward the argument that form and content are interconnected, and we should therefore look at how the creation of dead, multiple or triple endings – anything but the traditional restoration of the realist novel – is connected to changing attitudes to love and sexuality. As Peter Childs suggests, 'In the decade running up to 1970 there had been many self-conscious fictions which experimented with previous genres, toyed with literary theory, questioned traditional character-representations of a stable personal identity, and complicated familiar narrative organizations of space and time, expressing the liberationist impulse of the decade in prose techniques' (Childs 2005: 10). The sixties as a space of time is associated with both the Larkinesque loss of innocence that followed the introduction of the pill, which gave way to a new complex way of socio-sexual relations, and a claim to a new kind of innocence, with the hippie generation's utopian celebration of 'free love'. We will see that this enhanced interest in love and sexuality is accompanied by a narrative foregrounding not only of sex, as we saw in Chapter 3, but also of bodily materiality, and a claim by women of the need for bodily satisfaction. In general, the decade sees a steady increase in the pornofication of the human imaginary, with advertising companies and other capitalist enterprises manipulating human desire in order to sell goods. Anthony Burgess warned against what he termed 'pornotopia', 'where the only thought is lust and the only activity, orgasm' (Burgess 1973: n.p.). Burgess's definition builds on Susan Sontag's seminal essay 'The Pornographic Imagination' (1964), which analyses pornographic literature as a social, not a psychological, phenomenon:

> The books generally called pornographic are those whose primary, exclusive, and overriding preoccupation is with the depiction of sexual 'intentions' and 'activities.' [...] Pornography uses a small crude vocabulary of feeling, all relating to the prospects of action: feeling one would like to act (lust); feeling one would not like to act (shame, fear, aversion). There are no gratuitous or non-functioning feelings; no musings, whether speculative or imagistic, which are irrelevant to the business at hand. Thus, the pornographic imagination inhabits a universe that is, however, repetitive the incidents occurring within it, incomparably

economical. The strictest possible criterion of relevance applies: everything must bear upon the erotic situation. (Sontag 2002: 66)

The results of these changes in attitudes to pornography are different social and cultural narratives which, I argue, sixties fiction was keen to question and, in some case, subvert. Sixties narratives thwart the kind of straightforward endings found in realist, organicist literature geared towards easy gratification, and therefore postpone, cancel out or diverge textual orgasm. British fiction of the sixties distinguishes itself by aiming to achieve anti-climactic, anti-Spectacular, muted or deflationary conclusions.

Text, telos and the organic

Traditionally, narrative works of art have attempted to satisfy audiences through definitive closure, in the form of either marriage or the death of the protagonist. Such endings present the (re)organization of individuals within their families and/or the wider social constellations. Narrative outcomes are important as they provide the place where we can read most clearly the meaning of social and individual values at a particular time in place. In classic tragedies, tragic heroes such as Oedipus and King Lear succumb to the fate allocated to them by the Gods, as punishment for their hubristic attempts to rebel against the social order. In the Greek epic, heroes such as Odysseus return home to restore the order of things after a long period of unrest. Shakespeare's comedies and tragedies are also finely attuned to his audience's needs: in the comedies, the foolish (but often socially privileged) protagonists emerge from their mostly benign ordeals older and wiser, and married; the tragedies end with the stage as open-air mortuary. In the nineteenth century, Jane Austen's satires end in the pairing off of the protagonists, while Thomas Hardy's *The Mayor of Casterbridge* (1886) ends with the death of its tragic anti-hero, Henchard. Although in between the opening and final lines an infinite subtlety and ambiguity may manifest itself, these are the 'Traditional Happy Ending' and 'Traditional Unhappy Ending' that Braithwaite mentions, which have dominated narratives for centuries.

The function of such traditional endings is clear: individual people have a need to understand the world and their personal experience by consuming stories that through careful ordering illuminate the chaos and dizzying complexity of everyday life, and the world. Only by artificially imposing a spatio-temporal boundary on events can we make sense of our lives, which are themselves clearly delineated by that ultimate boundary, death. An integral part of this poetics was some kind of divine being (God), or collective of beings (the gods), who guarantee our continued existence after our expiration. Simultaneously, endings perform a wider social function by imitating the politico-economic and socio-cultural scripts – ideologies – that are embedded within, and that structure, the way we think about conventions in society. Such conventions are never neutral: both social and literary meanings are dependent on social instruments and legal apparatuses, such as the education system and the penal system, that determine and often limit our thinking by restricting the linguistic horizon. 'Traditional Happy Ending' (marriage) and 'Traditional Unhappy Ending' (death) are often conservative means affirming the order of things as morally correct: next to its anti-incest message, *Oedipus* teaches us that it is best not to rebel against one's fate and in *A Midsummer Night's Dream* Shakespeare's lovers learn that their fathers were right in the first place. Thus, the happy ending, with its conclusion in marriage, celebrates a society in which financial and emotional success are tied to successful integration into society through a heterosexual relationship, while death laments the loss, or decline, of social order through diminishing male authority.

Twentieth-century writers, and writers in the sixties in particular, have set out to rethink such patterns by presenting their characters with new opportunities and choices by rewriting traditional endings. Sixties fiction forms a concerted attempt to disrupt and reinvent the novelistic ending, and in doing so subverts the traditional Aristotelian relationship between the beginning, the middle and the end, and the idea of organic structure in a wider sense. In doing so, these authors not only reflect the changing organization of society as a narrative structure but also reflect, shape and reconfigure our thinking about society's changing social infrastructure. The sheer number of different narrative strategies that rewrite endings suggests that the narrative power behind these rewritings of traditional resolution lies in the emergence of a changing consciousness of society in which desires and destinies are ambiguous, plural and diverse.

An important new force for rethinking classical social and psychological structures came from within psychology. The tide against Freud was strong, with anti-psychiatrists such as R. D. Laing dismantling the rational logic behind psychoanalysis. An even stronger force came from France, first with Jacques Lacan and then with Gilles Deleuze and Félix Guattari destroying the geometrical patterns that Freud's thinking was based on. According to Deleuze and Guattari, this kept a privileged position for men, for capitalism and for the humanist views of the world and history that underpinned those structures. To work against such structures, they argued that we should let go of fantasies about organic structures, and replace them with subversive, anti-teleological forms. In *Difference & Repetition* (1968), Deleuze notes that 'The ultimate wish of the organic is to become orgiastic' (Deleuze 2004: 262). This orgiastic, teleological drive should be resisted, and new structures imposed, upon life, and representation. We should therefore not wish for a whole mind and body nor for a straightforwardly organic structure; the individual's psychology is not complete in the first place, so that striving for wholeness is a quixotic quest. Instead, we should accept the fragmented and incomplete nature of the world and human beings, and embrace anti-teleological forms of organization.

During the sixties, interest in, and play with, endings signals an increased problem with the nature of modern society. A hugely influential critic in Britain at the time, Frank Kermode, noted in *The Sense of an Ending* (1967) that modernity was characterized by a great sense of crisis that was technological, military and cultural in nature: this all-encompassing apocalyptic mindset created the sense that we are constantly on the brink of radical change of some sort, from the mass-slaughter during the First World War that shattered our belief in progress through to the Second World War and Cold War and the Vietnam War. We are continuously entering new eras, and we seem to need a sense of bracketing off periods. Kermode noted soberly that it was precisely the *continuity* of this sense of crisis that determines modern culture: 'the stage of transition, like the whole of time in an earlier revolution, had become *endless*' (Kermode 1966: 101). Indeed, discontinuity and difference are the determining factors within the modern consciousness. Furthermore, Kermode noted that:

> The fiction of transition is our way of registering the conviction that the end is immanent rather than imminent; it reflects our lack of confidence in ends, our mistrust in the apportioning of history to epochs of this and that. Our own epoch is the epoch of nothing positive, only of transition. Since we move from transition to transition, we may suppose that we exist in no intelligible relationship to the past, and no predictable relation to the future. Already those who speak of a clean break with the past, and a new start for the future, seem a little old-fashioned. (Kermode 1966: 101–2)

Therefore, we feel the need to constantly invent endings, so that we can categorize and neatly contain our world into surveyable, orderly periods. Indeed, this is perhaps why the space and time covered in the novel lends itself so well to thinking about society as an organic body. As Bernard Bergonzi notes:

This apocalypticism may, indeed, be inherent in the form. The novel is concerned, above all, with carving shapes out of history, with imposing a beginning, middle and an end on the flux of experience, and there might be obscure connections between the need for a novelist to find an end for his novel, and the preoccupation of critics with seeing an end for all novels. (Bergonzi 1970: 13)

Novelists in the sixties were keen to stress through subversive techniques that history and human experience were something to be played around with as way of escaping grand narratives about the order of the world and popular narratives about the sexual revolution. As we'll see below, literature found a much more playful, but seriously complex way of foregrounding endings in order to inscribe new values, often centred on, on the one hand, women's liberation and the role of the female body, and, on the other hand, the changing status of religion, its narratives and its institution, in the consciousness of British society.

Open-endedness

One popular way of ending, or rather, *not* ending, texts, was the use of an open ending. Maureen Duffy's *That's How It Was* (1962), which I briefly discussed in Chapter 4, forms an interesting case in point. The finale is one of the most powerful moments in post-war writing, a textual climax that emulates the ending of Joyce's *Ulysses* (1922). The plot and poetics of this semi-fictional autobiographical 'novel' are fairly uncomplicated due to its realistic narration and linear development of its plot and protagonist. The book occupies the traditional topos of the *Bildungsroman*, namely, the coming of age of a young person – in this case a girl, Paddy, tracing her birth, youth and adolescence, when she breaks with her working-class origins and transforms herself into a successful, young intellectual. Behind her achievements stands her strong-willed mother, Louey, who raises her as a single mother after her husband, the IRA member Patrick, deserts the family. *That's How It Was* is in many ways a classic narrative which establishes readerly empathy through focusing on the relationship between Paddy and her mother, whose sacrifices lead to the context that allows Paddy to transform herself into a successful young individual.

There is a teleological underpinning that drives the narrative towards its conclusion. The novel ends with the announcement, in the final, very short chapter, of the death of Paddy's mother, Louey, who, worn out by tuberculosis, collapses on the pavement while shopping. This announcement has an extraordinary power that sweeps the grounds beneath the reader's feet precisely because we have forgotten that this extremely strong woman could die in the first place. *That's How It Was* ends the penultimate chapter with a single question that drives home the importance of the uncertainty at the loss of this parent: 'And what the hell do I do now?' (Duffy 2002: 221). It is this deferral of the end that creates such a powerful sense of catharsis in the reader, who is at that moment denied a sense of closure or restoration: we are being asked to answer this question on behalf of Paddy, triggering a great sense of responsibility, but also a great rush of abandonment: just as Paddy is deprived of her mother, the reader is abandoned by the author. The challenge that Paddy faces, making sense of the world without her guardian, becomes ours, and there is a nauseous feeling of vertigo as the ground beneath our feet is swept away.

While the narrative is set in the 1930s and 1940s, the novel also makes a point about the time in which it was written. Duffy herself states that this kind of uncertain ending belongs to the spirit of the times:

> It can be called merely a fashionable device of openendedness but I suggest that such a label misses the point. I believe it is the contemporary equivalent of the Shakespearean endstop of order restored. As his was appropriate for his age with its particular philosophical and political cast so the ending which leaves the reader to answer is appropriate for our times of rapid change and the need for continual existential decision. (Duffy 2002: xi)

Although order is restored, the ending also captures the double sensation of an excitingly open future and the anxieties about an unreadable future. In the light of this reflection, the novel's ending in a sensation of suspension in a vacuum should also be read as an attempted reflection of the *zeitgeist*, which is determined by increased speed of developments leading to a great sense of uncertainty about the ways in which the modern subject occupies a position in the world. Whereas the naturalistic fabric of the text demands closure, its denial ruptures the traditional sense-making processes: the denial of the end result stands analogous to the idea that in the sixties rational logic leads not to resolution but to further complexities and uncertainties. By not 'properly' ending, Duffy highlights the idea that in modern culture there never is a sense of an end, but only perpetual transition.

Any discussion of closure in relation to sexuality cannot omit the work of John Fowles, whose sixties novels foreground an anxiety about narrative authority. Fowles's first novel *The Collector* (1963), greatly indebted to both Shakespeare and Modernism, tells the story of the reclusive young working-class orphan Fred Clegg, who wins the football pools and kidnaps a middle-class art student, Miranda Grey. We first read Clegg's first-person perspective, move to Grey's diary entries of her experiences and end again with Clegg's pathological narrative. The telos is provided by the reader's need to understand if and how Miranda will escape – how the ending will unfold. There is no satisfying ending, though, as even the unhappy ending unfolds in an unfulfilling manner. *The Collector* ends without Miranda escaping or the villain being captured, but in an unexciting variation upon an unhappy finale, when Miranda dies slowly of pneumonia. There is no escape or rescuing effort, nor a heroic return to society; the narrative simply peters out, giving Clegg a way of avoiding blame for his crime: 'I also thought that I was acting as if I had killed her, but she died, after all. A doctor probably could have done little good, in my opinion. It was too far gone' (Fowles 1964: 281).

What does *The Collector* mean, and how does the anti-ending fit in? Clegg's pathological mind is unable to distinguish between animal and human beings, and his collecting of butterfly corpses to create a greater, whole corpus, which forms a quest for an encyclopaedic knowledge, necessarily fails. The incorporation with an aim to find a complete, totalizing body is a masculine undertaking of conquering and submission, which in this new era of emancipation is blocked. Miranda's 'real' death, in the sense that it does not abide by the laws of fiction, signals the growing gap of misunderstanding that exists between men and women in the early sixties. Clegg's old-fashioned, Victorian attitude to women is partly what constitutes his psychopathology: 'It's a woman's job, really. I mean it was a time when women need other women' (Fowles 1964: 112). The point is of course that Fowles's work hopes to deconstruct and expose such attitudes as wrong, not for their intrinsic ideology but for their roots in mythologies. The inability of the narrative to find some kind of agency to resolve this matter embodies a kind of impotence, whereby even male violence is unable to bring the sexes together. One disturbing issue that the novel brings forward is the absence of any kind of authorial voice that places a verdict upon both Clegg and Grey. In Fowles's novel, such externally imposed authority is absent, throwing readers back on to their own perception to make judgements about the first-person narratives. On the one hand, these reconsidered endings form a comment on the changed role, and presence, of religion in society: fiction reacted to a steady secularization of culture in the west by rethinking the analogy between the provision of comfort in a meaningful ending by God and the conventional, organically structured narratives with their orgiastic ending. On the other hand, these anti-orgiastic restorations can then also be seen as a form of textual protest against the centring of the self as the source and object of bodily pleasure, the increasing 'liberation' and gratification of the individual desire as part of the sexual revolution and the end-thinking that dominated the sixties in general.

Needless to say, there were many novels which neatly sew up the narrative: one may think of Burgess's *A Clockwork Orange* (1962), where protagonist Alex DeLarge is cured and gets his comeuppance; and Doris Lessing's *The Four-Gated City* (1969), where we find an Appendix with future documents (dated between 1995 and 2000) that round off Lessing's immense project, including a description of Quest's death. Iris Murdoch's *Bruno's Dream* (1969) ends, as do most of Murdoch's novels, neatly rounded off, with the protagonist's death. Even in the anti-novel, many endings are relatively conventional. Eva Tucker's *Contact* (1966) ends with an affirmation of the troubled partners' belief in marriage, and a return to the marital home (see Chapter 5).

Yet, other authors resisted this pattern. Fowles's *The French Lieutenant's Woman* offers the reader multiple endings, following the Barthesian Death of the Author argument, and partially handed authorial power over to the reader. Ann Quin's *Berg* (1964) offers a curious, circuitous finale, whereby the ending loops back to the beginning: the protagonist has not actually resolved his quest, and is back to the proverbial square one. The protagonist, Berg/Greb, is unable to wrench himself loose from the power of Oedipal psychology, trapping him in a hell of repetition. J. G. Ballard's *The Drowned World* (1962) is interesting in this regard: the novel ends with the protagonist doing exactly the opposite of the reader's instincts. In a hostile world where the 'normal' logic is for people to seek refuge in the habitable parts of planet Earth, Ballard's anti-hero, Kerans, flees in the opposite direction. Kerans enters the jungle in order to find out the new psychological possibilities offered by this new, tropical climate, even though this means a certain death.

Crash, crash, crash

It is conspicuous that in the late sixties and early seventies we find a number of fictions that problematize various philosophical issues in which the car plays a central role. Margaret Drabble's *The Waterfall* (1969), Muriel Spark's *The Driver's Seat* (1970) and J. G. Ballard's cult novel *Crash* (1973) all think through the socio-psychological changes that society went through in the sixties. In these novels, the motor car and various crashes are used as metaphors for understanding the transformation that individuals had lived through. These novels are interested in and obsessed with the dangerous power of the imagination spawned by the revolution of the motor car as the pre-eminent sign of modernity, and its impact upon the way we conceive endings. Once again, it is the writer's engagement with rethinking the ending that allows us to pinpoint such changes, while understanding how the sexual relationship between the sexes played a central role in these changes.

Drabble's *The Waterfall* (see the earlier discussion in Chapter 2) contains three endings: a grand, dark finale; a surprisingly light epilogue; and a postscript, all of which are used by Drabble to theorize the possibilities of the end in the modern age. The result is that the reader is confronted with a heavily metafictional novel that paradoxically exposes, on the one hand, the machinery of its poetics while, on the other hand, affirming truth and reality as preferable over traditional Aristotelian poetics. Towards the end of Drabble's novel, the poet Jane Gray and her lover, the car salesman and husband of her best friend, James, drive to Norway during an illicit encounter and are involved in a car accident, killing another driver. In the immediate aftermath of the crash, she is at first convinced that James has been killed, reinforcing her Aristotelian views of 'divine providence, of the futility of human effort against the power that holds us' (Drabble 1980: 185). The description of this climactic event within their relationship, which threatens to reveal their secret, also challenges Jane's outlook on life and death in more general terms:

> I went back to the crashed car to collect my luggage. It was all crushed up: the suitcase had burst, and my things were lying about all over the place: I seemed to spend hours wandering around the road picking things up (though it cannot have taken more than a minute) and by the end I could not avoid the sight of the mingled blood and oil that was leaking from the other car to the ground. So liquid we are, inside our stiff bodies, so easily resolved into other elements. (Drabble 1980: 190)

For Jane, it is not the crash itself but the experience of having to imagine one's body being rent to pieces is one of pure horror: 'I am afraid of blood and flesh and gaping organs' (Drabble 1980: 188). The mingling of blood and oil presents us with a dangerous sexual image that imagines body fluids mixing together and equates the human body to a dead object, in a logic which for Drabble's protagonist can only symbolize death, punishment for her affair while underscoring Jane's frigidity, which after her miscarriage 'had set in relentlessly' (Drabble 1980: 100). At the heart of Jane lies the drive to keep the parts of which her body consists together in an organic, if imagined, whole; the threat of disintegration and death remains the great ending: 'if he [James] died, what right had I to deny those who belonged to him the spectacle of his end?' (Drabble 1980: 195).

However, the crash does teach her to reject this fantasy of Aristotelian organicity, yet a rationalization of the disaster is deferred as well: 'I was hoping that in the end I would manage to find some kind of unity. I seem to be no nearer to it' (Drabble 1980: 207). While watching over James, she later realizes that the comparison between her and the car is a perfectly valid one:

> 'He had talked of response, as the car took off along the road, as her body flung itself from him, but what idiocy to equate a machine and a woman, neurotics though both of them were: a lump of expensive metal, a mechanical toy, and she herself not so much better, she herself responding unwilled like a machine' (Drabble 1980: 203).

Similarly she is no longer sure of the authenticity of her actions: 'Death. Murder. What had I to do with such things, I who had chosen to play the victim?' (Drabble 1980: 200). This results in a wholesale questioning of her relationship with her lover: 'Such a shallow, transient, selfish affair, so self-styled their love had been: it had seemed necessary, but it had not been so. A question of surfaces: of skin, of touch, of admiration for hands and eyes and faces. Scars, tattoos, surface scratches merely' (Drabble 1980: 204).

The implications for the narrative composition – and the novel's ending – are that they are divested in the multiple, and highly self-conscious justifications (Drabble 1980: 195), which undercut the possibility of a grand finale. When James finally awakes, for instance, he does so slowly instead of abruptly: although it 'would have been so much simpler if he had been dead: so natural a conclusion, so poetic in its justice [...] it would be hard for us to recognize the true moment of his recognition: there would be no moment of revelation, no sudden light' (Drabble 1980: 189; 217–18). Indeed, the first-person narrator confesses that to this novel

> There isn't any conclusion. A death would have been the answer, but nobody died. Perhaps I should have killed James in the car, and that would have made a neat, a possible ending.
>
> A feminine ending?
>
> Or I could have maimed James so badly, in this narrative, that I would have been allowed to have him, as Jane Eyre had her blinded Rochester. But I hadn't the heart to do it, I loved him too much, and anyway it wouldn't have been the truth because the truth is that he is recovered [...] But it's hardly a tragic ending, to so potentially a tragic tale. In fact, I am rather ashamed of the amount of amusement that my present life affords me, and of how much I seem to have gained by it. (Drabble 1980: 231–32)

Indeed, after the crash Jane continues her affair with James and she narrates an epilogue in which she and James go away together for a weekend in Yorkshire: 'It was so lovely [...] that I can't resist attempting to evoke it, gratuitously, as a finale, however irrelevant' (Drabble 1980: 235). The short narrative boasts a sublime experience during which Jane and James climb the Goredale Scar in the Pennines, 'a lovely organic balance of shapes and curves, a wildness contained within a bodily limit' (Drabble 1980: 236). This tricks the reader into thinking a restoration or reaffirmation of the organic structure is taking place; however, when Jane accidentally spills talcum powder into the whiskey they drink in the hotel room, the foul taste 'of dust and death' provides a 'fitting conclusion to the sublimities of nature' (Drabble 1980: 238). Drabble makes it clear, then, that although she aligns herself with the feminist objectives of the realist narratives of women writers, and the Brontës in particular, she reimagines the end in modern terms, thus emphasizing the growing self-consciousness of women during the decade. This is underscored by another, third ending to the novel – 'I can't leave it without a postscript, without formulating that final, indelicate irony' (Drabble 1980: 238) – in which Jane notes that she has stopped taking the pill because she could possibly have died of thrombosis brought on by its chemical components: 'Nowadays it is [...] thrombosis or neurosis: one can take one's pick. [...] I prefer to suffer' (Drabble 1980: 239). Although this appears to again revert back to an affirmation of the natural, and to reject the scientific and technological innovations that shape modern life, and, more importantly, the female body, the paradoxical nature of the novel's form suggests otherwise.

The organic, humanist poetics that Drabble's naturalistic prose seems to support, and which seems to project an image of the human body as a structure for the novel, are merely a smokescreen for a highly complex vision of the modern subject. The irony that undercuts the narration is, however, indicative of her self-consciousness, while her building of a happy ending into the body of the novel provides a sense of a new beginning for Jane.

Only a few years later, this renegotiated humanist vision of the world and the self was itself coldly challenged, even potentially inverted, by J. G. Ballard's *Crash*, in which the problem of the orgasmic is centralized as well, and similarly structured around the 'sensational disaster' (Drabble 1980: 215) of the car crash. The novel is narrated by a fictional television producer, 'Ballard', who, after killing another driver in a car crash, is awakened to the transcendental nature of the technological landscape of London's periphery at Heathrow airport. He falls under the spell of the stunt driver and 'TV scientist', Vaughan, who re-enacts famous car crashes in which Hollywood stars such as James Dean and Jayne Mansfield, writer Albert Camus and President Kennedy died. In Ballard's novel,

> All of us who knew Vaughan accept the perverse eroticism of the car-crash, as painful as the drawing of an exposed organ through the aperture of a surgical wound. I have watched copulating couples moving along darkened freeways at night, men and women on the verge of orgasm, their car speeding in a series of inviting trajectories towards the flashing headlamps of the oncoming traffic stream. Young men alone behind the wheels of their first cars, near-wrecks picked up in scrap-yards, masturbate as they move on worn tyres to aimless destinations. (Ballard 1995: 17)

Ballard's *Crash* is also obsessed with the achievement of the orgasmic ending, and proposes that during the twentieth century an inversion of reality and fiction has taken place due to the increasing presence of technology in our understanding of the world around us. Yet, while within the novel Vaughan's climax is achieved, this is narrated indirectly by 'Ballard': the text itself, as a warning against apocalyptic and Spectacular thinking, presents us with a world of surfaces and a deflatory ending. Once again, the uncertain, open ending presents modernity as a crisis whereby the meaning, purpose and the direction of the lived experience is indeterminate, as we saw in the previous chapter.

The pornographic gaze

Ballard's connection of the car crash with latent sexuality is one of the finest expressions of the violence at the heart of twentieth-century experience, and it allows us to read the novel as a direct assessment and criticism of the changing nature of sexuality. Indeed, Ballard claims that *Crash* is the 'first pornographic novel based on technology' (Ballard 1995 [1973]), and we can use this fictional narrative to understand the implications of the sexual revolution that was at the heart of the various transformations that the sixties entailed.

It is a truth universally acknowledged that in the wake of the Lady Chatterley obscenity trial in 1960, sexual permissiveness took hold in both society and its representation in literature. The lifting of censorship changed perceptions of class, gender, sex, sexual preference and attitudes to liberalism at the level of content and form in fiction. Combined with the introduction of the pill in 1962, attitudes and behaviour were changing rapidly, and a perceived golden era of sexual liberation manifested itself in the popular imagination, with guilt-free enjoyment of one's body without the danger of the responsibility of pregnancy. The purported control that science gave over the women's body via the contraceptive pill is a much more complex issue: while women were able to enjoy their youth and not sacrifice themselves into marriage, (young) men saw the pill as an opportunity for sex without consequences. A survey suggested that women were having sex at a younger age, and more of it, but the more important issue was that men were often pressuring girls into sex, via 'violence, blackmail, or getting them drunk' (Marwick 1998: 387–88). There was also a want of knowledge about how to avoid pregnancy, so that the 'combination of greater sexual adventurousness with ignorance about contraception inevitably entailed a good number of unintended births' (Marwick 1998: 388). Randall Stevenson notes:

> Its much-vaunted sexual liberation, in particular, soon seemed seriously asymmetric. Greater freedoms included still freer exploitation of the female form [...] Supposed 'freeing or unbinding of social energies' often left women more subordinate than ever; more starkly objectified by unconstrained male desires. (Stevenson 1986: 39)

This observation that the sexual revolution led to collateral damage, or even worked against the emancipation of women, is nothing new either. In *The Vital Illusion* (2000), Jean Baudrillard explores the 'ambiguous repercussions [that] may be completely opposed to the goals of the sexual revolution itself':

> The first phase of sexual liberation involves the dissociation of sexual activity from procreation through the pill and other contraceptive devices – a transformation with enormous consequences. The second phase, which we are beginning to enter now, is the dissociation of reproduction from sex. First, sex was liberated from reproduction; today it is reproduction that is liberated from sex, through asexual, biotechnological modes of reproduction such as artificial insemination or full body cloning. This is also a liberation, though antithetical to the first. (Baudrillard 2000: 10)

What is interesting, though, is that there is a deep, long-standing level of interconnection between sexual, social and psychological economies, which fiction allows us to probe.

Lusty affairs that result more generally in the collapse of the institution of marriage, along with their concomitant questions of guilt, are explored by many authors, from Drabble and Dunn to Mackay and Angela Carter. If *Up the Junction* (1963) shows impartially the impact of social changes in the late fifties and early sixties, *Poor Cow* (1967) is more critical of this newness, and this novel represents a first wave of feminism in which women are more knowledgeable

to the historical events in which they are swept up. Dunn reduced the level
of fragmentation, yet retains many of the qualities that make *Up the Junction*
formally exciting and innovative, such as the dark irony and observation of signs
as means of connecting the human economy to desire and death. Although by
choosing a fictional character as the protagonist, Dunn places an authorial
distance between herself and the narrative, authenticity remains an important
motivation. In a confessional note, Joy confides in the reader about her sexual
life: 'If houses could tell secrets – no kidding – this house would have had more
sex in it than any other house in London' (Dunn 1968: 33). Male desire too is
represented with a post-coïtal sense of frankness. Dave tells Joy:

> I think about sex for about half an hour when I wake up in the morning and
> then it passes then later on I think about it again going over the exact details
> of when I last seduced you, that takes me another two hours and then I might
> think about it for another hour or so in the afternoon. In all I think about sex for
> about four hours a day. (Dunn 1968: 34)

Female desire and 'perversity' too are discussed unflinchingly. Joy becomes
friendly with the Saloon barmaid Beryl, who works as a prostitute for
customers who wanted to be whipped. She states, 'I don't mind them beating
you with a couple of plastic roses' (Dunn 1968: 46). Later on in the novel, in a
chapter entitled 'Turned On', Joy is sucked into the 'kinky scene' (Dunn 1968:
65), sleeping with a variety of men, changing her definition of, and condition
for, having sex dramatically: 'Proper lusty I was getting – it used to be love but
it's all lust now – it's so terrific with different blokes. Sometimes you fancy it all
soft and other times you want them to fuck the life out of you. Well you can't
get that from the same bloke can you' (Dunn 1968: 64).

This control over the female body is mirrored by its appropriation in language.
Joy uses the words 'fuck' and 'cunt', the use of which becomes increasingly overt
as the narrative progresses, showing a frustration at being imprisoned in her
body and direct environment. Joy states, 'What's the matter with me, I'm a
cunt aren't I? I was never a lover of sex in the beginning – it's taken a hold of
me' (Dunn 1968: 101). Around the same period, Germaine Greer advocated a
similar strategy in *Oz* magazine and *The Female Eunuch* (1970), published by
the same house as Dunn's work (MacGibbon & Kee), whereby women should
reclaim male-dominated power over the female body by foregrounding the
female body itself and by appropriating and actively using the c-word: 'the
emphasis should be taken off male genitality and replaced by human sexuality.
The cunt must come into its own' (Greer 2006: 356). It is striking therefore that

Joy also applies the c-word also to her jailed lover ('Dave why did you leave me you rotten cunt?' (Dunn 1968: 108)), which counteracts the offensive strategy of referring to women by their reproductive organs by applying it to men.

Indeed, writers also explored how liberation could easily spill over into perverse forms of sexuality. In Duffy's *The Microcosm*, for instance, one of the main characters, Ms Stephens, the head of department at a secondary school, observes of one of her pupils who she later seduces: 'That child has all the makings of masochist already. When she's a bit older she'll be crying out for someone to whip her. Unless it's all a deep laid out plot, an excuse to hang around after school and walk me to the station' (Duffy 1988: 33). Later on, she is accused of perversion: 'Seducing the innocent that's what you're contemplating Stevens. People like you should be locked up before you contaminate society. I am society. You're sick. So is society' (Duffy 1988: 49). This constant undercutting of hegemonic ideology by reframing the so-called deviant or pathological behaviour as not outside the social sphere, but as part of and produced by this very sphere, is a powerful strategy.

In the same year as the Chatterley trial the protagonist of Burgess's *The Doctor Is Sick* (1960) refuses the invitation of the gangster and whip-fetishist Bob, to whip him:

> 'You will. You must. Look.' Bob began to tear his upper clothes off. 'I'll show you,' he said, muffled by his shirt. 'Now then,' he said, throwing his shirt away. 'Look at that. I've had fifty stitches in my back. *Fifty.*' He displayed a broad back gnarled and wealed with lashes. 'But I don't care. You can do it as hard as you like. I don't care. Go on. GO ON!' he yelled. (Burgess 1960: 146)

In Burgess's typical mode of farce, Edwin Spindrift's revulsion turns into anger, reinforcing the perverse cycle: 'Edwin felt the joy of the sadist rising in his loins. This would not do. Angry with himself, he cracked the lash again' (Burgess 1960: 147).

Towards the later stages of the sixties, the aura of innocence has started to fade and to make way for a much harder realization about the effects of social change, combined with commercial exploitation and a new mass mediascape, upon human behaviour and consciousness. We see the formation of a pornographic gaze, through which women again would be imprisoned, ideologically and physically. This latter indictment of the emergence of the pornographic gaze is connected to the development of the industrial capitalist system into one which requires the citizen to submit herself or himself to observation purely at the level of signs, divorced from the very realities of human relationships.

Many writers warned against the rampant desire that often seemed to move through society.

Ballard's *The Atrocity Exhibition* forms a dubious case in point. The *Atrocity*-project first emerged as a series of short texts intermittently published during the 1960s in the *New Worlds* magazine for *avant-garde* science fiction and speculative fiction under the editorship of Michael Moorcock. It was first published as a collected text with the title *The Atrocity Exhibition* in 1970, but subsequently it was published in a variety of forms. A revised, expanded and illustrated version appeared with Re/Search in 1990, with Annotations and Commentary by Ballard and a Preface by William Burroughs; another revised, expanded, annotated and illustrated version came with Flamingo in 2001 (including a large format edition); and 2006 saw a new HarperCollins paperback edition which included an Appendix with two additional texts, and a short story, 'The Smile'. Continuously evolving, always unfinished, *The Atrocity Exhibition* is the ultimate text of *Becoming* rather than of *Being*.

The process of 'condensation', which sees all materiality taken out of the novels until we only have left the platonic Idea behind the 'flesh', is the guiding principle of *The Atrocity Exhibition*; this process destroys organic plotting, linear continuity and traditional notions of causality. Instead, it foregrounds randomness as a mode that suspends the possibility of a retrievable, organic structure with a beginning and an end. Just as in Italo Calvino's *Invisible Cities* (1974), which presents a similar mathematical sequence of text that boils the materiality of cities down to the Idea, what we are left with is the residue of materiality. Ballard thus literalizes a process of anti-materiality, which chimes in with the utopian spirit of the sixties. It is this anti-Aristotelian mode that gives the book its imaginative potential, and it is why *The Atrocity Exhibition* should, first and foremost, be read at the level of process and form, which is itself a *function* that does not express or reinforce the subject matter: process and form are the subject matter, and itself capture a peculiar sixties subjectivity.

We find one of the more accessible examples of condensation in the often-quoted 'Sex Kit' passage in Chapter 6, 'The Great American Nude', in which Talbert has condensed his love/lust object, Dr Karen Novotny, to its bare essentials:

> **The Sex Kit**. 'In a sense,' Dr Nathan explained to Koester, 'one may regard this
> as a kit, which Talbert has devised, entitled "Karen Novotny" – it might even
> be feasible to market it commercially. It contains the following items: (1) Pad of

pubic hair, (2) a latex face mask, (3) sex detachable mouths, (4) a set of smiles, (5) a pair of breasts, left nipple marked by a small ulcer (6) a set of non-chafe orifices, (7) photo cut-outs of a number of narrative situations – the girl doing this and that, (8) a list of dialogues samples, of inane chatter, (9) a set of noise levels, (10) descriptive techniques for a variety of sex acts, (11) a torn anal detrusor muscle, (12) a glossary of idioms and catch phrases, (13) an analysis of odour traces (from various vents), mostly purines, etc. (14) a chart of body temperatures (auxiliary, buccal, rectal), (15) slides of vaginal smears, chiefly Ortho-Gynol jelly, (16) a set of blood pressures, systolic 120, diastolic 70 rising to 200/150 at onset orgasm ... ' Deferring to Koester, Dr Nathan put down the typescript. 'There are one or two other bits and pieces, but together the inventory is an adequate picture of a woman, who could easily be reconstituted from it. In fact, such a list may well be more stimulating than the real thing. Now that sex is becoming more and more a conceptual act, an intellectualization divorced from affect and physiology alike, one has to bear in mind the positive merits of the sexual perversions. Talbert's library of cheap photo-pornography is in fact a vital literature, a kindling of a few taste buds in the jaded palates of our so-called sexuality.' (Ballard 2006: 84–85)

This provocative passage is relatively easy to read. In his devising of the 'Sex Kit', Talbert has destroyed Novotny's body by reducing its materiality to a collection of signs, which present us with fragmented images that express the functioning of male desire. The idea that Novotny 'could easily be reconstituted from' this kit reminds us of *Ulysses* – which itself emerged as a work in progress, and aimed to 'to give a picture of Dublin so complete that if the city one day suddenly disappeared from the Earth, it could be reconstructed out of [Joyce's] book' (Budgen 1989: 69). Implicit in Ballard's text is the idea that the relationship between the modern experience and representation has become even more complex. Novotny is presented through her fragmented body, but also by its effects upon Talbert's psyche. The body parts are mixed up with the images of the machinery (such as a heart-rate monitor and thermometer) that clinically measure and analyse desire and sexual activity (such as 'an analysis of odour traces'; 'charts of body temperatures'; 'a set of blood pressures'). Ballard's lists are post-Joycean, anti-encyclopaedic, heteroglossic – random rather than totalizing collections that imaginatively de-order the 'real'.

Nonetheless, Travers has engaged in an imagined renting apart of Novotny's body, leaving behind her *disjecta membra* in dematerialized form in order for it to be reconstructed in the imagination. The division of the subject was first put forward in Freud's dream analyses – a profound influence upon Ballard's thought, suggesting that the threat of fragmentation undermined the essentially whole self. However, *The Atrocity Exhibition* sees a shift away from Freudian psychoanalysis, with its centring on the bounded, complete subject, towards an acknowledgement of a post-Freudian model which is not necessarily organic and anthropomorphic, but an investigation of how desire structures the subject via intersubjective connections that are constructed in the imagination. In the Sex Kit, there is no unitary, organic body for us to invest desire in, but merely body and machine parts, which no longer function as signifiers of a whole organism that can potentially be retrieved.

In 'A Lover's Discourse' (1978), Barthes analyses the deadly impact of the male gaze and notes a shift from classical modes of perception to a distinctly modern one, a renegotiation of the relationship between subject and object, the violence of which expresses itself in a renegotiation of a classical topos, the female nude:

> However, there is an odd turnaround here: in the ancient myth, the ravisher is active, he wants to seize his prey, he is the subject of rape (of which the object is a Woman, as we know, invariably passive); in the modern myth (that of love-as-passion), the contrary is the case: the ravisher wants nothing, does nothing; he is motionless (as any image), and it is the ravished object who is the real subject of the rape; the *object* of capture becomes the *subject* of love; and the *subject* of the conquest moves into the class of loved *object*. (Barthes 2009: 433)

Barthes captures the passive, depersonalized gaze of Travis well, but this emphasis on clinical vision also suggests that the list is not composed through free association but by careful and rational analysis of how desire functions, suggesting how images mediate between the collective and society, and the individual. Ballard reimagines this fragmented body within the clinical vision and discourse of the scientist, which takes us another step away from the formal language of psychoanalysis. Note 'the small ulcer', a deliberately plotted fiction to heighten the sense of 'the real', drawing materiality into conceptual play, in its turn emphasized by the 'face mask'. The anal detrusor muscle is 'torn', introducing carefully calculated shock. This list starts with, and is haunted by, the curious inclusion of a 'Pad of pubic' hair, once a classic, biblical signifier of shame and innocence, the body's own attempt to cover up our private parts and instil guilt in us perhaps, but now mocked and put on display as a ludicrous anachronism through its commercial marketing, which also adumbrates the increasing obsession with the removal of body hair within the porn industry and society at large. Ballard is assessing the sixties, and mocks the fetishization of innocence and the politicization of female body hair by placing these in the wholly artificial and postlapsarian environment of the scientific laboratory.

Another important aspect of this list is Talbert's emphasis on the ways in which this process of condensation affects language. Two entries within the list ('a list of dialogues samples, of inane chatter' and 'a glossary of idioms and catch phrases') suggest that the pornographic gaze leads to a standardization or reduced richness of language and the subject's capacity to express itself, and to connect to others, in a meaningful manner. Ballard's text dramatizes the intense commercial and public marketing of sexuality in the sixties, which reduces making love to a clinical set of standard ingredients – pornography. Mass mechanical 'reproduction' results in collectively shared sexual codes leading to an emerging form of a collectivized social pornography that transgresses the boundaries between the individual and society, a pornotopia. The pornotopia forms the process by which society engages in an unwitting, public pedagogy that conditions a perpetual state of arousal through the form and not the content of reifying images. Ballard's distanced and distancing, depersonalized zero-degree writing counters this conditioning by constantly postponing a narrative climax and by withholding conventional processes of readerly identification. The repetitive, closed circuit of disjointed imagery demands from us for a multiple, fragmented emotional and sexual investment that in fact cancels out desire. *The Atrocity Exhibition* is profoundly anti-pornographic, and anti-pornotopic in its effect on the reader: 'the text of bliss is never a text that recounts the kind of bliss afforded literally by an ejaculation. The pleasure of representation is not attached to its object: pornography is not *sure*' (Barthes 2009: 409). In the light of our earlier discussions in Chapter 3, this passage is thus a knowing, yet provocative, example of ejaculative projectionism – constructed through a hyperfocused act of the male gaze. In a note to this entry Ballard 'explains':

> Sex, which many enthusiasts in the 1960s thought they had invented, then seemed to be the new frontier [...] the mass media publicly offer a range of options which previously have been available only in private. Thanks to the press, film and television, sex has become a communal and public activity for the first time since the Edens of a more primitive age. In a sense we now all take part in sex whether we want to or not. Many people, like the characters in *The Atrocity Exhibition*, use sex as a calculated means of exploring uncertainties in their make-up, exploiting the imaginative possibilities that sex provides. [...] The test of a language is how well it can be translated into other tongues, and sex is the most negotiable language of all. (Ballard 2006: 89–90)

This emphasis on language, metaphor and the possibility of translation is important, because rather than the emphasis on Ballard's use of visual material, from surrealist painting to pop art, it stresses Ballard's awareness of the medium in which he works, while pointing to the Modernist interest in approaching modernity as a linguistic problem.

Beyond such theorizing, there are questions of the motivation of such provocative, perhaps misogynist depictions and a wider literary context here – ethical question about the power of representation. Ballard's condensing of materiality of the female body to some critics might smack of a logic that is driven by an anxiety about the changing power dynamic between men and women in the sixties, that is, of men fearing the loss of power over women. Hence, we see fantasies of reasserting male power and the former privileged position. If we look at some other male fictions, such as *The Collector* and *A Clockwork Orange*, we might suspect that there indeed is a crisis of masculinity taking place. In *The Collector*, butterfly collector Frederick Clegg abducts Miranda Grey, treating her like another insect, resulting in her death. *A Clockwork Orange* contains rape scenes, including that of a ten-year-old girl, and the murder of women. These novels can be read as a backlash against the empowerment of women around this time by often writing fantasies in which men reappropriate power over women and their bodies.

One of the finest novels reacting against such fantasies is Muriel Spark's *The Driver's Seat*, discussed in Chapter 3. In the novel we find a woman who instigates her own murder at the hands of a man: this control over her body and death, but also creating power over man's sexual desire, shows how women felt the need to empower themselves in extreme ways. Similar to Ballard, Spark uses the metaphorical analogy that exists between sex and death, but only to appropriate it in tragic terms: 'As the knife descends to her throat she screams, evidently perceiving how final is finality' (Spark 1970: 159). Although Spark seemingly draws us back into an Aristotelian framework – the novel ends with references to 'fear and pity, pity and fear' (Spark 1970: 160) – the meaning of the novel is obscure and uncertain, and leaves the reader in a state of metaphysical shock. This effect is one which radically disrupts the representational framework, and the confusion articulates the troubled relationship and power balance between men and women in the late sixties.

Conclusion
The Future of the Sixties

The collision of Eros and Thanatos

This book has shown that writers during the sixties produced exciting and provocative literature, making the decade one of the most interesting periods in recent literary history. The sixties saw some of the greatest authors emerge, or mature, writing some of their best work; they include Doris Lessing, Angela Carter, Muriel Spark, John Fowles, J. G. Ballard, Iris Murdoch and A. S. Byatt. The year 1969 in particular was an *annus mirabilis*, with the publication of Angela Carter's *Heroes and Villains* and *Several Perceptions*, John Fowles's *The French Lieutenant's Woman*, B. S. Johnson's *The Unfortunates*, Doris Lessing's *The Four-Gated City*, Michael Moorcock's *Behold the Man*, Iris Murdoch's *Bruno's Dream* and J. G. Ballard's *The Atrocity Exhibition*. We have also uncovered an interconnected network of experiments that pitted its aesthetic against the mainstream conservative conventions and realism that traditionally run so strong in English literature. We also find writers with a hyperactive, nomadic and immensely prolific spirit such as Anthony Burgess and Michael Moorcock, whose frantic energy encapsulates the *Zeitgeist* of the sixties.

If one rereads these works of fiction now, the level of thinking about 'big' political and philosophical issues, such as the nature of reality, changing ways of representation of that reality, the nature of the self, free will and the onslaught of technology on authenticity, is astoundingly high. Literature considered forms of justice, and gave voice to marginalised individuals and groups. We encounter a society whose traditional footholds are dropping away: from religion and patriarchal dominance to humanism and heteronormative values. The intellectual context saw the rise of the New Left, and generated fierce debates, both within and outside the academe: post-Freudians such as R. D. Laing and Jacques Lacan ensured that madness was part of the public debate, while the new wave of philosophy and literary theory from France had a huge impact on thinking. The many social changes and events during the decade, from the introduction of the pill and the mass introduction of the fridge to social protest over education and the Vietnam War and the anxieties generated by the Cold War, created a climate in which the perception of human experience was heightened and more intense. Literature was opinionated – interested in, but also critical of, the ways in which human thinking was shifting during this period of social and cultural change. In a sense, the body of work assembled here can be viewed as a collective cognitive experiment that pinpoints how the human mind and behaviour was affected by these changes.

What is striking about this fascinating body of fictions is that, despite the revolutionary, incendiary aura of the sixties in the popular imagination, literary fiction of the period is often characterized by quiet, thoughtful and complex stories that reject the Spectacular narratives and mythologizing modes we find in the mainstream media. These novels have given us, besides their intellectual content, a kaleidoscopic sensibility that captures the decade's structure of feeling, which could be viewed as the collision of Eros and Thanatos. From newfound sexual liberties to the eroticisation of the public realm through, for instance, manipulation of the general public's unconscious by advertising agencies, new thinking and enactments of love and sex permeated almost every section of society. One aspect of this sensibility is a new openness and frankness about sexuality: an honesty about the human body and its desires. What is particularly striking is the violence and eroticism of the struggle between the sexes that emerges in these novels, from the depiction of rape to the protracted love-making session in Maureen Duffy's *Wounds*. Simultaneously, various forms of death took hold: from the spiritual death of a seemingly increasingly superficial world through to the tearing down of former institutional structures, which made way for new forms, embodied by Brutalist architecture and high-rises.

Sixties novels often let go of their historical dimension, and focus directly on contemporary issues. Of course authors such as Doris Lessing and John Fowles kept situating personal situations against a historical backdrop, and trace characters through time and space, yet one might think of Nell Dunn's work, Maureen Duffy's and Angela Carter's novels as well as those of Colin MacInnes, to name but a few who embraced the contemporary with a new eagerness. This shift towards investigating the present is interlinked with the emergence of social documentary. Other new genres emerged as well, the most interesting of them the new sf published in *New Worlds* magazine. Many writers started experimenting with the rewriting of the canon and mixing genres, such as the Gothic and the fairy tale, appropriated by Angela Carter, for instance; we also see the campus novel flourish in the work of Malcolm Bradbury and find echoes in the works of Jonathan Franzen and Zadie Smith in the twenty-first century.

This book has also developed fresh critical perspectives on existing material, moving beyond the techniques which have come to be known as postmodern to draw on the cognitive turn of the early twenty-first century. We have seen how women appropriated new technology to give new shape to literature: by using portable tape recorders, they were able to collect (women's) voices and to reimagine them in the more permanent medium of the written book, leading to new formal experiments that challenge established notions of representation and materiality. Women also used the materiality of the book to overthrow the masculine tradition of realism, by creating skinny fictions that aligned themselves with the alternative literary tradition known as 'minor literature'. Even within the works of authors who would generally classify themselves as realist, we see an increased level of reflection about the (changing) nature of storytelling, and how representation and 'the real' were increasingly merging, their relationship becoming much more problematic. We have seen how London becomes a battleground, with the influx of immigrants from the colonies in the fifties, leading to racism and anti-immigrant protest. In fiction, we see a response that tries to come to terms with this rapidly changing demography, while often reinforcing stereotypes. This book has also unearthed forgotten (experimental) writers, such as Eva Tucker, Rayner Heppenstall and Alan Burns. Many of these experimental fictions tried to find a way of representing the 'crisis' of humanism. In doing so, these experiments often gave us alternative ways of seeing and thinking the world; some of this writing adumbrates or bleeds into what would become postmodern fiction, but some visionary writers, such as B. S. Johnson and J. G. Ballard, anticipated our twenty-first digital experience. We have also seen how the sixties acted as a space where radical experimentation, such as that of Ballard's *The Atrocity Exhibition*, stretched – or perhaps, overstretched – the limits of the novel. Heightened self-consciousness about narration led to play with the endings of narratives; this signalled a change in storytelling, while also emphasizing change in the established order of things. These endings were anti-Spectacular, anti-orgiastic, and refused to give readers a climactic pay-off. These postponements or diversions of textual orgasm were strategically used by writers to provide new readerly experiences, and to comment on an increasingly sexualized society, its newfound permissiveness allowing for a new literary openness about sexuality, but also creating a pornification of the gaze and human behaviour.

The death of literature (again)

I want to look briefly at the literary sixties from two vantage points: from the immediate reassessment in the late sixties and early seventies, and from our twenty-first-century point of view. In doing so, we could ask a number of questions: how has the critical reception of sixties fiction changed? And, more importantly, what is the future of the legacy of British fiction of the sixties? In short, what do the sixties mean to us today? At the end of the sixties, critics voiced disappointment with the state of literature, which seemed unable to keep up with the radical transformation of society. Anthony Burgess pointed to Mary Quant OBE's invention of the miniskirt as a revolution that literature could only dream of:

> It's something we've always wanted; and she, probably through insensitivity, was able to push it through and was surprised at the response because she wasn't sensitive enough to expect a response. I don't know. These are no major achievements. The major achievements of a race are great architecture, great music, great literature. These are not coming out of England as far as I can see at the moment. (Quoted in Lewis 2002: 251)

In 1968, Anthony Burgess left England, in part for tax reasons, but also, he claimed, for the poor writing climate:

> It's not only to get away from British taxes, although that's part of it. We [writers] are not wanted here, you see . . . . We might as well get out. This is the story of English letters today. What a bloody shame. What a bloody nuisance. Here we have to do journalism to live. (Burgess 1968: 97)

From a contemporary perspective, when the average writer is unable to make a living and needs to seek refuge in Creative Writing departments, Burgess's comments seem rather privileged. Although published when, in many ways, the sixties was still in full swing, the June 1970 edition of the literary magazine *Encounter* – which turned out to have been sponsored by the CIA to promote western ideologies – was an intellectual stocktaking of what the decade's literature had yielded. In a special section on 'Literature and Criticism' spearheaded by Malcolm Bradbury, Martin Dodsworth, Paul Fussell, John Holloway, Rayner Heppenstall and Martin Seymour-Smith reflected on the recent upheavals that threatened to challenge the British literary tradition. Seymour-Smith's article 'Whose Shakespeare?' argues against the appropriation of the bard for loose, postmodern interpretations produced by misapplied reverence and 'the deliberately subjective approach' (Seymour-Smith 1970: 56).

In 'Dickens' Word-World', John Holloway worried about not only the careless republication of Dickens's novels during the centenary but even more about the tendency for promiscuous interpretation. In Gradgrindian fashion, Holloway argues against the dangers of deconstructive wordplay:

> The function of words may indeed be to render a valid account of reality (whatever that may mean); but they can just as easily do the other thing. From the plain man's standpoint, man bites dog runs counter to a specification of the greatest organising principle validated by the *facts*. So it can only be a joke, or a piece of nonsense. From the standpoint of language, it is merely one more lexical permutation among patterns one may largely reshuffle as one likes. (Holloway 1970: 66)

Paul Fussell's less conservative contribution meditates on reinterpretations of eighteenth-century literature in light of a new irony: 'we easily recognise now that perfectly responsible and well-educated people are dramatically capable of inattention, laziness, and disingenuousness, and that texts prepared when rosier views of human nature were presiding need to be scrutinised with a special scepticism' (Fussell 1970: 69–70). In a review of Susan Sontag's *Styles of Radical Will* (1969), Martin Dodsworth reverts to a Leavisite idea of the function of the English Department as a centre of consciousness for the community, providing 'that proper use of literacy so badly needed' (Dodsworth 1970: 80). There was, it seems, a knee-jerk reaction to experimental literature, and to the new genres and early postmodern game playing that were rapidly gaining popularity.

These responses are interesting from our contemporary point of view, and we will agree on some points. Critics such as Seymour-Smith and Holloway are anxious about the status of the English canon, and anticipated that for the postmoderns, who would rule culture and literature for the next twenty years, nothing would be sacred. Postmodern interpretations of Shakespeare, Defoe, Dickens and Conan Doyle, for instance, have given us masterpieces: fictions by Angela Carter, Salman Rushdie, J. M. Coetzee, J. G. Ballard and Jeanette Winterson, to name but a few. The democratisation of the literary canon has, on the whole, been a good development, and in universities we now teach Beowulf, Shakespeare, Milton and Austen next to lesser-known and perhaps perishable names. At the moment, immersed in the digital revolution, we experience another reconsideration of the nature of the canon. Now we are not questioning which single writer is important in hierarchical ranking of Great Literature, but we try to make sense of the endless archives and search methods that we are accruing. These offer new possibilities as well.

The position of English literature and the humanities in the twenty-first century is radically different. Whereas before the sixties English was still central to the university, and to a degree to public life, this has radically changed. Following a period in which English literature was still exciting and 'important', offering the key to understanding the changing nature of our culture, and the subsequent waning of postmodernity, literature seems less important. Science has made various leaps forward; in that respect, the anxieties articulated by Dodsworth about letting go of traditional, organic ideas about society seem prescient. This shift started in the sixties, as John Sturrock notes:

> The divergence and fragmentation of human knowledge are usually interpreted as a cause for alarm and confusion, but they can also converge into a single conviction – that when knowledge is so compartmentalized then there are no gods among us, but only men ... The age is one that favours the redefinition of spheres of influence and authority. The New Novelist, then, is intent on showing in his novels that he is simply a man, equipped with the universal human power of imagination. (Sturrock 1969: 14–15)

These desperate sounding voices suggest that during the sixties traditional society and its concomitant poetics had gone out of the window, triggering a knee-jerk reaction and return to a conservative, traditional middle ground. In his excellent study *The Situation of the Novel* (1970), Bernard Bergonzi too is dismissive of recent experiments within the novel form:

> There are times when to be English is, it seems, to be destined for endless humiliations. In these circumstances I do not think it surprising that many English writers, and some of the most talented among them, have exhibited the classical neurotic symptoms of withdrawal and disengagement, looking within themselves, or back to a more secure period in their own lives or the history of their culture, making occasional guesses about a grim and apocalyptic future. If I refer to these writers in this clinical way it is not to dismiss them; it is rather in the spirit of those modern psychologists who suspect that the schizophrenic may be right and the society in which he has grown up wrong, and who urge us to listen to his apparent babblings, since he may have something urgent to tell us. (Bergonzi 1970: 57)

Bergonzi, a thorough critic, got this wrong. The schizophrenic in postmodern literature has given us some of the most insightful views on our western cultures, from Pynchon and Delillo to Rushdie and Moorcock. Postmodern literature, however, was often slick and cool, and we should separate it from the deliberately 'difficult' experimental literature of the Calder stables. Today there is a niche market for the experimental fiction of writers such as Kenneth Goldsmith, Christian Bök and Vanessa Place, but often the ideas lying behind their projects are relatively narrow, leading to empty formalisms. There is also a strong experimental mainstream fiction, such as Tom McCarthy's *Satin Island* (2015), Eimar McBride's *A Girl Is a Half-Formed Thing* (2014) and Ali Smith's *How to Be Both* (2015): these novels are experiments, conditioned by postmodern coolness, very readable and appealing to a mainstream audience. We find an interesting parallel between sixties and current publishing in their shared interest in the exploitation of the materiality of the book. Subversive sixties interventions such as B. S. Johnson's hole-in-a-page in *Albert Angelo* (1963) and book-in-a-box *The Unfortunates* (1974), and Marc Saporta's *Composition No. 1* (1962) find their equivalents in Anne Carson's Japanese-style accordion album *Nox* (2009), Jonathan Safran Foer's reworking on Bruno Schultz's *Street of Crocodiles* in *Tree of Codes* (2010) and Adam Thirlwell's *Kapow!* (2014). These explorations of materiality are not only experiment in cognitive states, as I argued in Chapter 5, but also protests against the new ways of reading generated by technologies such as e-reader and the mobile phone.

The state of fiction, and the nature of thinking about what literature is capable of doing, has changed. In the sixties, with Roland Barthes and his Death of the Author at the intellectual helm, writers believed that the text was an indeterminate place, a force field where many different influences would collide, producing an atopic or heterotopic space that could be a cognitive playing field whereby the reader could unleash her interpretations, clashing and blending with the text into a cognitive play consisting of a maze of loops, backtrackings, jammings and circuits that had a unique life of its own. In the early twenty-first century, we have now returned to the cult of the celebrity writer, of a proliferation of literary festivals at which a hungry audience is determined to 'find the author', of asking what the text is 'about' and of performing authors carefully weaving in various bits of personal information into their discussion of the book. This is fine, and not surprising, given the precarious state in which literary production finds itself and how the landscape of the literary authors has changed so drastically.

We have lost a certain utopian spirit, both in society and in the arts, and a belief that literature and the literary imagination, which forms a contract between writer and reader, has a special place in society, where problems can be thought through in creative, aesthetic patterns that have their own magical logic. If the world is a place partly generated through the imaginary spaces of reflection provided by literary art, the sixties are a complex one, often contradictory and always ambiguous. This is nothing new, of course; every age is made up of subtle ambivalences, and yet the sixties are interesting for their compression of intensities and clashing ideological conflicts. What comes to mind is Foucault's heterotopia as formulated in *The Order of Things* (1966), a belief in idealism, in spaces of the imagination and in the power of ideas to have tangible effects on material reality.

One interesting continuity, however, takes place in feminist politics. We have seen that the sixties were, when it came to the position of women in society, a time when idealism was married up with a material impetus; the drive to make changes in the 'real' on behalf of human bodies – especially those of women. They were caught up in, and often trampled over by, a world which was dominated by the rigid inherited structures of old powers that would not give up their privileged position without a fight. Today, the importance of materiality is very much back on the agenda: after the postmodern obsession with considering the body a discursive construct, we are now coming to understand the importance of women's bodies as a material reality, ranging from action on female genital mutilation to neuroscientific books that (provocatively) claim there is such a thing as a female brain.

What is conspicuous about the sixties is the way in which new technologies and science very rapidly created a new context in which conceptions of our lived experience had to be renegotiated. The arrival of mass media in the late fifties and sixties was a major cause for concern to many critics, from Guy Debord's dismissal of the capitalist consumer society that created a Society of Spectacle to Marshall McLuhan's attempts to understand how new media were becoming extensions of the mind and body of man, making us vulnerable to manipulation by external forces. Whether we accept these nightmare visions of our world is besides the point: what is clear, however, is that cognitive extensions have only increased and intensified at the start of the twenty-first century. New technologies, driven by scientific innovation, have more and more turned people into a hybrid of machine and human body, and have extended and distributed cognition. The results are astonishing, in both good and bad ways, and the possibilities for creative engagement have increased significantly. For writers and literary critics, the question is how literature is able to adapt itself to these new contexts and demands. The regressive attitude that seemed to hold sway at the end of the sixties was unwise: the experimental mode in which many of the writers worked was important in its attempt to find new forms of expression for these changing shape of lived experience. Today, we can see many writers once again attempting to capture these new modes of living, no longer merely commenting (critically or celebratory) but finding new forms of expression, and making a claim for literature as a space of the imagination where the stories of our lives can be made sense of. Literature is not simply a competitor of new technologies that are changing the way we think about human beings. If it wants to, it can make a claim for its own ability to help adapt consciousness to new demands and pressures. The novel is, itself, an adaptable form that helps us to look over the horizon, towards new goals and achievements. In 1967, Anthony Burgess ushered the readers of his exhaustive study of contemporary fiction, *The Novel Now*, out on the following, hopeful note. His words resonate for today's literature:

> The contemporary novel is not doing badly. Soon, when we least expect it, it will do not merely better but magnificently. And one of us [novelists] may, astonishingly, prove the vehicle of some great expected masterpiece which will burn up the world (meaning the people who read). That dim hope sustains us. (Burgess 1967: 213)

Bibliography

Ackroyd, Peter, *Notes for a New Culture: An Essay on Modernism*. London: Vision Press, 1976.

Ackroyd, Peter, *London: The Biography*. London: Vintage, 2001. First published in 2000 by Chatto & Windus.

Aldiss, Brian and David Wingrove, *Trillion Year Spree: The History of Science Fiction*. London: Gollancz, 1986.

Amis, Martin, *Money*. London: Penguin, 1985. First published in 1983.

Amis, Martin, *Experience*. London: Cape, 2001.

Appleyard, Bryan, *The Pleasures of Peace: Art and Imagination in Post-War Britain*. London: Faber & Faber, 1989.

Ballard, J. G., 'Subliminal Man', *New Worlds*, No. 1, January, 1963.

Ballard, J. G., *The Kindness of Women*. London: HarperCollins, 1991.

Ballard, J. G., *Crash*. London: Vintage, 1995, unpaginated. First published in 1973.

Ballard, J. G., 'Time, Memory and Inner Space', in *A User's Guide to the Millennium*. London: Flamingo, 1996, p. 200. Originally published in *The Women's Journalist*, 1963.

Ballard, J. G., *The Drowned World*. London: Gollancz, 1999. First published in 1962.

Ballard, J. G., *The Atrocity Exhibition*. London: Harper Perennial, 2006. First published in 1970 by Jonathan Cape.

Barnes, Julian, *Flaubert's Parrot*. London: Vintage, 2002. Originally published in 1984.

Barthes, Roland, *The Fashion System*. New York: Hill and Wang, 1983.

Barthes, Roland, *Mythologies*. Translated by Annette Lavers. London: Vintage, 2000a.

Barthes, Roland, *A Roland Barthes Reader*. Edited by Susan Sontag. London: Vintage, 2000b.

Barthes, Roland, *A Roland Barthes Reader*. Edited by Susan Sontag. London: Vintage, 2009.

Baudrillard, Jean, *The Vital Illusion*. New York: Columbia University Press, 2000.

Baxter, Jeannette, *J. G. Ballard: Spectacular Authorship*. Farnham: Ashgate, 2009.

Beesley, T., Brierley, V. and Griffiths, S., 'The First Lady of Fashion', Concrete, UEA, Norwich, 2005.

Benjamin, Walter, 'The Work of Art in the Age of Mechanical Reproduction', *Illuminations*. London: Pimlico, 1999.

Bentley, Nick, 'Translating English: Youth, Race and Nation in Colin MacInnes's *City of Spades* and *Absolute Beginners*', in *Connotations*, Vol. 1–2, 2003–2004, http://www.connotations.de/pdf/articles/bentley01312.pdf (Accessed 4 October 2012).

Berger, John, *Ways of Seeing*. London: Penguin, 2006. First published in 1972.

Bergonzi, Bernard, *The Situation of the Novel* (1970; revised edn). London: Macmillan, 1979.

Birch, Sarah, *Christine Brooke-Rose and Contemporary Fiction*. Oxford: Oxford University Press, 1994.

Bloom, Paul, *How Pleasure Works*. London: Vintage, 2010.

Boccardi, Mariadele, *A. S. Byatt*. Houndmills: Palgrave Macmillan, 2013.

Bode, Christoph, 'Maureen Duffy: A Polyphonic Subversion of Realism', in *(Sub) Versions of Realism - Recent Woen's Fiction in Britain*, Irmgard Maasen and Ann Marie Stuby (eds). Heidelberg: Winter, 1997.

Bradbury, Malcolm, *The Novel Today: Contemporary Writers on Modern Fiction*. Washington, DC: Fontana Press, 1977.

Bradbury, Malcolm, ed., *The Novel Today*. London: Fontana, 1990.

Bradbury, Malcolm, 'The Sixties and After', in *The Modern British Novel*. London: Secker and Warburg, 1993, pp. 335–393.

Bradbury, Malcolm, *Eating People Is Wrong*. London: Picador, 2012. First published in 1959.

Braine, John, *Room at the Top*. London: Arrow, 1989. First published in 1957.

Brimstone, Lindy, '"Keepers of History": The Novels of Maureen Duffy', in *Lesbian and Gay Writing*, Mark Lilly (ed.). Basingstoke: Palgrave MacMillan, 1990, pp. 23–46.

Brooke-Rose, Christine, *Out, Such, Between, Thru* Omnibus. London: Carcanet, 2006. Originally published in 1964, 1966, 1968 and 1975, respectively.

Brophy, Brigid, *Flesh*. London: Allison & Busby, 1979. First published in 1962.

Brophy, Brigid, *In Transit*. London and Victoria, TX: Dalkey, 2006. First published in 1969.

Budgen, Frank, *James Joyce and the Making of* Ulysses. Oxford: Oxford Paperbacks, 1989.

Burgess, Anthony, *The Doctor Is Sick*. London: Heinemann, 1960.

Burgess, Anthony, *Honey for the Bears*. London: Heinemann, 1963a.

Burgess, Anthony, *Inside Mr. Enderby*. London: Heinemann, 1963b.

Burgess, Anthony, *The Wanting Seed*. London: Pan, 1965. First published in 1962.

Burgess, Anthony, *Tremor of Intent*. London: Heinemann, 1966.

Burgess, Anthony, *The Novel Now: A Student's Guide to Contemporary Fiction*. London: Faber, 1967.

Burgess, Anthony, *Enderby Outside*. London: Heinemann, 1968.

Burgess, Anthony, *Obscenity and the Arts*. Valletta: Malta Library Association, 1973.

Burgess, Anthony, *A Clockwork Orange*. London: Penguin, 1998. Originally published in 1962.

Burgess, Anthony, *The Novel Now: A Student's Guide to Contemporary Fiction*. London: Faber, 1981.

Burns, Alan, *Europe after Rain*. London: Calder, 1965.

Burns, Alan, *Celebrations*. London: Boyars, 1967.

Burns, Alan, *Babel*. London: Calder and Boyars, 1969.

Burroughs, William, *The Ticket That Exploded*. London: Calder and Boyars, 1968.

Byatt, A. S., *The Shadow of the Sun*. London: Chatto & Windus, 1964.

Byatt, A. S., *The Game*. London: Chatto & Windus, 1967.

Byatt, A. S., *The Game*. Harmondsworth: Penguin, 1983. First published in 1967 by Chatto & Windus.

Carr, Helen, *Jean Rhys*. London: Northcote House, 2012.

Carré, John Le, *The Spy Who Came in from the Cold*. London: Penguin, 2010. First published in 1963.

Carter, Angela, *The Magic Toyshop*. London: Virago, 1981. First published in 1967.

Carter, Angela, 'Notes for a Theory of Sixties Style', in *Nothing Sacred: Selected Writings*. London: Virago, 1982. Originally published in *New Society* in 1967.

Carter, Angela, *Nothing Sacred*. London: Virago, 1992.

Carter, Angela, *Shadow Dance*. London: Vintage, 1995. First published in 1966.

Carter, Angela, *Several Perceptions*. London: Virago, 1997. First published in 1969.

Carter, Angela, *Heroes and Villains*. London: Penguin, 2011. First published in 1969.

Childs, Peter, 'Ordinary Sublime: The Frustration of Life and Art in Rachel Cusk's Domestic Novels', in *Women's Fiction and Post-9/11-Contexts*, P. Childs, C. Colbrook, and S. Groes (eds). London: Lexington, 2014, pp. 95–106.

Clark, Andy and David Chalmers, 'The Extended Mind', in Andy Clark, *Supersizing the Mind*. Oxford: Oxford University Press, 2011. Loc.4378–4626. Originally published in 1998 in *Analysis*, Vol. 58, No 1, January, pp. 17–19.

Coe, Jonathan, *Like a Fiery Elephant: The Story of B. S. Johnson*. London: Picador, 2004.

Cohen, Stanley, *Folk Devils & Moral Panics: The Creation of Mods and Rockers*. Oxford: Martin Robinson, 1980.

Colebrook, Claire, *Gilles Deleuze; Essential Guides for Literary Studies*. London: Routledge, 2002.

Colebrook, Claire, *Gilles Deleuze*. Abingdon: Routledge, 2006. First published in 2000.

deBeauvoir, Simone, *The Second Sex*. London: Penguin, 1960. First published in 1949.

Debord, Guy, *The Society of the Spectacle*. Translated by Donald Nicholson Smith. New York: Zone, 1994.

Deheane, Stanlislas, *Consciousness and the Brain: Deciphering How the Brain Codes Our Thought*. London: Penguin, 2014.

DeKoven, Marianne, *Utopia Limited*. Durham: Duke University Press, 2004.

Deleuze, Gilles, 'Postscript on Control Societies', in *CTRL Space: Rhetorics of Surveillance from Bentham to Big Brother*, Thomas Y. Levin, Ursula Frohne, and Peter Weibel (eds). London: MIT Press, 2002, pp. 316–321.

Deleuze, Gilles, *Difference and Repetition*. London: Continuum, 2004. First published in 1968.

Deleuze, Gilles and Guattari, Félix, *Kafka: Towards a Minor Literature*. Translated by Dana Polan. Minneapolis and London: Minnesota University Press, 1986. Originally published in 1975.

Deleuze, Gilles and Guattari, Félix, *A Thousand Plateaus*. London: Athlone, 2000. Originally published in 1980.

Deleuze, Gilles and Guattari, Félix, *Anti-Oedipus: Capitalism and Schizophrenia*. Translated by Robert Hurley, Mark Seem, and Helen R. Lane. London and New York: Continuum, 2004. Originally published in 1977.

Delville, Michel, *J. G. Ballard*. Plymouth: Northcote House, 1998.

Dodsworth, Martin, 'Uses of Literacy', in *Encounter*, Melvin J. Laskey and Nigel Dennis (eds). June 1970, pp. 75–80.

Drabble, Margaret, *The Millstone*. London: Weidenfeld and Nicolson, 1965.

Drabble, Margaret, *Jerusalem the Golden*. London: Weidenfel and Nicolson, 1967.

Drabble, Margaret, *The Waterfall*. London: Penguin, 1980. First published in 1969.

Drabble, Margaret, 'Introduction' to *Poor Cow*. London: Virago, 1988.

Drabble, Margaret, *Angus Wilson*. London: Secker and Warburg, 1995.

Duffy, Maureen, *Wounds*. London: Mandarin, 1984. First published in 1969.

Duffy, Maureen, *The Microcosm*. London: Virago, 1988. Originally published in 1966.

Duffy, Maureen, *The Microcosm*. London: Virago, 1989. First published in 1966 by Hutchinson.

Duffy, Maureen, *England: The Making of the Myth from Stonehenge to Albert Square*. London: Fourth Estate, 2001.

Duffy, Maureen, *That's How It Was*. London: Virago, 2002, First published by in 1962 Hutchinson.

Dunn, Douglas, *Terry Street*. London: Faber and Faber. First published in 1969.

Dunn, Nell, *Freddy Get Married*. London: MacGibbon & Kee, 1968.

Dunn, Nell, *Up the Junction*. London: Little & Brown, 1988. First published in 1963 by MacGibbon & Kee.

Dunn, Nell, *Poor Cow*. London: Virago, 1988. First published in 1967.

Dunn, Nell and Henri, Adrian *I Want*. London: Jonathan Cape, 1972.

Elias, Amy J., *Sublime Desire: History and Post-1960s Fiction*. Baltimore: The Johns Hopkins University Press, 2001.

Empson, William, 'Proletarian Literature', in *Some Versions of Pastoral*. London: Chatto & Windus, 1935, pp. 1–35.

Figes, Eva, *Winter Journey*. London: Faber, 1967.

Figes, Eva, *Equinox*. London: Panther, 1969. First published in 1966 by Secker and Warburg.

Figes, Eva, *Patriarchal Attitudes*. London: Faber, 1970.

Figes, Eva, *B*. London: Faber, 1972.

Forster, E. M., *Howards End*. London: Penguin, 1992. First published in 1910.

Foucault, Michel, *The Order of Things: Archaeology of the Human Sciences*. London: Routledge, 2002. First published as *Les Mots et les Choses* in 1966.

Fowles, John, *The Aristos*. London: Cape, 1964.

Fowles, John, *The Collector*. London: Triad/Granada, 1976. First published in 1963.

Fowles, John, *The French Lieutenant's Woman*. London: Triad/Granada, 1981. First published in 1969.

Fowles, John, *The Magus*. London: Vintage, 2004. First published in 1965.

Furtado, Peter, *The Culture of Youth*. Abingdon: Equinox, 1994.

Fussell, Paul, 'The New Irony & the Augustans', in *Encounter*, Melvin J. Laskey and Nigel Dennis (eds). June 1970, pp. 68–75.

Gąsiorek, Andrzej, *Post-War British Fiction: Realism and After*. London and New York: Edward Arnold, 1995.

Gąsiorek, Andrzej, *J. G. Ballard*. Manchester: Manchester University Press, 2005.

Gibbons, Alison, *Multimodality, Cognition, and Experimental Literature*. London: Routledge, 2012.

Gibbs, Raymond W., 'Embodiment in Metaphorical Imagination', in *Grounding Cognition: The Role of Perception and Action in Memory, Language, and Thinking*, D. Pecher and R. A. Waan (eds). Cambridge: Cambridge University Press, 2005, pp. 65–92.

Gibson, A., 'Altering Images', in *London from Punk to Blair*, J. Kerr and A. Gibson (eds). 2003. London: Reaktion, 2003, pp. 292–300.

Gitlin, Todd, *The Sixties: Years of Hope, Days of Rage*. New York: Bentham, 1993.

Gould, Tony, *Insider Outsider*. Harmondsworth: Penguin Books, 1986.

Gray, Nigel, *The Silent Majority: A Study of the Working Class in Post-War British Fiction*. London: Vision, 1973.

Green, Jonathan, *All Dressed Up: The Sixties and the Counter-Culture*. London: Jonathan Cape, 1993.

Green, Jonathan, *It: Sex since the Sixties*. London: Secker & Warburg, 1993.

Green, Jonathan, *All Dressed Up: Sixties and the Counterculture*. London: Jonathan Cape, 1998.

Greer, Germaine, *The Female Eunuch*. London: Paladin, 1971.

Greer, Germaine, *The Female Eunuch*. London: HarperPerennial, 2006. First published in 1970.

Groes, Sebastian, 'Nell Dunn'. *The Literary Encyclopedia*. First published 21 October 2007. http://www.litencyc.com/php/speople.php?rec=true&UID=1351 (Accessed 9 October 2015).

Groes, Sebastian, 'Ian McEwan and the Modernist Consciousness of the City in *Saturday*', in *Ian McEwan: Contemporary Critical Perspectives*, Groes, Sebastian (ed.). London and New York: Continuum, 2009, pp. 99–114.

Groes, Sebastian, *The Making of London*. London: Palgrave Macmillan, 2011.

Groes, Sebastian, Jon Cook and Victor Sage, 'Journeys without Maps: An Interview with Ian McEwan', in *Ian McEwan: Contemporary Critical Perspectives*, Sebastian Groes (ed.). London and New York: Bloomsbury Academic, 2013, pp. 144–155.

Groes, Sebastian, 'The Prosthetic God: Psychosomatic Extensions in the Digital Age', *Californica*, 24 October, 2014. http://californica.net/2014/10/24/the-prosthetic-god-psychosomatic-extension-in-the-digital-age/ (Accessed 10 February 2015).

DeGroot, Gerard, *The 60s Unplugged: A Kaleidoscopic History of a Disorderly Decade*. London: Macmillan, 2008.

Harrison, Nancy R., *Jean Rhys and the Novel as Women's Text*. Chapel Hill, NC: University of North Carolina Press, 1988.

Hayles, N. Katherine, *How We Became Posthuman: Virtual Bodies in Cybernetics, Literature and Informatics*. Chicago: University of Chicago Press, 1999.

Hayles, N. Katherine, *Writing Machines*. Cambridge, MA: MIT, 2002.

Head, Dominic, *The Cambridge Companion to Modern British Fiction, 1950–2000*. Cambridge: Cambridge University Press, 2002.

Head, Dominic, *Cambridge Introduction to Fiction 1950–2000*. Cambridge: Cambridge University Press, 2008.

Heath, Stephen, 'Ambiviolences: Notes for Reading Joyce', in *Post-structuralist Joyce: Essays from the French*, Derek Attridge and Daniel Ferrer (eds). Cambridge: Cambridge University Press, 1984, pp. 31–68.

Hekman, Susan, 'Constructing a Ballast: An Ontology for Feminism', in *Material Feminisms*, Stacey Alaimo and Susan Hekman (eds). Bloomington: Indiana University Press, 2008, pp. 85–119.

Henri, Adrian, Roger McGough and Brian Patten, *Penguin Modern Poets. No. 10: The Mersey Sound*. London: Penguin, 1967.

Heppenstall, Rayner, *The Connecting Door*. London: Barrie & Rockliff, 1962.

Hitchins, Peter, *The Abolition of Britain*. London: Quartet, 1999.

Holloway, John, 'Dickens' Word-World', in *Encounter*, Melvin J. Laskey and Nigel Dennis (eds). June 1970, pp. 63–68.

Howard, Ebenezer, *Garden Cities of Tomorrow*. London: Faber, 1985. First published in 1902.

Hucklesby, David, 'B. S. Johnson, Giles Gordon, and a "New Fiction": The Book, the Screen and the E-book', in *B. S. Johnson and Post-War Literature: Possibilities of the Avant-Garde*, Martin Ryle and Julian Jordan (eds). London: Palgrave Macmillan, 2014, pp. 202–216.

Huntley, Jake, 'Disquieting Features: An Introductory Tour of *The Atrocity Exhibition*', in *J. G. Ballard: Contemporary Critical Perspectives*, Jeannette Baxter (ed.). London and New York: Continuum, 2008, pp. 23–33.

Inwood, Stephen, *A History of London*. London: Papermac, 2000.

Jameson, Fredric, 'Periodising the Sixties', in *Social Text, No. 9/10, The 60's without Apology (Spring–Summer, 1984)*. Abingdon: Routledge, 1988, pp. 178–209.

Jephcott, Pearl, *A Troubled Area: Notes on Notting Hill*. London: Faber and Faber, 1964.

Johnson, B. S., *Travelling People*. London: Transworld, 1964. First published in 1963.

Johnson, B. S., *The Unfortunates*. London: Picador, 1999. First published in 1969.

Johnson, B. S., *Albert Angelo*, in Picador Omnibus *Albert Angelo, Trawl, House Mother Normal*. London: Picador, 2004. First published in 1964 by Constable.

Johnson, B. S., *Trawl*, in Picador Omnibus *Albert Angelo, Trawl, House Mother Normal*. London: Picador, 2004. First published in 1966.

Johnson, B. S., *House Mother Normal*, in Picador Omnibus *Albert Angelo, Trawl, House Mother Normal*. London: Picador, 2004. First published in 1971.

Joyce, James, *Ulysses*. London: Penguin, 1992. First published in 1922.

Kermode, Frank, *The Genesis of Secrecy*. Harvard: Harvard University Press, 1980.

Kermode, Frank, *The Sense of an Ending: Studies in the Theory of Fiction*. Oxford: Oxford University Press, 1966.

Kermode, Frank, *The Sense of an Ending*. Oxford: Oxford University Press, 2000. First published in 1965.

Koolhaas, Rem, 'Junkspace', *October*, Volume 100, 'Obsolescence', Spring, 2002, 175–190.

Koolhaas, R. and B. Mau, *S,M,L,XL*. Köln: Taschen, 1995. First published in New York by The Monacelli Press, 1995.

Laing, R. D., *The Divided Self: An Existential Study in Sanity and Madness*. London: Penguin, 1965. First published in 1960.

Laplanche, Jean, *Essays on Otherness*. Translated by John Fletcher. Abingdon: Routledge, 1999.

Latour, Bruno, *We Have Never Been Modern*. Harvard, MA: Harvard University Press, 1993. First published in 1991.

Leavis, F. R., *The Great Tradition*. Cambridge: Cambridge University press, 1948.

Leeming, Glenda, *Margaret Drabble*. Tavistock: Northcote, 2006.

Lessing, Doris, *The Four-Gated City*. London: Grafton, 1988. First published in 1969.

Lessing, Doris, *The Golden Notebook*. London: Fourth Estate, 2013. First published in 1962.

Levy, Shawn, *Ready, Steady, Go!: The Smashing Rise and Giddy Fall of Sixties London*. London: Doubleday, 2002.

Levy, Shawn, *Ready, Steady, Go!* London: Fourth Estate, 2003.

Lewis, Roger, *Anthony Burgess*. London: Faber and Faber, 2002.

Lodge, David, *The Novelist at the Crossroads*. London: Routledge and K. Paul, 1971.

Luckhurst, Roger, *The Angle between Two Walls: The Fiction of J. G. Ballard*. Liverpool: Liverpool University Press, 1997.

Macaulay, Rose, *The World My Wilderness*. London: Virago, 1988. First published in 1950 by Collins.

McEwan, Ian, 'Intersection'. *Tri-Quarterly*, Fall, 1975, pp. 63–86.

McEwan, Ian, 'Save the Boot Room, Save the Earth', *The Guardian*, 19 March 2005. http://www.theguardian.com/artanddesign/2005/mar/19/art1 (Accessed 6 September 2013).

McEwan, Ian, 'Class Work', http://malcolmbradbury.com/uea_ian_mcewan_class.html (Accessed 14 March 2014).

McEwan, Ian, 'Class Work', http://malcolmbradbury.com/uea_ian_mcewan_class.html (Accessed 16 November 2014). First published in *Class Work*, Sceptre, 1995.

MacInnes, Colin, *Absolute Beginners*. London: Gibbon & Kee, 1959.

MacInnes, Colin, *City of Spades*. London: Allison & Busby, 1993. First published in 1957.

Mackay, Sheena, *Music Upstairs*. London: Vintage, 1998. First published in 1965.

McLeod, John, *Postcolonial London: Rewriting the Metropolis*. Abingdon: Routledge, 2004.

McLuhan, Marshall, *Understanding Media*. London: Penguin, 2003. First published in 1964.

Magrs, Paul, *Interview with Nell Dunn*. Reading and discussing work at the University of East Anglia in 1998. Cassette: 1/467.

Maitland, Sara, ed., *Very Heaven: Looking Back at the Sixties*. London: Virago, 1988.

Manovich, Lev, *The Language of New Media*. Cambridge, MA and London: MIT Press, 2001.

Marcuse, Herbert, *One-Dimensional Man*. London: Routledge, 2002. First published in 1964.

Marwick, Arthur, *The Sixties*. Oxford: Oxford University Press, 1998.

Minogue, Sally and Andrew Palmer, 'Confronting the Abject: Women and Dead Babies in Modern English Fiction', *Journal of Modern Literature*, Vol. 29, Nr, Spring 2006, pp. 103–125.

Moorcock, Michael, *Behold the Man*. London: Millennium, 1999. First published in 1969.

Moorcock, Michael, *London Bone*. London: Scribner, 2001.

Moore-Gilbert, Bart and John Seed, eds., *Cultural Revolution? The Challenge of the Arts in the 1960s*. London: Routledge, 1992.

Morphet, Janice, 'New Towns in the Novel: A Reflection on Social Realism', *Planning Practice & Research*, Vol. 18, No. 1, 2003, pp. 51–62.

Murdoch, Iris, *A Word Child*. London: Penguin, 1989. First published in 1975.

Murdoch, Iris, 'Against Dryness', in *The Novel Today*, Malcolm Bradbury (ed.). London: Fontana, 1990, pp. 1–16. First published in *Encoutner* in 1961.

Murdoch, Iris, *A Severed Head*. London: Vintage, 2001. First published in 1961.

Murdoch, Iris, *Bruno's Dream*. London: Vintage, 2001. First published in 1969.

Myer, Valerie Grosvenor, *Margaret Drabble: Puritan and Persmissiveness*. London: Vision, 1974.

Naipaul, V. S., *An Area of Darkness*. London: André Deutsch, 1964.

Norledge, Jessica, 'Thinking Outside of the Box: A Text World Theory Response to the Interactivity of B. S. Johnson's the Unfortunates', *Innervate*, Vol. 4, 2011–12. https://www.nottingham.ac.uk/english/documents/innervate/11-12/1112norledgecognitivepoetics.pdf (Accessed 17 march 2014).

Packard, Vance, *The Hidden Persuaders*. London: Penguin, 1960.

Peach, Linden, *Angela Carter*. Basingstoke: Palgrave Macmillan, 2009.

Perry, George, *London in the Sixties*. London: Pavillion Books, 2001.

Philips, Deborah, *Women's Fiction 1945–2005*. London and New York: Continuum, 2008.

Phillips, Charlie and Mike Phillips, *Notting Hill in the Sixties*. London: Lawrence & Wishart, 1991.

Porter, Roy, *London: A Social History*. London: Penguin, 2000. First published in 1994 by Hamish Hamilton.

Pressley, Alison, *Changing Times: Being Young in Britain in the '60s*. London: Michael O'Mara, 2000.

Quin, Ann, *Berg*. London: Grafton, 1989. First published in 1964.

Quin, Ann, *Tripticks*. London and Victoria, TX: Dalkey Archive Press, 2001. First published in 1972.

Quin, Ann, *Passages*. London and Victoria, TX: Dalkey Archive Press, 2003. First published in 1969.

Rabinovoitz, Rubin, *The Reaction against Experiment in the English Novel 1950–1960*. New York: Columbia University Press, 1967.

Reid Banks, Lynne, *The L-Shaped Room*. Harmondsworth: Penguin, 1976. First published in 1960.

Rhys, Jean, *Tigers Are Better-Looking*. London: Andre Deutsch, 1968.

Rhys, Jean, *Wide Sargasso Sea*. London: Penguin, 1970. First published in 1966.

Rhys, Jean, *Jean Rhys: Letters 1931–1966*. Selected and edited by Francis Wyndham and Diana Melly. London: Andre Deutsch, 1984.

Rhys, Jean, *Wide Sargasso Sea*. London: Penguin, 1988. First published in 1966.

Ridley, Matt, 'Ian McEwan and the Rational Mind', in *Ian McEwan: Contemporary Critical Perspectives*, Groes Sebastian (ed.). London and New York: Bloomsbury, 2014, pp. vii–x.

Sage, Lorne, ed., *Flesh and the Mirror: Essays on the Art of Angela Carter*. London: Virago, 1994.

Sage, Lorna, *Women in the House of Fiction*. Basingstoke: Macmillan, 1992.

Sandbrook, Dominic, *Never Had It So Good: A History of Britain from Suez to the Beatles*. London: Little and Brown, 2005.

Sandbrook, Dominic, *White Heat: A History of Britain in the Swinging Sixties*. London: Little and Brown, 2006.

Sandbrook, Dominic, *White Heat*. London: Abacus, 2009.

Sandbrook, Dominic, *Never Had It So Good*. London: Abacus, 2010.

Sarraute, Nathalie, *The Age of Suspicion*. Translated by Maria Jolas. London: Calder, 1963. First published as *L'Ère du soupçon* in 1956.

Sarraute, Nathalie, *Tropisms*. Translated by Maria Jolas. New York: George Braziller, 1967. First published in France in 1939.

Seymour-Smith, Martin, 'Whose Shakespeare?' in *Encounter*, Melvin J. Laskey and Nigel Dennis (eds). June 1970, pp. 56–63.

Showalter, Elaine, *A Literature of Their Own*. London: Virago, 1978.

Sinclair, Iain, 'Crowning Glory: Michael Moorcock's London', *The Guardian*, 23 November 2000 (Accessed 9 September 2013).

Sinclair, Iain, 'Primal Screen', *The Guardian*, 9 September 2006, http://film.guardian .co.uk/features/featurepages/0,,1868158,00.html.

Sinfield, Alan, *Literature, Politics and Culture in Post-War Britain*. London: Athlone, 1997.

Sizemore, Christine W., 'Reading the City as Palimpsest: The Experiential Perception of the City in Doris Lessing's *The Four-Gated City*', in *Women Writers and the City*, Susan Merrill Squier (ed.). Knoxville: University of Tennessee Press, 1984, pp. 176–190.

Smith, Patricia Juliana, ed., *The Queer Sixties*. London: Routledge, 1999.

Sontag, Susan, *Against Interpretation*. London: Penguin, 2009. First published in 1966.

Spark, Muriel, *The Girls of Slender Means*. London: Penguin, 1975. Originally published in 1963 by Macmillan.

Spark, Muriel, *The Prime of Miss Jean Brodie*. London: Penguin, 1997. Originally published in 1961.

Spark, Muriel, *The Girls of Slender Means*. London: Penguin, 1983. First published in 1963.

Spark, Muriel, *The Driver's Seat*. London: Penguin, 1998. First published in 1970.

Spark, Muriel, *The Prime of Miss Jean Brodie*. London: Penguin, 2001. First published in 1961.

Stephens, Chris and Katherine Stout, *This Was Tomorrow: Art and the Sixties*. London: Tate, 2004.

Stevenson, Randall, 'Beyond Fifties Realism: David Storey and Angus Wilson', in *The British Novel since the Thirties* (1997), Mike Storry and Peter Childs (eds). London and New York: Routledge, 1986, pp. 49–63.

Sturrock, J., *The French New Novel*. London and New York and Toronto: Oxford University Press, 1969.

Tauchert, Ashley, *Romancing Jane Austen: Narrative, Realism, and the Possibility of a Happy Ending*. Basingstoke: Palgrave Macmillan, 2006.

Thompson, E. P., *The Making of the English Working Class*. London: Penguin, 1963.

Torgovnick, Marianna, *Closure in the Novel*. Princeton, NJ: Princeton University Press, 1981.

Trocchi, Alexander, *Cain's Book*. London: Calder, 1962.

Tucker, Eva, *Contact*. London: Calder & Boyars, 1966.

Unsigned review, 'An English Anti-Novel', *Times Literary Supplement*, Vol. 3, 1962, p. 162.

Unsigned review, 'As Authentic as a Tape Recorder', *Times Literary Supplement*, 18 October 1963, p. 941.

Unsigned review, 'Vaguely Villainous', *Time Literary Supplement*, 21 November 1963, p. 941.

Unsigned review, 'Author as Obstacle', *Times Literary Supplement*, 6 August 1964.

Unsigned review, 'I Am a Photograph', *Times Literary Supplement*, 4 May 1967, p. 373.

Unsigned review, 'Nell Dunn', *Times Literary Supplement*, 17 May 1967, p. 373.

Vreeland, Diana, 'Swinging London', *TIME*, No. 15, 15 April 1966, pp. 16–34.

Wall, Stephen, 'New Novels', *The Listener*, 30 July 1964.

Waterhouse, Keith, *Billy Liar*. London: Penguin, 2010. First published in 1959.

Watt, I., *The Rise of the Novel*. London: Chatto & Windus, 1957.

Waugh, P., *Harvest of the Sixties*. Oxford and New York: Oxford University Press, 1995.

Waugh, Patricia, 'Kazuo Ishiguro's Not-Too-Late Modernism', in *Kazuo Ishiguro: Critical Visions of the Novels*, S. Groes and B. Lewis (eds). London: Palgrave Macmillan, 2011, pp. 13–30.

White, Jerry, *London in the Twentieth Century*. London: Viking, 2001.

Williams, R., *The Long Revolution*. London: Chatto & Windus, 1961.

Williams, Raymond, *The Long Revolution*. London: Pelican, 1971. Originally published in 1961 by Chatto & Windus.

Williams, R., *The Country and the City*. London: Chatto & Windus, 1973.

Wilson, Angus, *The Wild Garden*. Berkeley: University of California Press, 1963.

Wilson, Angus, *The Old Men at the Zoo*. London: Penguin, 1988. First published in 1961.

Wilson, Angus, *Late Call*. London: Penguin, 1998. First published in 1964.

Wilson, Angus, *Late Call*. London: House of Stratus, 2001. Originally published in 1964.

Wood, James, *The Nearest Thing to Life*. London: Jonathan Cape, 2015.

Woolf, Virginia, *Mrs Dalloway*. London: Penguin, 1992. First published in 1925.

Yarrow, R., ed., *European Theatre 1960–1990*. London: Routledge, 1992.

Zunshine, Lisa, *Why We Read Fiction*. Columbus: Ohio State University Press, 2006.

Index

CPSIA information can be obtained
at www.ICGtesting.com
Printed in the USA
LVHW08s0813171018
593811LV00006B/93/P

9 781350 054196